WHAT
HAPPENED
TO
BERNIE
SANDERS

WHAT HAPPENED TO TO BERNIE SANDERS

JARED H. BECK, ESQ.

Hot Books

Hot Books may be purchased in bulk at special discounts for sales promotion, corporate gifts, fund-raising, or educational purposes. Special editions can also be created to specifications. For details, contact the Special Sales Department, Skyhorse Publishing, 307 West 36th Street, 11th Floor, New York, NY 10018 or info@skyhorsepublishing.com.

Hot Books® and Skyhorse Publishing® are registered trademarks of Skyhorse Publishing, Inc.®, a Delaware corporation.

Visit our website at at www.hotbookspress.com.

10 9 8 7 6 5 4 3 2 1

Library of Congress Cataloging-in-Publication Data is available on file.

Hardcover ISBN: 978-1-5107-3723-5
Paperback ISBN: 978-1-5107-3669-6
Ebook ISBN: 978-1-5107-3670-2

Printed in the United States of America

Dedicated to the memory of my grandfather Henry Lessick—who proudly defended his country in World War II and bore testimony to his grandchildren about the horrible suffering endured by the Japanese people on the Night of the Black Snow.

Table of Contents

Foreword

By David Talbot

THE WORLD IS BURNING, AND YET the firelight illuminates the way out. The times are dire, even catastrophic. Nonetheless we can sense a grand awakening, a growing realization all around the globe that "people have the power, to dream, to rule, to wrestle the world from fools" in the prophetic words of Patti Smith.

But in order to rouse ourselves from the nightmares that hold us in their grip, we need to know more about the forces that bedevil us, the structures of power that profit from humanity's exploitation and from that of the earth. That's the impetus behind Hot Books, a series that seeks to expose the dark operations of power and to light the way forward.

Skyhorse publisher Tony Lyons and I started Hot Books in 2015 because we believe that books can make a difference. Since then the Hot Books series has shined a light on the cruel reign of racism and police violence in Baltimore (D. Watkins' *The Beast Side*); the poisoning of U.S. soldiers by their own environmentally reckless commanding officers (Joseph Hickman's *The Burn Pits*); the urgent need to hold U.S. officials accountable for their criminal actions during the war on terror (Rachel Gordon's *American Nuremberg*); the covert manipulation of the media by intelligence agencies (Nicholas Schou's *Spooked*); the rise of a rape culture on campus (Kirby Dick and Amy Ziering's

The Hunting Ground); the insidious demonizing of Muslims in
the media and Washington (Arsalan Iftikhar's *Scapegoats*); the
crackdown on whistleblowers who know the government's dirty
secrets (Mark Hertsgaard's *Bravehearts*); the disastrous policies of the liberal elite that led to the triumph of Trump (Chris
Hedges' *Unspeakable*); the American wastelands that gave rise to
this dark reign (Alexander Zaitchik's *The Gilded Rage*); the energy
titans and their political servants who are threatening human
survival (Dick Russell's *Horsemen of the Apocalypse*); the utiliza-
tion of authoritarian tactics by Donald Trump that threaten to
erode American democracy (Brian Klaas's *The Despot's Appren-
tice*); the capture, torture, and detention of the first "high-value
target" captured by the CIA after 9/11 (Joseph Hickman and
John Kiriakou's *The Convenient Terrorist*); and the deportation of
American veterans (J Malcolm Garcia's *Without a Country*). And
the series continues, going where few publishers dare.

Hot Books are more condensed than standard-length books.
They're packed with provocative information and points of view
that mainstream publishers usually shy from. Hot Books are
meant not just to stir readers' thinking, but to stir trouble.

Hot Books authors follow the blazing path of such legend-
ary muckrakers and troublemakers as Upton Sinclair, Lincoln
Steffens, Rachel Carson, Jane Jacobs, Jessica Mitford, I.F. Stone
and Seymour Hersh. The magazines and newspapers that once
provided a forum for this deep and dangerous journalism have
shrunk in number and available resources. Hot Books aims to
fill this crucial gap.

American journalism has become increasingly digitized and
commodified. If the news isn't fake, it's usually shallow. But
there's a growing hunger for information that is both credible
and undiluted by corporate filters.

A publishing series with this intensity cannot keep burning
in a vacuum. Hot Books needs a culture of equally passionate

readers. Please spread the word about these titles—encourage your bookstores to carry them, post comments about them in online stores and forums, persuade your book clubs, schools, political groups and community organizations to read them and invite the authors to speak.

It's time to go beyond packaged news and propaganda. It's time for Hot Books . . . journalism without borders.

Preface

THIS IS THE STORY OF WHY Bernie Sanders lost the 2016 Democratic primaries. It is also the story of a class action lawsuit brought by donors to Sanders's campaign, who sued the Democratic National Committee—the DNC—and its former chairperson, Congresswoman Deborah Wasserman Schultz, for rigging the primary process in favor of Hillary Clinton. I am the attorney for the plaintiffs in this case, which is currently on appeal with the Eleventh Circuit Court of Federal Appeals after being dismissed by the district court.

Because the case was dismissed on preliminary grounds and well before proceeding to the merits—and because appellate courts rarely reverse cases—it is unlikely that my clients' claims will ever be tried before a jury. However, this reality does not mean the evidence—much of which is already a matter of public record—cannot be assembled, described, and set before the public in a cohesive manner. This, after all, is one of the main purposes of the legal trial—to arrive at the truth, through rigorous assessment of the evidence. The issues presented by the rigging of the 2016 primaries surely deserve, if not demand, a public hearing, and not all public hearings happen in a courtroom.

So, I have set upon this book with that goal in mind, recognizing, of course, that there are some inherent limitations. For example, only evidence that has been made public record can be cited, as our case was dismissed before the discovery process even got off the ground. And of course, I cannot present live witness testimony, which is the heart of any trial. In addition, the defendants will not have an opportunity to respond or present their own evidence. That said, I have tried to structure this book as I might a courtroom presentation, starting with an Opening Statement that charts the history of the lawsuit. Acts I and II present the evidence. This evidence shows—in my mind, irrefutably, but I will let the reader be the judge—that Bernie Sanders was destined to lose the race for the 2016 Democratic Party nomination even before he entered the race, because the DNC and its allies rigged the process for another candidate. These chapters move from close analysis of internal DNC documents—published by WikiLeaks and others—demonstrating how the very organization that was obligated, by its own Charter, with running the elections in a fair and evenhanded manner, did everything it could to ensure that Hillary Clinton would be the nominee. I examine the financial ties between Clinton's campaign and the DNC that rendered the latter nothing more than an arm of the former. I also pay close attention to the media landscape and how Sanders's candidacy was deliberately undermined by false narratives created in the mainstream corporate media by Clinton loyalists, as well as the superdelegate system, which has evolved over time to bar genuine progressive candidates, "another McGovern" such as Sanders, from ever attaining the nomination.

In a summation or closing statement, it is up to the attorney to recount all the important evidence that has been presented during the trial, address weaknesses or holes suggested by the other side, and, in the end, plead with the jury to return the verdict that he or she wants for the client. In my Summation, I am less concerned about asking for a legal judgment—something which can only be delivered by a court of law—and more focused on situating the questions of what happened to Bernie Sanders, and what we have learned from trying to prosecute election-rigging claims within the present-day American legal system, against the larger issues of how to think about the American political system. Does the term "democracy" even describe or relate to our political system in any meaningful sense? And if we are not a democracy, what kind of political system do we have, and what are the consequences? I firmly believe that these questions, in one form or another, are the most significant political issues presently before the American people, who will eventually have to return some manner of "verdict."

I believe understanding the plight of Sanders and his supporters is key to comprehending the current American political landscape along with the various, often conflicting forces swirling around it. Indeed, the presidential election of 2016 is unique, in the sense it is *still* being fought by the parties—even after we pass the one-year anniversary of Donald Trump's inauguration. While the 2000 election was the first to be litigated within the judicial system between the major party candidates following Election Day, the Supreme Court handed down *Bush v. Gore*—effectively deciding the election for George W. Bush—over one month before Inauguration Day. Further back in history, the notoriously controversial election of 1876 was settled by the Compromise of 1877, just days before Rutherford B. Hayes took office.[1]

In contrast, while the presidential torch has formally passed to Trump, as the Electoral College winner as certified in a joint session of Congress on January 6, 2017, a battle over the legitimacy of his election—and, indeed, his qualification to serve as president—continues to rage. The notion that Russia colluded with the Trump campaign to skew the election to Trump has become a prevailing mainstream media narrative,[2] and a mainstay talking point of the Democratic Party.[3] Numerous Democrats have loudly called for Trump's impeachment, and articles of impeachment have been introduced in Congress.[4] Meanwhile, Trump's Democratic opponent, Hillary Clinton, has publicly declared herself to be the real winner of the election,[5] [6] squarely pinning the result on "Russian interference" and "an opponent who broke all the rules."[7] The battle is not just rhetorical in nature: a special counsel has been appointed to investigate the allegations of collusion between Trump's campaign and Russia, and two separate grand juries, in Virginia and the District of Columbia, are now conducting criminal investigations.[8] On October 30, 2017, the first three indictments were announced by special counsel Robert S. Mueller III,[9] with more expected.[10] One month later, Trump's former national security adviser, Michael T. Flynn, pleaded guilty to lying to the FBI during its investigation into alleged collusion with Russia.[11]

The question of whether Trump's election was aided and abetted by Russia is beyond the scope of this book. As a lawyer, I have full confidence that the truth will ultimately emerge through the ongoing legal proceedings—and if not there, in the court of public opinion. In fact, both sides of the case have already been presented to the public in some detail.[12]

Instead, I would suggest that the key to understanding "what happened" in a general election that has sparked an ongoing public debate about the legitimacy of the election itself, is to first undertake an examination of the 2016 Democratic primaries, where forces menacing American political life operated more transparently. An honest assessment of these primaries—free from the hotly tinged rhetoric of Russian interference and threats to national security—shows that Bernie Sanders lost to Hillary Clinton because he *never had a chance to win*. In multiple ways, the process was rigged, and rigged for Clinton. These pages will document how a web of forces, emanating from elite interests through the mainstream media and Democratic political establishment, and fronted by the Democratic National Committee, operated to ensure that Clinton would secure the nomination. As such, not only did Clinton carry an overwhelming material advantage in funding and support from the political establishment into the primaries, but the contest occurred within a system that itself was structured to ensure her victory. In other words, the story of the 2016 Democratic primaries is the story of how corruption has critically eroded America's political institutions to the point of crippling democracy itself.

The assessment of what happened to Bernie Sanders—whose campaign inspired hope for so many through visions of a "Political Revolution" without recent precedent in U.S. political history—appears dark and foreboding. If there is any beacon of light, it is that the truth can no longer be fully hidden. Indeed, the truth already began to emerge in the summer of 2016, even before the Democratic National Convention in Philadelphia, with the publication by purported hacker Guccifer 2.0 and online publisher WikiLeaks of internal DNC documents supplying direct evidence of collusion by and among actors in the DNC, the Clinton campaign, and mainstream media, to elevate her to the nomination. Those documents have afforded Americans an extraordinary, behind-the-curtain view of how their political system actually functions.

Although the forces that prevented Bernie Sanders from winning are systemic in nature, they can no longer operate under cover of darkness. The Internet Age, and with it, the development of revolutionary publishers like WikiLeaks and new channels of dissemination embedded in social media, have brought a dawning of some transparency to bear on the workings of government. Every day, Americans gain consciousness regarding the true form of their governing institutions. If there is any glimmer of hope, it is that such consciousness is the very precondition for Americans to free themselves from those forces which have seized control of their political life and pushed it in an increasingly undemocratic direction.

OPENING STATEMENT
"Democracy Demands the Truth"

IN 2016, THE DREAM WAS SHARED by over twelve million Democratic primary voters, as well as nearly 2.5 million campaign donors, that for the first time in forty-four years, a genuinely progressive candidate might run for president of the United States as a major party candidate. These supporters of Bernie Sanders's historic candidacy genuinely believed in his vision of a "political revolution" whereby the United States would reverse its "drift toward oligarchy" while creating "a government which represents all the people and not just the few."[13]

This is about the death of that dream—or, more precisely, why the considerable faith, effort, and resources so many Americans put into Sanders's campaign was based on a false hope. In the end, Sanders lost the contest for the Democratic nomination because the Democratic Party, through its governing body, the Democratic National Committee, had determined that Hillary Clinton would be the nominee even before Sanders announced his candidacy. From the beginning, the "fix was in," so to speak, and not in a loose sense signifying the obvious outsized advantage in campaign funding and political connections that Clinton brought to the table. Rather, Sanders's candidacy proceeded within a primary electoral system that was designed and shaped with the specific purpose of excluding candidates in the mold of George McGovern—who unsuccessfully contended as the Democratic candidate for president in 1972—from ever acceding to the party's nomination again. Given the unprecedented ability to peer "behind the scenes" of the U.S. political process through the work of revolutionary media sources, most notably WikiLeaks, the contours of this electoral system, along with its inherent biases, can be diagrammed and described with more precision than ever before in modern American political history.

In seeking the explanation for how the dreams of millions of Americans came to be shattered in this manner, I have found it necessary to come to terms with the potential demise of my own dreamscape—one that has propelled my life path since my middle school days in a small suburban community outside of Albany, New York.

I believe the setting for this dreamscape was laid in 1991 when I was fifteen years old, and my hometown's proximity to the state capital allowed me (along with several eighth grade classmates) to work as an intern in a New York state assemblyman's office on selected days of the week[14]—an experience that didn't entail much more than licking stamps, stuffing envelopes, and occasionally fetching hot dogs from the carts outside the New York State Capitol for the assemblyman's brother, but which forged a budding fascination with my country's political institutions. In due course, this fascination led me to other experiences—for example, an opportunity to shake the president's hand when Bill Clinton visited Albany during my senior year of high school,[15] and led me to submit the winning entry in the 1994 New York State Democratic Committee Essay Contest.[16] The proceeds from the contest helped pay for my first year at Harvard College, where my studies focused on political theory and political philosophy, and I was able to ruminate on current politics as a writer on the staff of the student-run *Harvard Political Review*.[17]

By the time I graduated college in 1999, my undergraduate studies had transformed into a desire to study political theory in greater depth and, perhaps, eventually teach it at the university level. I was especially interested in theories of international law, and decided to pursue this further by applying to both law schools and graduate programs in political science. In the end, I decided to remain at Harvard and work toward a PhD in the Department of Government.[18]

Two years into the PhD program, after completing all the required coursework and tests, but before starting my dissertation, I made the decision to withdraw. Intellectually, my time in graduate school was fulfilling enough—it allowed me to take challenging graduate-level seminars taught by the discipline's best minds, including Stanley Hoffmann and Samuel P. Huntington, two luminaries in the field who are no longer with us.[19] But it took two years of graduate study to appreciate the fact that the academic discipline of political science is strangely separate from the actual practice of politics or functioning of government in the United States. With a few exceptions, there is typically very little interplay or discourse between professors of political science at American universities, and politicians or other participants in the political process itself.

Foreseeing that an academic career might be fulfilling only at an intellectual level, while neglecting other aspects of my underlying interest in politics, I turned to law school in search of more balance. The old adage—which was still widely believed at the time I attended law school, from 2001 to 2004—is that one can do practically "anything" with a law degree.[20] The experience promised three years of intense study of subjects relating to the American legal system—covering topics that would inevitably dovetail with my core interests in political theory—while culminating in a professional credential that, upon admittance to the relevant bar, would entitle me to be a practitioner within legal institutions that have served as the model for legal systems around the world for many years.[21]

I will have more to say about my time at Harvard Law School later on. For now, I will summarize by noting that I received my JD with honors, also served as an editor of the *Harvard Law Review*, and then began legal practice at Quinn Emanuel in Los Angeles, a large firm that specializes in litigating the interests of major corporations. I started work there as a "summer associate," during my second year of law school, and that is where I met my future wife Elizabeth, who was also a summer associate and studying law at Yale. We got married during our third year of law school, seven months after our first meeting, and then both started work as full-time associates attorneys at Quinn Emanuel in the fall of 2004.

It was only three years before we exited the world of corporate litigation. While the work was lucrative,[22] it could also be soul taxing. I was especially disenchanted with the work I was being asked to do, as an associate attorney at the Miami office of a large international firm, on behalf of a company whose core business model was to make the foreclosure process less costly and more efficient for banks by circumventing property records requirements.[23] The work pitted me directly against the interests of people who had lost their homes or were on the brink of being foreclosed upon. Many of them could not even afford an attorney. The work did not leave me fulfilled and seemed like a misuse of my law degree.

In June 2007, Elizabeth and I opened our own two-lawyer practice in a small, windowless office across the street from the courthouse in downtown Miami. We started with a grand total of two clients—both of whom were pro bono and transferred to us from our prior employers. The first few months were memorably lean, but before long, our phone was ringing off the hook, as the initial years of Beck & Lee's existence coincided with a period of extraordinary demand for a certain type of litigation service in South Florida that not all lawyers were willing to consider, and we were able to provide.

While the Great Recession is typically considered to have started in late 2007,[24] South Florida was already feeling the effects of a slumping real estate market as of late 2006.[25] Easy credit coupled with the traditional lure of Florida property as an investment vehicle had fueled a historic real estate boom beginning in 2005.[26] The boom attracted numerous speculators who saw opportunities to profit off of rapidly escalating prices by "flipping" (*i.e.*, holding for a short-term and then selling) real estate. By late 2006 and early 2007, many of these speculators, sensing the market was overheated and not based on a genuine demand for housing, had started to back away, leading to a substantial decline in prices.[27] The resulting real estate market crash, which was already in progress by the time we opened our firm, led many to seek legal representation.

After being in business for just a few months, our little law firm started to receive many calls and emails from a certain type of prospective client. Such people had signed a contract and paid a down payment, or deposit, to buy a condominium. At the time of the contract (which had typically been executed during the fevered 2004-06 real estate bubble timeframe), the condominium was not even built; this is known in the industry as a "preconstruction" contract, where a portion of the buyer's deposit is used to finance the construction of the building. During the boom, many speculators had signed such contracts, hoping to "flip" them to someone else at a higher price. A singe preconstruction condominium unit contract may have had multiple buyers in succession, each flipping to a subsequent one at increasingly higher prices, before the builders had even finished construction of the actual building. By flipping the contract, each buyer would realize a substantial profit without even having had to take title to the condominium.

But by mid-2007, with the market in decline, many of those who had entered into preconstruction contracts were starting to realize they were not going to find a new buyer to purchase the contract from them. Not only were they not going to make a profit as hoped, but they risked losing the entirety of their preconstruction deposit. And these deposits were not insubstantial—with many new South Florida condominiums priced at a minimum of $500,000 for even the more basic units, the deposit could run at least $100,000 and often much more than that.[28]

Buyers under preconstruction contracts were not only facing a substantial financial hit in the potential loss of their deposits. In some instances, the developers were threatening to sue them if they did not perform on the contract and close title to the condominium. But as the real estate market tumbled into free fall, it became virtually impossible to obtain mortgage financing to close on a condominium. The buyers were in a precarious legal position. They started seeking legal counsel. Almost everyone wanted a contingency arrangement (that is, No Win, No Fee basis), whereby the attorney would be paid for his or her legal services only if successful at recovering any monies.

Due to existing loyalties to their developer, construction or banking industry clients, many South Florida lawyers could not represent these buyers, while numerous others were simply unwilling to, due to the inherent risks for contingency work where the lawyer could not be sure he or she would receive payment. But as a new law office with few cases and no ties to the real estate, construction, or banking industries, Elizabeth and I had ample time, ability, and energy to take on many of these cases. We also had a small nest egg saved up from our few years of working at large law firms that allowed us to advance the legal costs of these lawsuits on behalf of our clients.

In developing a specialized practice providing legal representation to buyers of preconstruction condominiums, we served hundreds of people caught up in the deleterious effects of an unregulated industry.[29] It was a diverse group of clients cutting across geographic and most socioeconomic boundaries. Wealthy investors from around the world bought preconstruction real estate as did individuals of considerably more modest means. Among the many we assisted were police officers, teachers, small business owners, a postal worker, an entertainment promoter, lawyers, doctors, retirees, as well as an internationally renowned jockey. The income from these cases eventually enabled us to offer representation to clients in other under served areas of legal practice, including personal injury, police misconduct, and class action litigation on behalf of plaintiffs. In most of these cases, the client pays nothing, not even covering the legal costs, which we would advance out of pocket. Such costs are a permanent loss for us if we do not recover funds for the client.

By 2015, as Bernie Sanders was campaigning on the unfairness of America's "rigged economy" to packed venues across the country,[30] Elizabeth and I had come to see the legal system as equally rigged in favor of corporations and the wealthy. Alongside its campaign finance jurisprudence elevating the payment of money by corporations to privileged status among forms of "political participation,"[31] the Supreme Court, in recent years, has issued opinion after opinion making it increasingly difficult to hold corporations legally accountable. Nowhere is this trend more apparent than in class action law. Before and since the time Elizabeth and I switched from representing large corporations to bringing claims against them, the Supreme Court has made it ever increasingly difficult—and in many cases, impossible—to make use of one of the most potent legal devices available for redressing injuries on a large scale.

With its roots in the medieval English common-law notion of "group litigation,"[32] the modern American class action began to take shape in 1966. That year, the Advisory Committee on Civil Rules, a policymaking body charged with reviewing and recommending changes to the Federal Rules of Civil Procedure,[33] revised the rule governing class actions to, among other things, allow for the possibility of aggregating the damages claims of numerous claimants or "class members" within a single lawsuit.[34] The revisions were motivated by the desire to craft a "receptive procedural vehicle" for the many civil rights cases being filed in the wake of *Brown v. Board of Education*, as well as to facilitate the enforcement of public policy–driven laws in areas such as securities fraud and antitrust.[35] By allowing for a single lawsuit to pursue the claims of many similarly situated class members through one or several class representatives, the new class action rule defined a powerful procedural mechanism for bringing corporations to account for their misconduct—especially when that misconduct caused separate injuries to many different individuals with little incentive to file a lawsuit singly. The reporter to the Advisory Committee, Benjamin Kaplan, defended the new rule as part of the class action's "historic mission of taking care of the smaller guy."[36] Accordingly, a corporation's total liability measuring into the multiple millions or even billions of dollars, but spread out over many small-dollar individual claims, might be adjudicated in a single proceeding. Before the modern class action, there was no practical way of determining such a liability.

The efficacy of the modern class action procedure is well illustrated by the quickness of the backlash from corporate interests once the potential became apparent. In 1972, just six years after the Advisory Committee drafted the new rule, the corporate defense bar complained to the committee that class actions would lead to "judgments of astronomical size" and amounted to "legalized blackmail" and extraction of "ransom."[37] While, according to my old law professor Arthur Miller (who participated in the process leading to the 1966 amendments), for the two decades following introduction of the new rule class action litigation was allowed to "flourish[] in a rather unencumbered way,"[38] by the 1990s, corporate interests had mobilized and were determined to dismantle it.

As with campaign finance law, these interests accomplished their objectives largely through conservative judicial activism. Beginning with two decisions rejecting class-wide settlements of asbestos-related claims, in recent years, the Supreme Court has handed down a body of case law piling up increasingly weighty stumbling blocks to the successful prosecution of class actions.[39, 40] This line of precedent has culminated in the wholesale eradication of the right to even file class actions for certain types of claims. Unsurprisingly, many of the anti–class action opinions have been signed by the same Justices responsible for the Court's campaign finance jurisprudence placing corporate cash on the highest of pedestals.

In 2011, within a span of just under two months, and four years into our transition from corporate litigators to plaintiff's trial lawyers, the Supreme Court handed down two such opinions. Both dealt body blows to the continued viability of the class action procedure. Both were authored by Justice Scalia (who also joined the majority in *Citizens United* and *McCutcheon*, key campaign finance reform decisions which will be discussed further in Act II).

In *Wal-Mart Stores, Inc. v. Dukes*,[41] the Court overturned an order granting class certification in a nationwide sex discrimination suit against Wal-Mart. The plaintiffs presented evidence of significant pay and promotion differentials between male and female employees, as well as expert analysis demonstrating the existence of a corporate culture encouraging gender bias in employment decisions made throughout the company.[42] This evidence was sufficient for both the trial court and Ninth Circuit Court of Appeals to find the case appropriate for class action status, so that the discrimination claims of some 1.5 million female Wal-Mart employees could be decided in a single proceeding. In reversing the Ninth Circuit, the Supreme Court held that there was insufficient "commonality" for the class to be certified.[43] The heart of the Court's opinion comes in this striking sentence from Justice Scalia: "In a company of Wal–Mart's size and geographical scope, it is quite unbelievable that all managers would exercise their discretion in a common way without some common direction."[44] For the Court, speaking through Scalia, the existence of a common corporate culture shaping employee decision making is unfathomable. In its view, there is only one way for a corporation to induce desired behavior in its employees, and that is via "common direction." Power of suggestion—or just plain brainwashing, for that matter—can apparently play no role. As will be discussed further when I trace the legal development of the American election system, while *Citizens United* famously green-lighted unlimited campaign spending by corporations in its refusal to see political corruption in anything other than quid pro quo arrangements, *Wal-Mart* grants these same corporations a kind of blanket legal immunity with respect to the deleterious effects of any conduct that is not the result of explicit "direction." In the fantasy world spun by the Court, money never corrupts unless it is given directly for a favor, while corporations act only through express directives, never cultural or societal imperatives.

Citizens United and *Wal-Mart* are just two examples of the Supreme Court constructing the legal framework for a corporate oligarchy, based on a picture of human affairs which accords only with the reality that the oligarchs desire to create. *AT&T Mobility LLC v. Concepcion*,[45] decided just two months before *Wal-Mart*, followed this recipe to the letter when it granted corporations a way of avoiding class actions altogether through the vehicle of class action bans in arbitration clauses in contracts. What Justice Scalia's opinion in *Concepcion* fails to advise us, of course, is that the now-widespread use of arbitration clauses in contracts to preclude class actions was "[m]ore than a decade in the making" and "engineered by a Wall Street-led coalition of credit companies and retailers[.]"[46] One of those "engineers" who strategized from "law offices on Park Avenue and in Washington" on ways to shield companies from class actions was a corporate lawyer by the name of John G. Roberts Jr., who went on to become Chief Justice and one of the majority in *Concepcion* (as well as *Citizens United* and *McCutcheon*).[48] All of this seemingly relevant history is omitted from the opinion, where Justice Scalia repeatedly extols the virtues of private arbitration, noting arbitration's potential for "streamlined proceedings and expeditious results."[48]

The problem, however, is that "only a lunatic or a fanatic sues for $30"[49]—all the "streamlined proceedings" in the world are worthless to the small-dollar claimant without the ability to aggregate many small-dollar claims in a class action. A ban on class action litigation, like the one approved by the Supreme Court in *Concepcion*, is therefore nothing less than a ban on pursuing one's legal rights. As a result, in the wake of *Concepcion*, countless Americans—in cases ranging from consumer fraud, antitrust, employment discrimination on the basis of gender and race, and unfair business practices—have found themselves without a legal remedy against their banks, cable companies, credit card companies, phone companies, and employers.[50] That is to say, the corporations' war on class actions, as implemented through their legal representatives including now Chief Justice Roberts, worked to perfection.

I recall reading *Concepcion* on my computer screen the day it was posted to the Supreme Court website and marveling at how the opinion seemed so out of sync with the legal system I had studied in law school. The core premise is that a 1925 statute called the Federal Arbitration Act constitutes such a powerful embrace of enforcing private arbitration agreements—to the letter—so that this federal policy must take precedence over practically any other policy concern that could arise about these types of agreements.[51] But in studying law at Harvard, the "Vatican" of legal scholarship and teaching about the American legal system, I hardly got any sense *at all* that arbitration was such a preeminent feature of our legal system! Our basic courses always taught us cases handed down by courts, not by arbitration panels. As far as I can recall, there was just one course offered on arbitration (which I took in my second year)—International Commercial Arbitration and it dealt with the framework governing the arbitration of complicated international disputes, nothing close to the small-scale arbitrations that *Concepcion* conjures up as a means to do away with class actions. For such a supposedly critical feature of the American justice system and prominent matter of federal policy, arbitration was, curiously, barely discussed during my three years at one of the country's most prestigious law schools. And I don't remember a single question about arbitration appearing on the bar exam in either California or Florida.[52]

The truth, however, is that I, not the *Concepcion* Court, was the one who was out of sync with the realities of the American legal system, by virtue of what nine years at Harvard, including three years at Harvard Law School, had failed to teach me. The Supreme Court's anti–class action jurisprudence is just one in a quiver of arrows shot through the heart of the plaintiff's bar by the dedicated legal representatives of the corporate oligarchy populating courthouses and statehouses. This line of cases has evolved as part and parcel of a wider judicial assault on access to justice, embodied in Supreme Court decisions enabling the use of "summary judgment" as a vehicle to prevent plaintiffs from having their claims decided by juries,[53] alongside cases fabricating a heightened pleading standard in federal court that now routinely slams the courthouse door in the plaintiff's face before the case has even gotten off the ground.[54] To quote my old professor Arthur Miller, the question must be asked, "[I]s our American court system still one in which an aggrieved person, however unsophisticated and under-resourced he may be, can secure a meaningful day in court?"[55]

I believe that for anyone who has tried to represent an unsophisticated and/or under-resourced "aggrieved person" in the modern-day federal legal system, the answer to this question must be a resounding "No!" Having done so for the last ten years, I've lost count of the number of times my client's meritorious lawsuit was thrown out before trial because the court granted a defendant's request for dismissal or summary judgment. The opinions issued by these courts are often baffling, from the vantage point of logic or legal reasoning, and the judges will frequently incorrectly cite or misapply cases to make it appear that the decisions are supported by legal precedent. The defendant is almost always a well-heeled corporation represented by a team of many defense lawyers, often from more than one large law firm.

The practice of law in these circumstances is terribly unsatisfying and unrewarding because it entails the continual frustration of the very purpose of my role as lawyer—to ensure my client obtains his or her day in court and has a fair (if inherently imperfect) chance at obtaining justice. If there is any solace, it is in the fact that the public record now contains at least one admission, by a prominent judge, of what plaintiffs' lawyers have known for some time: that our legal system is decidedly rigged in favor of corporate interests.

On March 28, 2017, the recently retired federal appellate judge Richard Posner, in a keynote address to attendees of an academic conference on antitrust issues at the University of Chicago, pronounced that the U.S. judicial system is "very crappy," mediocre and "highly politicized." [56] Judge Posner laid the blame for this state of affairs on "the ownership of Congress by the rich," what he termed "[t]he real corruption." Observing that the allowance of unlimited campaign spending has made elected representatives "slave[s] to the donors," Judge Posner explained that because federal judges are appointed by these same representatives, cases are decided by "mediocre courts that are highly politicized. And that's what we have now in the Supreme Court: extremely reactionary Supreme Court justices, appointed by Bush mainly."[57]

Judge Posner's striking observations regarding the legal system in which he held court for thirty-six years came as he articulated his view, to a conference of antitrust scholars, that antitrust—the body of law concerned with promoting and protecting competition in the marketplace—is now "dead."[58] Like the demise of antitrust, the death of class actions and access to justice, among other legal mechanisms meant to protect the "smaller guy," can be traced to the political production of mediocre, politicized courts. As far as I know, Judge Posner is the only federal jurist who has publicly acknowledged the reality of our present-day federal courts and that they are the product of, and serve, oligarchic corporate interests. But Posner's words carry special weight: in addition to serving over three decades on the U.S. Court of Appeals for the Seventh Circuit in Chicago (he was appointed by Reagan in 1981), Posner has written over fifty books and more than five hundred articles exercising an enormous impact on legal scholarship, particularly in the fields of antitrust, and law and economics.[59] The *New York Times* has called him the "most dominant" figure in American law in the past half century, noting his "qualities of erratic genius, herculean work ethic and irrepressible ambition."[60] In short, Richard Posner was the cream of the judicial crop.[61]

By late 2015, our experience working within the legal system so aptly described by Judge Posner led Elizabeth and me to become enthusiastic supporters of Bernie Sanders's campaign. While his platform did not directly address the gross bias in our courts, his blunt attacks on the campaign finance system wrought by the Supreme Court hit at the very root of the overwhelming inequity in the federal judicial system.[62] Working to elect Sanders appeared to be the last viable avenue remaining to begin restoring fundamental fairness to our political system— and by extension, our legal system, where trying to represent the "small guy" has turned into an increasingly frustrating and fruitless endeavor.

Eight years of practicing law under the Obama administration had taught us not to expect any solutions from mainstream Democratic Party politicians. While Obama inherited the Great Recession from George W. Bush, his administration failed to make "even a single arrest or prosecution of any senior Wall Street banker for the systemic fraud that precipitated the 2008 financial crisis[.]"[63] Many of our clients had been direct victims of this crisis, losing their retirement investments or even their homes as a consequence of criminal malfeasance in the banking industry. Aside from the fact that the Obama administration's inaction will ensure that another, similar crisis happens again, it set the general tone for the continuation of a legal system which is rigged to guarantee that corporate interests will escape accountability time and again.

While *Citizens United* was the product of, to quote Judge Posner, five "extremely reactionary Supreme Court justices" appointed by Republican presidents (Chief Justice Roberts and Justices Kennedy, Scalia, Alito, and Thomas), the Obama administration failed to prioritize the making of appointments to the federal bench—the one branch of government which has the power to neutralize the deleterious effects of *Citizens United*, *i.e.*, by overruling the case. To the contrary, Obama left office with over one hundred judicial vacancies unfilled—nearly double what he inherited from his predecessor.[64] Obama's failure on judicial appointments is perhaps best encapsulated by the fact that he is the only president in U.S. history who proved to be incapable of filling a vacancy on the Supreme Court.[65]

Obama's lack of appreciation for the serious problems inherent in our "very crappy" judicial system seemed characteristic of the Democratic Party's general attitude. For example, while the class action–killing opinions, *Concepcion* and *Wal-Mart*, were issued in 2011 by the same cabal of "extremely reactionary" Justices responsible for *Citizens United*, unlike the latter, the class action–killing opinions turned on issues of statutory interpretation, not constitutional law. Accordingly—and unlike *Citizens United*—the negative effects of these ill-conceived decisions may be reversed by acts of Congress. Nonetheless, congressional Democrats (who controlled both the House and Senate up until 2012) made only half-hearted efforts to pass such legislation, culminating in the proposed Arbitration Fairness Act of 2011. The bill, which would have made arbitration clauses unenforceable with respect to most types of class actions, never even made it out of the Senate Judiciary Committee for a full vote.[66] Given the lackluster Democratic response to the judicial evisceration of individual rights vis-a-vis corporations, it was not hard to conclude that the mainstream wing of the Democratic Party is beholden to the same corporate interests motivating the Republican Justices who stripped away these rights to begin with.

Like many, Elizabeth and I initially supported Bernie Sanders by opening our wallets to his campaign.[67] Before long, Elizabeth was spending much of her time volunteering—attending organizational meetings in Miami including local "Bernstorms,"[68] helping with crowd control at a rally featuring Sanders, as well as phone banking and "text banking" to reach voters. Our little law office became a phone banking outpost, with volunteers crammed around the conference table, sometimes making calls late into the evening. Bernie posters and other paraphernalia filled the walls.[69]

At some point, it began to feel to me that our efforts—which were almost entirely Elizabeth's, as she enthusiastically embraced the urgency of spreading Sanders's campaign platform to the public—were frustratingly inefficient. One person can only reach so many voters—that is why, indeed, that the spending of money on mass media messaging has become the very fulcrum of our electoral politics. The "Magna Carta"[70] setting forth corporations' powerful rights vis-a-vis the U.S. political system, *Citizens United*, arose in the context of a corporation's desire to produce a movie critical of Hillary Clinton and advertise it on TV during the 2008 Democratic primaries. Needless to say, it was not a case about phone banks.

When the Supreme Court decided *Citizens United* it went out of its way[71] to rule that corporations cannot be stopped from making unlimited, independent expenditures on political campaigns.[72] In removing any limitations on what it referred to as "corporate speech,"[73] the Supreme Court laid the vital groundwork for what has become known as the Super PAC: political fundraising committees which can raise unlimited amounts of cash from corporations (as well as unions, associations, and individuals) for independent expenditures on campaigns.[74] Super PACs provided formidable support to Hillary Clinton's candidacy in 2016, with the largest, Priorities USA Action, taking in over $175 million and spending over $161 million to advance Clinton's candidacy.[75] By contrast, the largest Super PAC supporting Bernie Sanders (whose campaign repeatedly expressly attacked the very concept of Super PACs), National Nurses United for Patient Protection, raised $8.1 million.[76]

Professor Miller has called the best plaintiff's lawyers "incredibly inventive, talented, and tenacious—some might call them stubborn" people who "know how to find the back doors."[77] Elizabeth and I have always strived for this ideal in our practice. When it came to helping Bernie, we felt there might be a "back door" within *Citizens United* itself.

On February 22, 2016, Elizabeth and I became the directors of a new Super PAC.[78] The process of coming to control a vehicle that is permitted, by law, to inject unlimited amounts of money into U.S. elections was incredibly simple from a legal perspective. All we had to do was fill out a five-page form titled Statement of Organization ("FEC Form 1") on the Federal Election Commission website.[79] We initially chose the name "Do the Right Thing," in reference to Spike Lee having recently come out in support of Sanders.[80] Later, we changed it to JamPAC.[81]

The basic concept was this. Deploy the Super PAC not as a vehicle for funneling corporate dollars into mass media messaging for political campaigns favoring corporate interests, but as a network for collecting small-dollar donations from individuals, like the average Sanders donation, and then using the funds to advance progressive campaigns. At the same time, we hoped to deploy new forms and modalities of communication promoting norms of collaboration rather than manipulation. From a legal standpoint at least, the concept had the advantage of being at least a practical response to *Citizens United*;

rather than simply criticizing the decision as ill-reasoned and/ or ill-conceived and demanding it be overruled (highly unlikely anytime soon) or nullified via constitutional amendment (even more unlikely), we might at least try to harness some of the very potential unleashed by the Supreme Court's jurisprudence into a movement based, in large part, on reforming the campaign finance system. As I wrote about eight weeks after starting JamPAC, "perhaps the system can be hacked, and the hack can make the system better."[82]

Right off the bat, however, the implementation of this vision of a "hack" had a hurdle to overcome. Without access to spigots of corporate cash like the Super PACs supporting the Clinton campaign, we would have to find a way to have impact on the race on a very limited budget. While Elizabeth and I seeded JamPAC with twenty thousand dollars of our own savings, that could only go so far, and time was short. This meant, for example, that while the major Super PACs had ready access to legions of high-priced consultants to guide them on critical issues, our consultants were friends who graciously responded to our requests.[83]

After some quick telephone calls and brainstorming sessions, we settled on a strategy of producing and disseminating pro–Bernie Sanders messaging over the Internet, with the goal of launching one or more "viral videos." At the time, various anti-Sanders narratives were emerging in the mainstream media, which we knew to be untrue given our experiences on the ground in South Florida and through social media.[84] Chief among these were notions that "Black Voters Don't Feel the Bern"[85] and that Latinos had never been a core part of Bernie's constituency.[86] Knowing how laughably absurd such statements were in light of what we knew about the appeal of his campaign in our local and social media communities, we felt that they might easily be disproved through short videos, that could be produced quickly, at low cost, and then disseminated through social media channels.

Fortunately, we were able to persuade my old friend from college, Dan DeVivo, to serve as JamPAC's creative director. Dan, an independent filmmaker who has produced and directed two award-winning documentaries on the immigration debate,[87] put together JamPAC's first video himself[88] and then connected us with a network of independent filmmakers who were more than happy to lend their considerable talents in aid of Sanders.[89] The collective fruits of their labor can be viewed on JamPAC's YouTube channel.[90] Of the eight pro-Sanders videos JamPAC ended up producing,[91] five featured Latino supporters and included what we believe to be the first Spanish-language videos promoting his campaign.[92]

The anemic number of views on JamPAC's YouTube page bears testament to our failure to attain "viral" status on any of the videos. Most of the time, we worked to disseminate the videos through social media, including through paid Facebook "boosts" as permitted by our modest budget. Perhaps we didn't try hard enough, or perhaps the content of our videos wasn't viral-worthy, but at least one of our strategies was doomed to failure from the get-go: our attempt to get the mainstream media's attention for what JamPAC was trying to accomplish.[93]

For the same reason they were opposed to Sanders's candidacy, as will be discussed in detail in Act I, the interests served by the mainstream media were opposed to the concept of drawing any attention to JamPAC, its mission, or its implementation. Perhaps we were naive for even trying to attract its attention, or perhaps we overestimated our own ability to draw its interest given that Elizabeth had had a well-publicized dispute with Donald Trump in late July 2015 arising out of one of our pieces of condominium deposit litigation.[94] In any event, the mainstream media interest in what JamPAC was doing was practically nonexistent.[95] Determined, we retained the services of a public relations specialist, Charles Jones, who had previously worked with us in our legal practice. A veteran local TV news reporter with many industry contacts, Charles wrote us an ominous memorandum on March 17, 2016:

> I have been glued to the national media coverage for the past month. The coverage is shifting far away from being balanced. This is what I see:
>
> 1. The media focus changes by the day. What's hot news one day could be completely ignored the next.
> 2. The media is transfixed on anything related to Donald Trump. I mean anything.
> 3. The media is transfixed on [the] implosion of the GOP.
> 4. The media is building up for the GOP Convention in Cleveland. They want BLOOD . . .
> 5. The media is already convinced Clinton will get the party nomination, no matter what.
> 6. Every single campaign is complaining that their core campaign messages are not getting through via the national press. No one is covering real issues. Just the daily Trump report about how he's "winning or losing."
> 7. The media is completely ignoring all traditional ground and grassroots campaigns, unless it is an attempt to dismantle the Trump campaign.
> 8. The media does not care about debating the issues between Clinton and Sanders.
> 9. The media is completely ignoring the voice of millennials, minorities, women, etc. The focus is on angry white men: who they are going to support, what are they going to do with Trump, who else could lead them.

10. The media MIGHT come around once we are down to two (or three) candidates, unless there is a complete circus.

At this point, you can't rely on the media to focus on anything related to the campaign, unless it relates [to] Trump. What needs to happen now with the Super PAC is to focus on touching people directly face-to-face or through social media, email blasts, special events, etc. I could position Elizabeth as a talking head for the talk shows since they are actively looking for people who can speak about Trump, the GOP, and breaking developments in the major campaigns. . . . But it will take some time.[96]

Charles may have identified a litany of factors making the task we had set out for JamPAC nigh on impossible. At the same time, as we struggled to gain any bit of traction for the messages we so desperately wanted to reach the public, Dan De-Vivo reminded me to think of JamPAC as an "experiment." This perspective made me less prone to thinking in terms of successes and failures, and more open to appreciating whatever directions, however unexpected, toward which JamPAC might lead us.

Three days after Charles presented his ominous view of the media landscape, we encountered a twist in the road when Niko House walked into our conference room. An army veteran and political science major at the University of North Carolina at Chapel Hill, Niko had been a prominent student organizer for the Sanders campaign.[97] His enthusiastic support of Sanders had been featured in campaign coverage appearing in, among other places, the *New York Times*[98] and *McClatchy*.[99] By March, however, Niko was speaking out about his belief that Hillary Clinton loyalists had infiltrated the Sanders campaign in North Carolina, and he was making videos documenting his beliefs and posting them to Facebook and YouTube.[100] Jam-PAC's director of social media, Danielle Underhill, came across these videos and passed them to Dan. Dan called Niko, who happened to be visiting his brother in Miami and had been talking to a couple of independent journalists about what he had seen in North Carolina. We invited him to our office after Dan told us Niko was looking for a place where he could hold a press conference.

By the time we met Niko on March 20, 2016, the media narrative that the Democratic nomination had effectively been decided was starting to rigidify—even though there were 2020 of 4051 pledged delegates still up for grabs in the remaining three months of primaries and caucuses.[101] Phrases like "insurmountable lead" had begun to filter into the media ether, principally owing to Clinton's wide margins of victory in southern states such as Alabama, Mississippi, Louisiana, and North and South Carolina.[102] It was a restless and uncertain time to be a Sanders supporter. And here was Niko, a bright and ambitious volunteer organizer, sitting at our conference table and methodically explaining to two independent journalists on the phone how he had witnessed, with his own eyes, the infiltration of the Sanders campaign structure in North Carolina by a known Clinton loyalist. According to Niko, a Clinton acolyte had managed to become appointed as the campaign's state director and then engaged in acts of sabotage by stymieing the campaign from engaging in organizational opportunities and receiving key endorsements.[103] And Niko said the infiltration wasn't isolated—his own investigation had suggested there were other instances of infiltration of Sanders campaign offices in South Carolina and Wisconsin. He was personally convinced it was widespread enough in North Carolina to have "destroyed" Sanders's chances there.

Reports that there might be infiltration afoot with the Sanders campaign did not originate with Niko. In late December 2015, an unnamed advisor to the campaign was quoted as suggesting that the campaign's national data director, Josh Uretsky—who was fired three months into the job for accessing Clinton's confidential voter data from the DNC database[104]—was a DNC plant, whose actions allowed the DNC to cut off the Sanders's campaign access to voter data.[105] Niko's statement in our office, however, was singularly personal and poignant. After the press conference, I asked Niko whether in the event Sanders went on to lose the nomination, he would put the blame on the infiltration he had seen in North Carolina and uncovered elsewhere. But Niko wasn't ready to contemplate the possibility of Bernie not winning. "I'm not going to let Bernie Sanders lose this nomination," he said. "This is too important. I've just seen too much." Tears welled in Niko's eyes momentarily, and then he excitedly launched into praise for Sanders's platform on issues of race. Niko told us that if necessary, he was determined to do everything he could to convince Sanders to take legal action based on the events he had witnessed.[106]

Like Niko, at the time, we still had faith that Bernie could still pull off a victory, however "insurmountable" the odds were purported to be by this point. As for Niko's investigation, we thought it might make a compelling subject for a JamPAC video series with potential significance even beyond the 2016 presidential contest. Dan had a trailer edited, and we established a crowdfunding page.[107] While obsessively following the remaining primary contests, I ruminated for a bit on possible legal theories based on alleged infiltration of the Sanders campaign by Clinton loyalists. After searching around, I found a helpful legal treatise on federal election law crimes on the Justice Department website[108] and gave a copy to Niko (who had served as a paralegal in the Army) to get his thoughts.

It wasn't until June 15, 2016 (which happened to be the day after the last primary, in the District of Columbia) that I saw a legal pathway begin to take shape. By then, there had been widespread reports of irregularities at the polls, including in Arizona,[109] California,[110] New York,[111] and Puerto Rico,[112] among other places.[113] The concept of this being a "rigged" election had already started to germinate in discussions among Sanders's supporters.[114] But on that day in particular, a publicly accessible WordPress blog was established under the name "Guccifer 2.0,"[115] who took credit for having hacked the DNC's servers,[116] and released a series of DNC documents. Among them was a memorandum addressed to the Democratic National Committee, and dated May 26, 2015 (the "May 26 Memo").

Upon reading through the May 26 Memo for the first time, it struck me as the kind of "hot document" I was trained to spot as a first-year lawyer, when I was tasked with reviewing the copious email files of a group of executives at a large San Diego software company being sued for securities fraud.[117] As part of that assignment, I had to "flag" any emails or documents which might be used to show that the company's leadership had knowledge that its accountants were improperly booking and inflating its publicly reported revenues.[118] From a litigation perspective, such pieces of evidence are especially valuable given the well-known difficulty of proving the *scienter* element for claims sounding in fraud.

The May 26 Memo, however, constituted not just direct evidence of knowledge that the nominating process was being rigged for Hillary Clinton, but itself was a kind of blueprint for accomplishing the rigging. We will look at this and other internal DNC documents in closer detail in Act I, but to summarize, even before Bernie Sanders had announced his candidacy, this *single memorandum*—which just happened to be one of the documents released by Guccifer 2.0 on June 15—explicitly laid out how the DNC would work directly with the mainstream media to advance Clinton through the nomination process, via a tripartite strategy of what the author categorized as: (1) Reporter Outreach ("stories with no fingerprints"); (2) Releases and Social Media; and (3) Bracketing Events. In Act I, we will further explore the true meaning of these strategic concepts, which worked to ensure that the nomination would go to Hillary Clinton. Based on my professional experience as a business litigator, it seemed like the equivalent of a report to a corporation's leadership explaining how the company should go about falsifying its sales data.

Clear and direct evidence of fraud like the May 26 Memo may be rare, but it is not sufficient to bring a legal claim in court. That requires a plaintiff in addition to a viable cause of action. The plaintiff must have a sufficient stake in the matter to pursue a claim—what the law calls "standing." And there must be an actionable legal theory—it is not enough to identify something as "wrong" or "illegal," but the conduct in question must be capable of being described in terms of a recognized category of legal claims.[119]

Perhaps it was due to my own background in civil litigation, having first dealt with the possibility of "smoking gun" documents in the context of a massive securities fraud case, but what flashed in my mind upon considering the questions of plaintiffs and legal theory was an analogy to the typical securities fraud class action. In such cases, the plaintiffs are the company's shareholders—those who are injured by the company's misrepresentations because they have participated in the market for the company's stock, which they purchased at an inflated price. But the DNC, while it is a corporation, doesn't sell stock. It functions in the political market. And in the political market, as the Supreme Court has ensured through its holding in *Citizens*

United, the most privileged form of participation is the giving of money to political campaigns.

Analogy aside, from the vantage point of bringing a legally viable case based on the rigged primaries, it seemed that the best candidates to serve as plaintiffs were those who participated in the process as political donors. Indeed, the law has always recognized the loss of money as one of the "classic" instances giving rise to legal standing.[120] The analogy to securities fraud also suggested general causes of action to assert. A typical securities fraud case will plead claims based on material misrepresentations or omissions of the company. The plaintiff shareholders can also plead claims for breach of fiduciary duty against the company's officers and directors.

I believe that the conduct of the DNC and its then Chair, Debbie Wasserman Schultz, can readily be described according to these legal claims. By the time Guccifer 2.0 published the May 26 Memo, the DNC and Wasserman Schultz had already proclaimed their neutrality multiple times in the mainstream press.[121] Moreover, the Democratic Party's own Charter and Bylaws (which I was able to locate on the Internet without too much trouble) governed the DNC and explicitly required it (and its officers and staff) to exercise and maintain "impartiality and evenhandedness" during the nominating process. We will examine the meaning of the Charter and Bylaws in further detail in Acts I and II. Suffice it to say, the mandate to act in a "fair and evenhanded" manner with respect to the primaries is rather explicit, and it had been acknowledged by DNC officers publicly with respect to events in the 2016 primaries. By claiming it was acting in a neutral manner, the DNC was both painting a false picture and hiding the truth of the matter: that the organization was determinedly working to advance Hillary Clinton to the nomination from before the get-go. The May 26 Memo confirmed that.

Every claim based on fraud or misrepresentation must satisfy the element of injury. In this case, there was tangible injury in the form of over two hundred million dollars paid by donors to the Bernie Sanders campaign. Many of these donors paid small amounts—the "twenty-seven dollar donation" of Sanders's famous rallying cry[122]—which made the case tailor-made for a class action. And I firmly believe these donors have one very important thing in common: they never would have paid that money had they known the truth of just how rigged our political system is.

I firmly believe this because of the experience Elizabeth and I had as Bernie donors and supporters. Before the 2016 election, we believed what we had been taught in school about the fundamental democratic character of America's political institutions. Before the light began to trickle in with Niko's visit to our office along with the reports of rigging in the primaries, and then a whole bright ray of light with the release of documents by Guccifer 2.0 and WikiLeaks, our faith in the essential democratic character of America's political institutions had fueled our creation of JamPAC, its work in support of Sanders, and our own financial contributions to his campaign. When we began to learn just how far the DNC had gone to ensure Clinton would be the nominee, Elizabeth and I felt like victims of a massive Ponzi scheme.[123]

And we would learn in due course that we were not alone—not by a long shot. When Elizabeth posted to the JamPAC Facebook page and website[124] that Beck & Lee was conducting an investigation of possible legal claims against the DNC for rigging the primaries, the response was overwhelming. Our office became inundated with thousands of messages, emails, and calls from people around the country who supported Bernie Sanders and felt that the primary was a sham.[125] Many of them had given money to the campaign, and when we spoke or emailed with them, they sounded no different from the typical victim of fraud desperately seeking a legal remedy. The group of folks who consulted with us wanting to sue the DNC was a real cross section of the country. They hailed from every state, as well as from diverse socioeconomic backgrounds. Among those who contacted us were lawyers and doctors who had donated the maximum $2700 each to the campaign alongside folks on fixed incomes who had reached into their retirement accounts for a few hundred dollars, to the average donor of twenty-seven dollars— as well as homeless people who had reached into their pockets for a few dollars.[126] All of them had believed in American democracy, and in the real possibility of Sanders becoming president. And all of them were mistaken.

We discussed the possibility of filing a case against the DNC with our trusted colleagues, Tony Hernandez and Cullin O'Brien.[127] Once they came on board as co-counsel, we circulated contingency class action retainer agreements[128] to multitudes of folks who were contacting us at all hours of the day wanting to hire our firms to pursue legal action against the DNC. On June 28, 2016, *Carol Wilding et al. v. DNC Services Corporation d/b/a Democratic National Committee; and Deborah "Debbie" Wasserman Schultz*, Case No. 16-cv-61511-WJZ (S.D. Fla.) (often referred to as the "DNC Fraud Lawsuit"[129]) was filed in the U.S. District Court for the Southern District of Florida.[130] The Complaint was brought in the names of 120 representative plaintiffs[131]—our lead or "first-named" plaintiff, Carol Wilding, also just happened to live in Broward County—and against the DNC and its chair, and alleged claims for fraud, negligent misrepresentation, statutory unlawful trade practices, unjust enrichment, breach of fiduciary duty, and negligence.[132] It strives to succinctly explain how the DNC and Wasserman Schultz violated the charter commitment to neutrality in the presidential nominating process based on the facts as known at the time. Attached to the Complaint as Exhibit 1 is the May 26 Memo.[133]

The case has received very little attention in the mainstream media,[134] and this was especially true in the early going.[135] But from the outset, and as an offshoot of JamPAC's original commitment to cultivating social media forms of communication, there has been an active social media presence centered around the lawsuit, its objectives, and related issues, with key nodal points including the lawsuit's Facebook and Twitter accounts, as well as our own personal accounts.[136]

To find the most striking visible manifestation of the lawsuit's social media presence, one might look to the events of July 1, 2016. On that afternoon, the Complaint and summons were delivered at the DNC's headquarters in Washington, D.C., by a young man named Shawn Lucas, who was hired by One Source Process, Inc. ("One Source"), the Washington, D.C., legal services company we retained to serve the initial process.[137] While the case had only been filed with the court three days earlier, there was already burgeoning interest in the lawsuit on social media, and Elizabeth came up with the idea of live-streaming the serving of process on Facebook in order to enable our clients and any other potential class members and interested members of the public to witness the moment when the DNC and Wasserman Schultz would become subject to the jurisdiction of the court. As such, hundreds of viewers tuned in live to watch JamPAC filmmaker Ricardo Villalba record Shawn as he entered the imposing DNC building, legal papers in hand.[138]

Those who have watched the video, whether live or among the almost million who have viewed it since, witnessed Ricardo tell his audience that the DNC was about to be served with legal papers. Ricardo then walks across the street and meets Shawn outside the headquarters. They enter together. Shawn tells the guard at the security desk that they have legal papers to serve. The guard takes Shawn's ID card and proceeds to enter data into a computer. At this point, while waiting for the guard to complete the check-in process, Ricardo and Shawn have an animated discussion, where both express how happy they are about serving the DNC. Ricardo says that, "We're very excited because I feel like . . . we're gonna push the Democratic Party to . . ." And Shawn completes the sentence with "do the right thing."

After a few minutes, three additional security guards approach the desk. One asks Ricardo if he is taking video; Ricardo responds that he is live-streaming to Facebook. She requests that he stop recording. Another guard, an older male, approaches, points directly at Ricardo while exclaiming, "I need you to turn that off!" When Ricardo questions why, the guard circles out from behind the desk and gets right next to Shawn and Ricardo. "We don't allow cameras in this building," he tells them. A heated debate ensues, and eventually Shawn and Ricardo are told that they have to get preapproval from "the proper people" in order to film on the premises. At this point, Ricardo notes that there are now over three hundred viewers watching live on Facebook. He lets the audience know that he has to stop live-streaming because they must go through the necessary procedures. He apologizes, and the camera shuts off.

When the live-stream resumes, the camera is angled up at the security desk; Ricardo appears to be in a seated position while filming surreptitiously. Shawn informs the audience that, "contact has been made and there is someone on the way down to receive us." While they wait, Shawn and Ricardo engage in quiet discussion. Shawn tells Ricardo that he volunteered to be the process server for One Source in this case. Doing this job, Shawn says, is like his "birthday, Christmas, and Canada Day all coming together at the same time."

Eventually, a woman emerges from the vestibule visible behind the security desk; she turns in their direction and Shawn and Ricardo rise to greet her. Shawn shakes her hand and she introduces herself as "Becca," "with the DNC upstairs." Shawn proceeds to hand Becca separate packages for the DNC and Wasserman Schultz with the words, "You guys have been served . . . See you in court." Becca takes them, responding "Perfect" and "Ok," and walks back to the vestibule.

Once outside, Shawn and Ricardo are plainly jubilant. "That was probably the most gratifying thing I've ever done," says Shawn. "Democracy has prevailed today." The sentiments are echoed in many viewer Facebook comments from that day, for example:

> "HAPPY 4th . . . A chance for Democracy!!!";
> "Omgomgomgomg! POWER TO THE PEOPLE BERNERS";
> "Let's hope something good comes out of this."[139]

In the practice of litigation, service of process is typically a routine matter, especially when the recipient is a large organization. Before this case, I couldn't recall a time when a large corporate defendant had made service an issue in court. The great enthusiasm exhibited by the public in witnessing Shawn and Ricardo serve the DNC, and their own enthusiasm in carrying out this otherwise mundane legal task, made me realize that this lawsuit was going to be like no other.

Still, all of us on the plaintiffs' legal team were surprised when, on July 22, 2016, the defendants filed a motion to dismiss the case based on insufficient process—a request making the contention that Shawn had not served the correct DNC employee.[140] Not only are such motions exceedingly rare, but we had something almost never available with respect to the issue of service—that is, video evidence which showed unequivocally that the DNC had sent an employee named "Becca" down to receive the legal papers from Shawn, who told her he had legal papers for both defendants, whereupon Becca accepted them, saying "Perfect." There was no mention from Becca that she was unauthorized to accept legal service on behalf of the DNC, or Wasserman Schultz. Nonetheless, the defendants filed a memorandum arguing that Becca, whose full name is Rebecca Herries, was a mere "special assistant" and was never authorized to receive legal papers. It attached an affidavit from Herries acknowledging that she had received the papers from "two men" who "were refusing to leave," but because it was "the Friday right before the Fourth of July weekend," there was no one in the office with actual authority to accept the papers.[141]

The legal team conferred and began to prepare our response.[142] In addition to making the Court aware of the video evidence, which was posted on Facebook and YouTube, Cullin suggested we obtain a sworn declaration from the process server. We were in the process of drafting one up for Shawn's review when the unthinkable happened.

I got news of Shawn Lucas's death on August 3, 2016. It first came through social media; I bolted up from my chair and yelled in the direction of Elizabeth's office, "Someone's telling me the DNC process server is dead!" After some loud, rapid discussion, Elizabeth found the number for One Source in D.C. and placed a call. The terrible news was true: a shaken Brandon Yoshimura, the owner of One Source who had given Shawn the DNC job, confirmed that Shawn had been found dead the day before. At the time, with no other details available, it seemed impossible that the young man whose contagious enthusiasm lit up our Facebook and YouTube pages just a month earlier was suddenly no longer with us.

Further clouding the mood was the fact that on the day we received news that Shawn was dead, there was already an atmosphere of considerable tension surrounding the DNC Fraud Lawsuit—outside of the degree which might be considered "normal" for major litigation. Just twenty-four days earlier, the DNC's voter expansion data director, twenty-seven-year-old Seth Rich, had been shot dead on the street outside his D.C. apartment.[143] While Rich's murder was initially characterized by the police as a "botched robbery" (even though his possessions, including a wallet, wristwatch, and phone, were left on his body), there was almost immediate speculation that Rich had been responsible for leaking the internal DNC emails published by WikiLeaks, and that he had been assassinated as a result.[144] (Over 18 months later, Rich's murder remains unsolved—although the mainstream media has clung stubbornly to the official narrative that he died in a mugging gone wrong. At the same time, evidence suggesting Rich was connected to the documents published by WikiLeaks, as well as unanswered questions pertaining to this evidence, have mounted.[145])

Within a day of Shawn's death, Elizabeth was able to obtain a police report from the D.C. Metropolitan Police Department, which indicated that Shawn's girlfriend had found him lying unconscious on his bathroom floor on August 2, shortly after 7 p.m.[146] We filed it with the court,[147] along with a legal memorandum opposing the defendants' motion to dismiss the case.[148] In our opposition memorandum, we advised the court of the video taken on July 1, which showed Shawn handing the legal papers to the DNC staffer sent downstairs to receive them. Now that Shawn was no longer alive and therefore obviously unable to provide his own sworn testimony about what transpired, the video would have to suffice as evidence of proper service. Upon receiving the opposition papers, which contained the notice of our process server's sudden death, Judge William S. Zloch promptly issued an order scheduling an evidentiary hearing.[149]

Judge Zloch set the hearing for August 23, 2016, at 11 a.m. in his courtroom in Fort Lauderdale. He advised the parties to "be prepared to present testimony and/or physical evidence" regarding the defendants' motion to dismiss for failure to make proper service.[150] That left us with two weeks to gather all the evidence we needed and make arrangements for any necessary witnesses. We had the video, of course, but we also required witness testimony to authenticate the video.[151] Ricardo Villalba was understandably nervous in the wake of Shawn's death but agreed to come down from D.C. for the hearing. Lead named plaintiff Carol Wilding, a retired flight attendant who lived nearby and had watched the service of process on live-stream while it was happening, also agreed to testify if necessary. In addition, we wanted to present any evidence to rebut the DNC's contention that Rebecca Herries was just a lowly "assistant" not authorized to receive legal papers; by that time of course, WikiLeaks had published a significant quantity of internal DNC emails,[152] which our legal team began to scour.

A hearing on the technical issue of proper service is not generally the type of legal proceeding one would expect to pack in the galleries, but this case was an exception. Judge Zloch's small courtroom became crammed with riveted spectators, who watched each side make their presentations. Cullin, who is the most accomplished and versatile courtroom lawyer on our team,[153] led the charge for the plaintiffs. A large chunk of the nearly two-hour hearing was spent playing the video and then eliciting testimony from Ricardo on the relevant events. The defendants' lead attorney, Bruce Spiva, spent no time attacking the admissibility of the video or Ricardo's testimony, although on cross-examination, he tried to raise eyebrows about the fact that Ricardo filmed the event surreptitiously after the DNC's guards had ordered him to stop.[154] On re-direct, Ricardo gave

the following response to Spiva's insinuation he had done something wrong by live-streaming that day:

> As a filmmaker, I believe that it was necessary to document this
> event, not just for me, but also for the audience that we have.
> Prior to tuning out the live-streaming, we had over three hun-
> dred viewers, and I needed to bring closures to them.
>   At the same time, Mr. Lucas and I had a conversation. The
> building, the DNC building, has several cameras. They video-
> tape us going into the building. They videotape us approaching
> the building. So there's a lot of cameras in the building as well.
> So I felt that it was necessary for us to continue videotaping. I
> didn't see any signs saying that I couldn't videotape.
>   When I first walked in, none of the officers—the first secu-
> rity officer saw me videotaping. They didn't say nothing. This
> happened after the other supervisors came out. The reason why
> I couldn't videotape, I felt it wasn't reading law or reading rule.
> I felt they were just making things up, and that's the reason why
> they asked me to stop.[155]

Spiva's main complaint at the hearing was a technical one:
even though the video clearly depicted Herries accepting legal
papers on behalf of the DNC and Wasserman Schultz from
Shawn (after he had advised the security desk exactly what
he was there to do), she was just a "low level employee" who
was never "authorized" to receive them.[156] In response, Cullin
pointed out that the defendants hadn't even bothered to bring
Herries to the hearing to testify, and that the declaration she
submitted with the motion to dismiss contained material con-
tradictions with the video.[157] He also disputed the idea that she
was just a "low level" employee,[158] proffering an email from
WikiLeaks showing her title to be "Special Assistant to the
CEO Democratic National Committee" in which she invited

the entire DNC staff to an afternoon meeting in the "Wasserman Conference Room."[159]

Observing the proceedings from plaintiffs' counsel table, I sensed a tense but solemn atmosphere in the room which belied the banality of the precise legal issue being addressed. During the hearing itself, Judge Zloch, who stoically oversaw the proceedings from the bench, commented that this was a case of "magnitude."[160] Many, if not most, of the spectators either considered themselves to be proposed class members or supported Sanders in ways other than donating money, and the nomination of Hillary Clinton had formally occurred just one month earlier in Philadelphia.[161] That and the sudden resignation of Wasserman Schultz as DNC chair on the eve of the convention were still fresh in their minds.[162] A number approached us before the hearing, as well as during breaks and afterward, thanking us for taking on the case. Their demeanor was uniformly grave, even sad, but focused on the proceedings at hand. Joe Kreps, a senior advisor to law professor Tim Canova's unsuccessful grassroots campaign to unseat Wasserman Schultz from Congress, shook my hand while looking especially glum.

Eight months later, I was back in Judge Zloch's courtroom. The service of process issue having been resolved,[163] I was again seated at the plaintiffs' counsel table, watching the DNC's counsel make new arguments for dismissing the case. The court had scheduled the hearing in response to the defendants' second motion to dismiss complaint,[164] which proffered a whole new slew of grounds for why Judge Zloch should throw out the case without even getting to the discovery phase, i.e., the process by which litigants accumulate potential evidence through such discovery tools as document requests and depositions. Among them was the contention that courts should not intrude in cases involving mere "political promises"; the defendants compared the promise of neutrality in the Democratic the Party's Charter to George H. W. Bush's notorious broken campaign promise of "Read my lips: no new taxes," arguing that if Sanders's donors have standing to bring suit, so too would have Bush's donors.[165] Spiva has been going over this line of reasoning with Judge Zloch, warning the Court that it should not "wade into the political thicket."[166] Now the judge alluded to the example of Bush, previously argued by the defendants in their moving papers:

> THE COURT: Is there a difference between a campaign promise made by a political candidate and a promise that pertains to the integrity of the primary process itself?
>
> In other words, President George H. W. Bush's –
>
> MR. SPIVA: "Read my lips."
>
> THE COURT: — promise—"read my lips, no new taxes," and then he raised taxes. Well he could not be sued for raising taxes. But with respect to the DNC charter, Article V, Section 4, is there a difference between the two?
>
> MR: SPIVA: Not one—there's obviously a difference in degree. I think your Honor—I'm not gonna—I don't want to overreach and say that there's no difference. But I don't think there's a difference that's material in terms of how the Court should decide the question before it in terms of standing, in that this, again, goes to how the party runs itself, how it decides who it's going to associate with, how it decides how it's going to choose its standard bearer ultimately. In case after case, from *O'Brien, to Wymbs*, to *Wisconsin v. LaFollette, Cousins v. Wigoda,*

the Supreme Court and other courts have affirmed the party's right to make that determination. Those are internal issues that the party gets to decide basically without interference from the courts.

And the fact that money has—I know that my distinguished colleague on the other side has several times said that, Well, money makes this different, and it really doesn't in this context. You know, again, if you had a charity where somebody said, Hey, I'm gonna take this money and use it for a specific purpose, X, and they pocketed it and stole the money, of course that's different. But here, where you have a party that's saying, We're gonna, you know, choose our standard bearer, and we're gonna follow these general rules of the road, which we are voluntarily deciding, we could have — and we could have voluntarily decided that, **Look, we're gonna go into back rooms like they used to and smoke cigars and pick the candidate that way. That's not the way it was done. But they could have. And that would have also been their right,** and it would drag the Court well into party politics, internal party politics to answer those questions.[167]

In his response to Judge Zloch's question, loaded with the image of Tammany Hall–esque figures smoking cigars, Spiva only confirmed what we, our clients, and so many of Sanders's supporters have felt in our guts for months—that the DNC's obligation to be neutral is a sham, making the primaries a sham as well. To hear the DNC's lawyer admit this fact in open court was still shocking though. When it was my turn to speak, I rose and told Judge Zloch that if what Spiva has said "is true, then I think it's a really sad day for democracy in this country. Because what essentially the DNC has now stated in a court of law is that it believes that there is no enforceable obligation to run the primary elections of this country's democracy in a fair and impartial manner."[168]

One does not typically see lawyers defending multi million-dollar corporations from fraud claims get up in court to proclaim that their clients have no obligation to follow the commitments set forth in their governing documents. Yet that was precisely the tactic adopted by Spiva at the hearing. And it was not the only jarring or unexpected statement of the day. At one point, he suggested that our case could never be certified as a class action because donors to the Sanders campaign would have still given money to him—indeed, been more likely to donate—had they known the process was rigged.[169] At another, Spiva told Judge Zloch there was no way for the Court to even define what the Charter means by "evenhanded and impartial."[170] Such terms weren't the only key components of our case incapable of definition, according to Spiva. Earlier in the hearing he had suggested it would be impossible for the Court to "define who is a member of the Democratic Party nationwide."[171] At the start of his presentation, Spiva even accused our lawsuit of being "a political weapon against the DNC and its former chairperson, Congresswoman Debbie Wasserman Schultz"[172] and that we were the ones "threaten[ing] some serious First Amendment injury to the defendants[.]"[173]

Spiva's brazen comments felt like a form of gaslighting, a psychological tactic to distract from the core legal arguments at issue that long afternoon.[174] But the comment about smoking cigars in backrooms was like a punch in the gut—an in-your-face statement by Spiva that his clients would say and do as they pleased, and there was nothing we, our clients, or anyone else could do about it.

My closing comments to Judge Zloch reflected the foreboding feeling I was having at the time, as I noted that if Spiva were right—that there was no legal remedy for the DNC having rigged the primaries—then "that's a really dire road for this country to be on."[175] If people participating in the political process who get defrauded as a result, such as Sanders's campaign donors, can have no relief, then "the prospects for democracy in this country are dark indeed."[176]

In the thick of Judge Zloch's brief parting remarks before adjourning the hearing came a second proposition about the nation's democracy: "Democracy demands the truth so people can make intelligent decisions."[177]

I can tell you that Judge Zloch's words were ringing in my ears as I left the courthouse that day, and ever since, from time to time, they reenter my mind. I will have more to say about the progress of the lawsuit in my summation, where I will try to assess the evidence presented and draw some conclusions. But for now, it is time to dive into the question at hand: What happened to Bernie Sanders?

ACT I
Stories with No Fingerprints

On April 30, 2015, the senior senator from Vermont, Bernie Sanders, announced his candidacy for the Democratic nomination for president.[178] But while the Iowa Caucus was still ten months away, his fate in the Democratic Party's nominating process, along with those of all of its contestants, was already sealed. Just one week prior to Sanders's announcement, an email had circulated among a group of Hillary Clinton campaign strategists, including campaign manager John Podesta, scheduling a conference call. There were to be three agenda items, including a "DNC plan."[179] Attached to the email was the following memorandum addressed to "The Democratic National Committee":

To: The Democratic National Committee
Re: 2016 GOP presidential candidates
Date: April 7, 2015

Friends,

This memo is intended to outline the strategy and goals a potential Hillary Clinton presidential campaign would have regarding the 2016 Republican presidential field. Clearly most of what is contained in this memo is work the DNC is already doing. This exercise is intended to put those ideas to paper.

Our Goals & Strategy

Our hope is that the goal of a potential HRC campaign and the DNC would be one-in-the-same: to make whomever the Republicans nominate unpalatable to a majority of the electorate. We have outlined three strategies to obtain our goal:

1) Force all Republican candidates to lock themselves into extreme conservative positions that will hurt them in a general election;
2) Undermine any credibility/trust Republican presidential candidates have to make inroads to our coalition or independents;
3) Muddy the waters on any potential attack lodged against HRC.

Operationalizing the Strategy

Pied Piper Candidates

There are two ways to approach the strategies mentioned above. The first is to use the field as a whole to inflict damage on itself similar to what happened to Mitt Romney in 2012. The variety of candidates is a positive here, and many of the lesser known can serve as a cudgel to move the more established candidates further to the right. In this scenario, we don't want to marginalize the more extreme candidates, but make them more "Pied Piper" candidates who actually represent the mainstream of the Republican Party. Pied Piper candidates include, but aren't limited to:

- Ted Cruz
- Donald Trump

- Ben Carson

We need to be elevating the Pied Piper candidates so that they are leaders of the pack and tell the press to them seriously.

Undermining Their Message & Credibility
Most of the more-established candidates will want to focus on building a winning general election coalition. The "Pied Pipers" of the field will mitigate this to a degree, but more will need to be done on certain candidates to undermine their credibility among our coalition (communities of color, millennials, women) and independent voters. In this regard, the goal here would be to show that they are just the same as every other GOP candidate: extremely conservative on these issues. Some examples:

- Jeb Bush
  - o What to undermine: the notion he is a "moderate" or concerned about regular Americans; perceived inroads with the Latino population.
- Marco Rubio
  - o What to undermine: the idea he has "fresh" ideas; his perceived appeal to Latinos
- Scott Walker
  - o What to undermine: the idea he can rally working- and middle class Americans.
- Rand Paul
  - o What to undermine: the idea he is a "different" kind of Republican; his stance on the military and his appeal to millennials and communities of color.
- Bobby Jindal
  - o What to undermine: his "new" ideas
- Chris Christie
  - o What to undermine: he tells it like it is.

Muddying the Waters

As we all know, the right wing attack machine has been building its opposition research on Hillary Clinton for decades. The RNC et al has been telegraphing they are ready to attack and do so with reckless abandon. One way we can respond to these attacks is to show how they boomerang onto the Republican presidential field. The goal, then, is to have a dossier on the GOP candidates on the likely attacks HRC will face. Based on attacks that have already occurred, the areas they are highlighting:

- Transparency & disclosure
- Donors & associations
- Management & business dealings

In this regard, any information on scandals or ethical lapses on the GOP candidates would serve well. We won't be picky.

Again, we think our goals mirror those of the DNC. We look forward to continuing the conversation.

Two aspects of the memorandum stand out.

First, and as a predicate to defining the DNC's strategy, the memo articulates the "hope" that "the goal of a potential [Hillary Rodham Clinton] campaign and the DNC would be one-in-the-same[.]" While the document goes on to discuss matters of DNC strategy in relation to candidates for the Republican nomination, the significance of this identity of purpose between the DNC and the Clinton campaign cannot go underemphasized. For one, as a legal matter, the proposition contradicts the Charter and Bylaws of the Democratic Party, the legal document which governs the conduct of the DNC during the nominating process.[180] To quote Article 5, Section 4 of the Charter:

> The National Chairperson shall serve full time and shall receive such compensation as may be determined by agreement between the Chairperson and the Democratic National Committee. In the conduct and management of the affairs and procedures of the Democratic National Committee, particularly as they apply to the preparation and conduct of the Presidential nominating process, the Chairperson *shall exercise impartiality and evenhandedness* as between the Presidential candidates and campaigns. The Chairperson shall be responsible for ensuring that the national officers and staff of the Democratic National Committee *maintain impartiality and evenhandedness* during the Democratic Party Presidential nominating process. (emphasis added)

There is no way to read this provision other than as requiring the DNC to maintain a neutral posture with respect to the candidates for the nomination. The mere suggestion that "the goal of a potential [Hillary Rodham Clinton] campaign and the DNC would be one-in-the-same" violates the charter obligation of the DNC on its face.

Of further significance is what the memo offers regarding its stated purpose of making "whomever the Republicans nominate unpalatable to the majority of the electorate." On this point, it sets forth what has become known as the DNC's "pied piper strategy"[181]—that is, "elevating" the "extreme" candidates in the GOP field for purpose of stacking the general election contest in its favor. The memo names Ted Cruz, Donald Trump, and Ben Carson as examples of pied piper candidates. How to "elevate" these candidates? The Clinton campaign's message to the DNC is blunt: "tell the press to [take] them seriously." Again, the memo postulates the proper role of the DNC as something other than running the primaries in an "impartial and evenhanded manner"—but not only is it improper for the DNC to have a unity of purpose with the Hillary Clinton campaign, the latter is now directing the DNC to elevate the status of specified "extreme" GOP candidates in the public perception. In other words, the memo orders the DNC to shape the mainstream media landscape in whatever manner maximally benefits the Clinton campaign, presenting the pied piper strategy as one specific avenue for accomplishing this goal.

On May 26, 2015—approximately one month after Sanders announced his candidacy—a second memorandum was addressed to the Democratic National Committee, this one stamped with a "confidential" watermark.[182] It is reproduced in full below:

To: The Democratic National Committee
Re: 2016 GOP presidential candidates
Date: May 26, 2015

Below, please find a suggested strategy for positioning and public messaging around the 2016 Republican presidential field. Ultimately, we need to

Our Goals & Strategy
Our goals in the coming months will be to frame the Republican field and the eventual nominee early and to provide a contrast between the GOP field and HRC. Over the long-term, these efforts will be aimed at getting us the best match-up in the general election, and weakening the eventual nominee through the course of the primary. We have outlined three strategies to obtain our goal:

1) Highlight when GOP candidates are outside of the mainstream on key issues, ideally driving the rest of the field to follow with positions that will hurt them in a general election;

2) Damage Republican presidential candidates' credibility with voters by looking for targeted opportunities to undermine their specific messaging;

3) Use specific hits to muddy the waters around ethics, transparency and campaign finance attacks on HRC

Operationalizing the Strategy

Highlighting Extreme or Unpopular Positions

There are two ways to approach the strategies mentioned above. The first is to use the field as a whole to inflict damage on itself similar to what happened to Mitt Romney in 2012. The variety and volume of candidates is a positive here, and many of the lesser known can serve as a cudgel to move the more established candidates further to the right. In this scenario, we don't want to marginalize the more extreme candidates, but make them more "Pied Piper" candidates who actually represent the mainstream of the Republican Party. In these issues, we would elevate statements and policies from any candidate— including second and third-tier candidates—on issues that will make them seem too far to the right on social issues and too far from the priorities of everyday Americans on economic issues.

Undermining Their Message & Credibility, Based on our General Election Priorities

In addition to pinning down the field on key issues, we will work to undermine the Republican candidate's specific messaging, while keeping in mind which candidates and which messages we believe are most powerful. These messages and the responses to them will change given new campaign positioning and new learnings from polling and research, but on these issues, we will keep the focus on the most likely candidates to allow some possibility for growth with the weaker candidates.

- Jeb Bush
    - o What to undermine: the notion he is a "moderate" or concerned about regular Americans; perceived inroads with the Latino population.
- Marco Rubio
    - o What to undermine: the idea he has "fresh" ideas; his perceived appeal to Latinos and younger voters
- Scott Walker
    - o What to undermine: his Wisconsin record, particularly on jobs; the idea he can rally working- and middle class Americans.
- Rand Paul
    - o What to undermine: the idea he is a "different" kind of Republican; his stance on the military and his appeal to millennials and communities of color.
- Chris Christie
    - o What to undermine: his success as governor, his hypocrisy in telling it like it is vs. his ethical issues and acts of a typical politician.

Muddying the Waters
As we all know, the right wing attack machine has been building its opposition research on Hillary Clinton for decades. HRC's critics have been telegraphing they are ready to attack and do so with reckless abandon. While reporters have much less of an appetite for ethics stories about GOP candidates, we will utilize the research to place highly targeted hits—for example, GOP candidates taking positions supported by their major super PAC donors.

Tactics

Working with the DNC and allied groups, we will use several different methods to land these attacks, including:

- **Reporter Outreach:** Working through the DNC and others, we should use background briefings, prep with reporters for interviews with GOP candidates, off-the-record conversations and oppo pitches to help pitch stories with no fingerprints and utilize reporters to drive a message.
- **Releases and Social Media:** Where appropriate these attacks can be leveraged for more public release, particularly the attacks around specific issues where a public release can point out that Republicans are outside of the mainstream.
- **Bracketing Events:** Both the DNC and outside groups are looking to do events and press surrounding Republican events to insert our messaging into their press and to force them to answer questions around key issues.

We look forward to discussing this strategy further. Our goal is to use this conversation to answer the questions who do we want to run against and how best to leverage other candidates to maneuver them into the right place.

Like the one circulated to the DNC on April 7, the May 26 Memo articulates the goal of the DNC as advancing Clinton's candidacy, starting with the primaries. From this vantage point, the DNC's task is to wage battle on Clinton's behalf from Day 1—"to frame the Republican field and the eventual nominee early and to provide a contrast between the GOP field **and HRC**." (emphasis added). By fighting for Clinton in the primaries, the DNC will facilitate "getting us the best match-up in the general election, and weakening the eventual nominee through the course of the primary."

Absent from both the April 7 and May 26 memoranda is any discussion of how the stated strategic goals for the DNC could possibly square with the DNC's obligation, under its own Charter, to "maintain impartiality and evenhandedness during the Democratic Party Presidential nominating process." In actuality, they are diametrically opposed: the DNC could not possibly pursue a media strategy tailored to the goals of the Clinton campaign while maintaining a neutral posture with respect to the Democratic primary candidates. As seen, the April 7 memo makes the DNC's wholesale disregard of its responsibility to be neutral quite explicit when it asserts that "the goal of a potential HRC campaign and the DNC would be one-in-the-same[.]"

Upon reaffirming the role of the DNC as an arm of the Clinton campaign, the May 26 Memo reiterates the pied piper strategy. The urgency of serving as an attack vehicle for Clinton during the primaries is underscored when the memo's author notes that "the right wing attack machine has been building its opposition research on Hillary Clinton for decades" and "HRC's critics have been telegraphing they are ready to attack and do so with reckless abandon." It then goes on to describe "tactics" within the overall media strategy under the headings, "Reporter Outreach," "Releases and Social Media," and "Bracketing Events."

These three sets of "tactics" might be regarded as the channels or vehicles by which the desired media narratives are to be created. "Reporter Outreach" encompasses direct use of reporters with the aim of generating "stories with no fingerprints"—narratives that do not bear indications of authorship by the DNC, but would have the appearance of news generated organically via the conventional practice of journalism. Tellingly, the memo regards reporters as assets to be "utilize[d]" for the purpose of injecting narrative into media. "Release and Social Media" also describes narrative-creation by the DNC, but the narrative is then subject to "public release," *i.e.*, disseminated via the DNC's own voice. "Bracketing Events" denotes the formation of narratives through staging of events by the DNC and "outside groups," with the ultimate goal of "insert[ing] our messaging into their [Republican] press."

Taken together, the two DNC memos depict a network of power operating by and between the Clinton campaign, DNC, and mainstream media that would work to ensure Bernie Sanders could not win the Democratic nomination, and which was activated even before Sanders announced his candidacy. To be sure, the name "Bernie Sanders" appears nowhere in the documents.[183] However, Sanders's literal invisibility only reflects the invisibility of his significance with respect to the primaries themselves. Sanders, the candidate, was a nonperson given that "the goal of a potential [HRC] campaign and the DNC would be one-in-the-same." There was simply no room for an alternative viable candidate when the overarching purpose of the DNC was to elevate Hillary Clinton to the presidency. The fate of Sanders as a presidential candidate took shape in the absence of his name.

The strategy outlined in these memos was destined to elevate Clinton to the nomination because the Clinton campaign and DNC could rely on the American mainstream media to be dependable allies and assets. To see why, it is necessary to view the events of 2016 against a more general understanding of the role and function of the mainstream media in the present-day United States.

In his landmark analysis of the American media industry,[184] the late Ben Bagdikian, Pulitzer Prize–winning journalist and dean of the University of California at Berkeley Graduate School of Journalism, reported the extraordinary fact that by 2003, "Five global-dimension firms, operating with many of the characteristics of a cartel, own[ed] most of the newspapers, magazines, book publishers, motion picture studios, and radio and television stations in the United States."[185] As a consequence of this exceptionally tight compression of media assets in the hands of essentially five individuals,[186] the American mainstream news media has come to concern itself principally with the production of news narratives favorable to a narrow band of corporate interests. At the same time favorable narratives are cultivated and disseminated, news unfavorable to these interests is suppressed. Writing in 2004, Bagdikian illustrated this dynamic with examples including the media's wholesale failure to investigate the U.S. government's announced rationale for invading Iraq in 2003 and dissemination of a false narrative around the capture of Private Jessica Lynch to promote the ensuing war effort.[187]

Bernie Sanders's campaign was built, in principal part, on the notion that the United States has "a rigged economy, which works for the rich and powerful, and is not working for ordinary Americans."[188] As he explained shortly after announcing his candidacy,

> [T]here are millions and millions of people who are tired of establishment politics. Who are tired of corporate greed. Who want a candidate that will help lead a mass movement, in this country, of millions of people who essentially say what people are saying is "enough is enough." The billionaire class cannot have it all.[189]

It stands to reason, then, that the mainstream media, representing the very interests condemned and singled out for progressive action by Sanders's candidacy, would readily fall in line with the DNC's determined strategy to elevate his opponent to the nomination. And as it would turn out, the mainstream media proved itself to be a most dependable ally in the DNC's strategy to elevate Clinton.

In June 2016, the Shorenstein Center on Media, Politics and Public Policy of the Harvard John F. Kennedy School of

Government released a twenty-one page study of the media during the "invisible primary"—that is, the period of campaign preceding the actual primaries and caucuses.[190] The Shorenstein study prefaced its analysis with the observation that "how well the candidates position themselves in the year leading up to the Iowa caucus" is a "better indicator of who will win the nomination" than whether a candidate wins the caucus itself or the New Hampshire primary.[191] Moreover, "[o]f all the indicators of success in the invisible primary, media exposure is arguably the most important."[192] As the Shorenstein study went on to note, media exposure is "essential if a candidate is to rise in the polls. Absent a high poll standing or upward momentum, it's difficult for a candidate to raise money, win endorsements, or even secure a spot in the presidential debates."[193]

The Shorenstein study made significant findings regarding media exposure concerning both the Democratic and Republican "invisible primaries," based on data drawn from the reporting of eight news outlets.[194]

Its conclusions regarding media coverage of Bernie Sanders are noteworthy and unambiguous. For one, as the study noted, the Democratic race, as a whole, "got much less media attention than did the Republican race when Hillary Clinton led Bernie Sanders by nearly 60 percentage points in the polls." The study concluded that in 2015, "the Democratic race got less than half as much news exposure as the Republican race."

Second, this dramatic differential in coverage "worked against Bernie Sanders' efforts to make inroads on Clinton's support." Because Sanders was a virtual nobody as far as the mainstream media was concerned—which viewed him as "barely more than that of the other lagging Democratic contenders, former Maryland Governor Martin O'Malley and former Virginia Senator Jim Webb" early in the race—mainstream coverage of Sanders did not begin to "pick up" until it was too late to compensate for the earlier lack of coverage. The Shorenstein study's findings on this score are stark: Not only did he get less coverage than **five** Republican contenders (Trump, Bush, Cruz, Rubio, and Carson), but Clinton received **three times** the media exposure as Sanders. Moreover, the mainstream media's treatment of Sanders ensured, as the Shorenstein study found, that from the very beginning in his campaign, any coverage of him was "in the unenviable position of a likely loser."[195]

"Media power is political power," wrote Bagdikian.[196] This is so because media frames the public perception of what is possible in the political realm. It creates the reality in which political outcomes happen. The media's capacity to exclude certain possibilities is what allows it to exert its power.

Over the course of the invisible primary, the media worked to exclude the possibility of Bernie Sanders being a viable candidate for the nomination—sealing the fate portended for him by his literal exclusion from the DNC strategy memos. Sanders was framed as a "likely loser" by the media precisely because it wanted and needed him to lose—and he was thus destined to lose. As we have seen, the media speaks for interests that were diametrically opposed to the central thrust of Sanders's campaign—"the billionaire class cannot have it all!" As we shall explore further, the media, Democratic Party, and larger American political establishment are structurally intertwined in a manner guaranteeing that the goals of the media and the DNC were one and the same. Thus, Sanders's near invisibility during the invisible primary—bear in mind, as the Shorenstein study found, he trailed five Republican candidates while at the same time being buried by coverage of Hillary Clinton at the rate of three to one—was guaranteed by his omission from the DNC strategy memos circulated with the Clinton campaign. Accordingly, the enormous swell of fundraising, along with overflow crowds, attracting itself to Sanders on the campaign trail, were largely shielded from public view during the critical time span when coverage would have been necessary to boost Sanders's momentum in the published polling. As such, in August 2015—in the midst of the invisible primary—the *Washington Post* seemed almost dumbfounded in its headline, observing that "100,000 people have come to recent Bernie Sanders rallies" and asking, "How does he do it?"[197] Eight months later, NPR would headline a story with another question: "Why Don't Bernie Sanders' Big Rallies Lead To Big Wins?"[198] Unsurprisingly, of course, missing from among the four answers suggested was the one borne out by the Shorenstein study: namely, that critical information about Bernie Sanders and his enormous and growing base of support across the country had been withheld from American voters, blacked out behind a blizzard of media coverage of the Republican primary candidates and Hillary Clinton.[199]

In addition to oversized crowds at his campaign stops, another highly significant measure of Sanders's burgeoning grassroots support—his unprecedented fundraising prowess, based on small donations from individuals around the country—was also excluded from the prevailing media campaign narratives. By the middle of the invisible primary (*i.e.*, the summer of 2015) it was apparent that Sanders was about to close the "fundraising gap" with Clinton; in the third quarter of 2015 alone, Sanders raised twenty-six million dollars to Clinton's twenty-eight million.[200] But even though this extraordinary influx of donations to Sanders had been happening for months—*i.e.*, throughout practically the entire invisible primary—news of the phenomenon did not begin to receive widespread media attention until the tail end.[201] By then, it was too late to make up for the lack of reporting on Sanders during the invisible primary period—the measure of what the Shorenstein study identifies as the most important indicator of who will ultimately win the nomination.[202]

Media blackout was not, of course, the only tactic leveraged against the doomed Sanders. The unspoken tactic of media blackout/exclusion of any candidate who is not Hillary Clinton exists, in the May 26 Memo, alongside explicit directives, including the creation of "stories with no fingerprints." The overarching strategy envisioned, in other words, the active creation of a media narrative landscape populated by stories favorable to Clinton and unfavorable to her opponents, stories which could not readily be traced back to the DNC or the Clinton campaign.

The Bernie Bro Myth is perhaps the most notorious of such stories that were inserted into the media narrative against Sanders. According to the myth, which began to appear in the media in fall of 2015,[203] Sanders's supporters were both predominantly male and "uniquely abusive and misogynistic in their online behavior."[204]

To quote journalist Glenn Greenwald, "[t]he concoction of the 'Bernie Bro' narrative by pro-Clinton journalists" was a "potent political tactic."[205] As Greenwald relates, the notion that Sanders's supporters were largely young, white, aggressively misogynistic men—which began to filter into media coverage in October 2015, just as the visible manifestations of Sanders's support were becoming undeniable—was created and propagated out of whole cloth by pro-Clinton journalists with no basis in fact. While minimizing and eviscerating the "literally millions of women" who preferred Sanders to Clinton,[206] the profusion of the Bernie Bro Myth played a "crucial" tactical role, in Greenwald's account, by painting all of Sanders's supporters as either: (1) sexist; or (2) insensitive to sexism, to the extent they were unwilling to accept the Bernie Bro Myth as fact or engaged in actively trying to refute it.[207]

The Bernie Bro Myth, writes Greenwald, demonstrated "that Clinton media operatives are campaigning for the candidate under the guise of journalism and social issue activism."[208]

Indeed, as we have already seen, this is exactly what the DNC strategy memos prescribed: to deploy journalists as operatives with the mission of creating and disseminating pro-Clinton narratives. The Bernie Bro Myth was not just bad or irresponsible journalism. It was the product of a conscious implementation of strategy and intent that was outlined by the DNC and Clinton campaign in black and white but kept hidden from the eyes of the public until WikiLeaks and Guccifer 2.0 released it for all the world to see.

If there is anything missing from Greenwald's passionate dissection, it is a sense of how the seamless implementation of this strategy, as embodied in the Bernie Bro Myth, was facilitated by the tightly interlocked network of interests comprising the Democratic political establishment and mainstream media. Greenwald locates an origin of the myth's persuasive force in a single tweet from *New Yorker* TV critic Emily Nussbaum remarking that "the Feel the Bern crew (as opposed to Bern himself) is such a drag. Say anything pro-Hil & they yell 'bitch' & 'psycho.'"[209] Examples of the Bernie Bro Myth appearing in mainstream media are legion, however, and include the following examples: (1) An article appearing on CNN.com proclaiming in its headline, "Are accusations that Bernie Sanders is sexist fair?," and concluding, based on no evidence whatsoever, that Sanders is "sexist" and that Sanders had not done enough to address the baseless allegations that he is;[210] (2) an in-depth November 20, 2015 article from *Politico* using more unsupported allegations of sexism, emanating from Hillary Clinton's campaign, to portray Sanders as "suddenly on the defensive";[211] (3) and, of course, the original "Bernie Bro" fable—which appeared in the *Atlantic* on October 17, 2015, and rather unironically, but in a strange and unjournalistic, almost bitter tone, described what it fantasized to be the quintessential supporter of Sanders as "male . . . Very male."[212]

In Greenwald's account, the *New Yorker*'s Nussbaum is one in a constellation of "Clinton media operatives . . . campaigning for their candidate under the guise of journalism and social issue activism." While consistent with the DNC strategy memos' view of media as an extension of the Clinton campaign (just as the DNC was itself an extension of the Clinton campaign), Greenwald's characterization falls short of grasping the complete texture of forces aligned against Sanders. Digging deeper, one learns that Emily Nussbaum is not just a writer for the *New Yorker* but also the daughter of attorney Bernard W. Nussbaum, who served as White House Counsel to Bill Clinton and was a fierce defender of the Clintons during the Whitewater investigation.[213] Viewed in this light, the production of anti-Sanders narratives in the media was not merely the inevitable result of a media ecosystem logic based upon the concentration of media assets in a few, oligopolistic hands. Rather, it depended upon the active participation of individuals networked within and across institutions of government, media, and civil society in a configuration that has corrupted these institutions, rendering them incapable of fulfilling the role of a free press in a democratic political system.[214]

The Bernie Bro Myth was hardly the only example of an anti-Sanders narrative fabricated out of whole cloth by the media. In 2015, for example, lengthy putative "analyses" appeared in places like the *Washington Post*[215] and *ABC News*,[216] claiming that Sanders had "deep" and "pause"-worthy problems connecting with black and Hispanic voters. Stories like these were echoed in news studios and publications around the country—all based on rampant speculation, quotes from nonexperts on the demographics of Sanders's support base, and other transparent fallacies. As I recounted in my Opening Statement, such stories were so laughably untrue and contrary to our direct experiences as Sanders supporters in our local community that Elizabeth and

I were inspired to form JamPAC and release videos portraying a more realistic picture of what types of folks were moved by his message.

Just as the DNC memo published by WikiLeaks revealed the strategic architecture framing the media construct by which the truth of Bernie Sanders's candidacy was effectively concealed from public view, the revolutionary publisher would also reveal key moments in the actual deployment of the strategy. On October 11, 2016, WikiLeaks released an email[217] from John Podesta's files showing that Donna Brazile—Vice Chair of the DNC, Democratic political consultant and CNN contributor who would become interim chair of the DNC after Debbie Wasserman Schultz resigned in the wake of the prior WikiLeaks release in July, right before the Democratic National Convention—had provided the Clinton campaign with advance notice of a question to be used at CNN's town hall debate in Ohio.[218]

Re: From time to time I get the questions in advance

From:jpalmieri@hillaryclinton.com
To: donna@brazileassociates.com, balcantara@hillaryclinton.com
CC: john.podesta@gmail.com, Minyon.Moore@deweysquare.com
Date: 2016-03-12 19:41
Subject: Re: From time to time I get the questions in advance

Hi. Yes, it is one she gets asked about. Not everyone likes her answer but can share it.
Betsaida - can you send her answer on death penalty?

Sent from my iPhone

On Mar 12, 2016, at 4:39 PM, Donna Brazile
<donna@brazileassociates.com> wrote:

Here's one that worries me about HRC.

DEATH PENALTY

19 states and the District of Columbia have banned the death
penalty. 31 states, including Ohio, still have the death penalty.
According to the National Coalition to Abolish the Death Penalty,
since 1973, 156 people have been on death row and later set
free. Since 1976, 1,414 people have been executed in the U.S.
That's 11% of Americans who were sentenced to die, but later
exonerated and freed. Should Ohio and the 30 other states
join the current list and abolish the death penalty?

Sent from Donna's I Pad. Follow me on twitter @donnabrazile[219]

What is striking about the Brazile affair is not so much the nature of the act, which bears a juvenile quality, reminiscent of
a high school or college student stealing the questions for the
final examination out of the teacher's desk. Indeed, one will
never be able to ascertain whether having advance knowledge of
the question—which asked whether the death penalty should be
abolished—even materially altered Clinton's presentation at the
town hall in question.[220] While its actual effect may have been
relatively insignificant, what stands out about Brazile's conduct
is its brazen and unapologetic quality. The email correspondence
itself—headed by Brazile's blunt statement that "From time to
time I get the questions in advance"—makes no attempt to either: (1) disguise her identity; or (2) conceal the fact that she
received the question ahead of the debate because it had been
given to her through a CNN contact.[221] These circumstances

constitute compelling evidence to suggest that at the time of the email, Brazile detected no legal or ethical breaches—emanating, for example, from her long-time association with CNN as a weekly contributor and political commentator on various programs, the fact she obtained the information through a CNN contact, or that she was then serving as vice chair of the DNC—that might preclude her from promptly passing along the question to Clinton's camp.

It is an astounding proposition. Recall that as an officer of the DNC, Brazile was bound by Article 5, Section 4 of the DNC Charter, requiring her to "maintain impartiality and evenhandedness during the Democratic Party Presidential nominating process." Let us also consider that at the time, Brazile was not just vice chair of the DNC, but a longstanding political commentator on the very news channel responsible for producing the Ohio town hall debate. Yet, neither the explicit language of the DNC Charter, nor the implicit expectation that a debate cannot be impartial if the media entity producing it is placing a thumb on one scale,[222] gave rise to even a modicum of doubt in Brazile as to the propriety of her deeds. Tellingly, even after CNN announced it had accepted her resignation for leaking the questions, Brazile was publicly unapologetic, appearing on the radio to proclaim that her conscience was "very clear," and that "if I had to do it all over again, I would know a hell of a lot more about cybersecurity."[223]

In law, the term "scienter" denotes the "degree of knowledge that makes a person legally responsible for the consequences of his or her act or omission; the fact of an act's having been done knowingly."[224] Courts have time and again recognized that scienter is "difficult to prove with direct evidence," meaning that intent in fraud cases is typically established through circumstantial evidence together with inferences drawn from these circumstances.[225] In this respect, WikiLeaks's publication of Brazile's emails, together with her ensuing comments regarding the appropriateness of her actions at the time, provide a rare window into the state of mind of a high-ranking DNC official and member of the mainstream media, willfully and knowingly taking measures to advance Hillary Clinton's nomination at the expense of Sanders and his supporters.

In publishing the DNC's internal correspondence, WikiLeaks flashed a tiny sliver of light on a domain hitherto inaccessible to public view. It is a domain characterized by the fingerprints of scienter: conscious and deliberate activity by members of the political elite class and the mainstream media taken to elevate a presidential candidate while still cloaking themselves in the twin pretenses of fair elections and objective journalism. In a world where discussions and transactions are largely conducted on the phone, in person, and by text in addition to over email, it is noteworthy just how many examples of such "fingerprints" (in addition to the Brazile affair) have been found in the comparatively small sample of DNC emails confined to a discrete period of time[226] in the WikiLeaks release. Among the most glaring examples:

1. On May 5, 2016, DNC Chief Financial Officer Brad Marshall emailed three fellow high-level DNC executives[227] seeking to raise, prior to the Kentucky and West Virginia primaries, the issue of whether Bernie Sanders, as an ethnic Jew, believes in God. Marshall, who attended college in Kentucky, writes that if Sanders is shown to be an atheist, "[t]his could make several points difference with my peeps. My Southern Baptist peeps would draw a big difference between and a Jew and an atheist":

Re: No shit

From:DaceyA@dnc.org

To: MARSHALL@dnc.org, MirandaL@dnc.org,
PaustenbachM@dnc.org
Date: 2016-05-05 12:23
Subject: Re: No shit

AMEN

Amy K. Dacey I Chief Executive Officer
Democratic National Committee
430 S. Capitol Street, SE Washington, D.C. 20003
202-528-7492 (c) I 202-314-2263 (o)
DaceyA@dnc.org

On 5/5/16, 1:33 AM, "Brad Marshall" <MARSHALL@dnc.org>
wrote:

>It's these Jesus thing.
>
>> On May 5, 2016, at 1:31 AM, Brad Marshall <MARSHALL@
    dnc.org> wrote:
>>
>> It might may no difference, but for KY and WVA can we get
    someone to ask his belief. Does he believe in a God. He had
    skated on saying he has a Jewish heritage. I think I read he
    is an atheist. This could make several points difference with
    my peeps. My Southern Baptist peeps would draw a big
    difference between a Jew and an atheist.[228]

CEO Amy Dacey's response to Marshall's suggestion: "AMEN."

2. On May 18, 2016, Maria Cardona, a Democratic political consultant and commentator on CNN, forwarded a draft opinion piece to DNC communications director Luis Miranda and DNC director of party affairs Patrice Taylor for approval before

submitting for publication by CNN.[229] Miranda signed off on the piece, which appeared on CNN's website the same day.[230] In the view of the *Washington Post*'s media critic, Eric Wemple, the fact that Cardona precleared her piece with the DNC shattered the concept of "actual journalism."[231] As Wemple explained,

> [T]here's a brand promise inherent in CNN, as in any other legitimate news organization. When it presents an op-ed to the public, there's a built-in presumption that this piece of journalism comes off the keyboard of the writer and is amended by the professional editors of CNN. In this case, it appears to have been edited by partisan activists as well. That means that the product is not, in fact, an op-ed, as it's categorized. *It's an op-propaganda-ed.*[232]

The subject of CNN's "op-propaganda-ed" was itself the product of dubious "journalism." In the piece, Cardona slammed Sanders and his supporters for "ugly displays of disrespect" and "uncontrolled anger," encapsulated by an alleged chair-throwing incident and death threats made to the chair of the Nevada Democratic State Party Convention.[233] But as reported the same day in *CounterPunch*, there was one not insignificant difficulty with this story being wielded as a cudgel by CNN and the DNC against Sanders and his supporters: it never happened. *CounterPunch* traced the "faux fracas in Nevada" to Jon Ralston—a writer for the Gannett-owned *Reno Gazette Journal*—who, practically out of whole cloth, manufactured reports that Sanders's supporters had thrown chairs and made death threats to Nevada chair Roberta Lange.[234] Nonetheless, the false reports were repeated as fact in the mainstream media on multiple occasions.[235] And DNC Chair Wasserman Schultz—after, ironically enough, affirming that the DNC had a "neutral" position with respect to the candidates—took the false allegations of violent conduct as opportunity to issue a scathing rebuke to Sanders and his supporters on MSNBC.[236] In one fell swoop, the "op-propaganda-ed" and its underlying false narrative integrated all three "tactics" set forth in the confidential DNC memo of May 26, 2015: (1) a "story with no fingerprints" (Cardona's piece itself); (2) "public release" (Wasserman Schultz's statements on MSNBC); and (3) staging of an "event" (false report, and subsequent media amplification, that Sanders's supporters threw chairs and made death threats).

3. The third example is notable more for the contours of the fingerprint than the story it is attached to—a comparatively mundane item forwarded to several DNC operatives, including Wasserman Schultz and Miranda, on May 21, 2016.[237] The item is a blurb reporting that Sanders vowed, in an appearance on CNN, not to reappoint Wasserman Schultz as chairperson should he win the presidency. In response to a suggestion by Miranda for pushing back on the story, Wasserman Schultz answers with just two short sentences: "This is a silly story. He isn't going to be president."

At the time Wasserman Schultz wrote these eleven words, there were still 781 pledged delegates up for grabs, across nine primaries and caucuses to be decided including the largest (California). But the timing of her observation was irrelevant. As we have seen, any story suggesting that Bernie Sanders could win the presidency was "silly," at least from the point of view of those elite political insiders working on behalf of Clinton, because *they knew* that those in charge of the political process itself were working every day to ensure he could not win the nomination. The DNC, the organization responsible for overseeing the nominating process in an impartial and evenhanded manner, was, in actuality, an arm of the Hillary Clinton campaign, charged with advancing Clinton's nomination. And as we have seen, the DNC worked closely with Clinton's allies in the mainstream media to ensure that she won the crucial "invisible primary," through a combination of blacking out news of Sanders's rapidly burgeoning movement and, later on, peppering the media ether with anti-Sanders fiction.

Perhaps "silly" was the right word to describe Sanders's chances from the perspective of those in the political and media establishments who worked together seamlessly so that his opponent would be the Democratic Party nominee. But for those millions of Americans who fervently supported Sanders— whether by phone-banking, volunteering, donating, voting, or simply believing in Sanders's transformative vision of a progressive "Political Revolution"—the notion that their candidate could become president of the United States was anything but "silly." No, the list of Sanders's donors, which has been called "[o]ne of the most valuable donor lists ever,"[238] is a testament to the nearly 2.5 million individual donors responsible for pouring over $228 million into his campaign.[239] This put Sanders on par with Barack Obama's historic 2008 campaign, and, according to some reports, Sanders outpaced Obama's previous fundraising pace at various key junctures.[240] It is ludicrous to suggest that those who believed in Sanders—and expressed themselves so forcefully with their voices, efforts and wallets—were any less inspired by Sanders than those Obama faithful who galvanized under the banner of "hope and change."

Many of those who fiercely committed themselves to Bernie Sanders were doing so as first-time participants in the political system. As a whole, his supporters crossed economic, geographic, and demographic lines to share in a common vision of America's political future. The treatment of Sanders in the mainstream media—which, as we have seen, alternatively blacked out news of Sanders's movement and disseminated patently false stories about the candidate and his campaign—came as a rude and unwelcome lesson about the realities of the American electoral system.

While Americans are accustomed to regarding their elections as a function of democratic government, they were actually borne out of America's republican tradition, which dominates the nation's constitutional origin. One might be surprised to read that the Constitution nowhere uses the terms "democracy" or "democratic"; rather, Article IV, Section 4, expressly "guarantee[s] to every State in this Union a Republican Form of Government[.]" Meanwhile, the Electoral College system for electing the president, also set forth in the Constitution, has its roots in the medieval bodies used to elect European kings and popes, which themselves were descendants of institutions in the Roman Republic such as the *comitia centuriata*, [241] or Centuriate Assembly, which "decided on war and peace, passed laws, elected consuls, praetors, and censors, and considered appeals of capital convictions."[242] In this ancient Roman assembly, plebeians and patricians both voted, but the wealthiest members' votes outweighed those of the poor. A foreshadowing, perhaps.

At the fount of the republican tradition stands Plato's *Republic*, which presents the political question of what sort of government is best alongside the epistemological question of how human beings acquire knowledge about the world. Plato explains the problem of human knowledge through his famous Allegory of the Cave: what the political theorist Hannah Arendt called "a kind of concentrated biographer of the philosopher" that "unfolds in three stages, each of them designated a turning point, a turning-about, and all three together form . . . that turning-about of the whole human being which for Plato is the very formation of the philosopher."[243]

Plato illustrates the first stage in the development of philosophy with the image of a group of prisoners in an underground cave, chained together so that they can see only a screen in front of them on which the shadows of various objects (statues of animals and people and the like) are maneuvered by puppeteer-like figures and illuminated by an unseen fire. The first motion of philosophy—and toward enlightenment—is taken by the prisoner who, when the prisoners are finally freed from their shackles, swivels around to see the fire casting its light upon "the things in the cave as they really are"[244]—what he previously experienced as mere shadows on the screen.

Plato's shadows are akin to the mainstream media's coverage of the 2016 Democratic presidential campaign. These shadows were created by puppeteers in the DNC and media with the aim of casting Hillary Clinton as the inevitable nominee and relegating Bernie Sanders (as well as any other threat to Clinton's campaign) to invisibility or triviality. If, as the *Republic* teaches, the path to being well governed begins with philosophy, *i.e.*, the quest for knowledge about the world, then perhaps WikiLeaks's publication of internal DNC documents has allowed us to take the first step toward grasping those forces which crushed Bernie Sanders, and have come to debilitate America's democratic institutions.

But to stop our account now, after having assessed what happened to Bernie Sanders through the lens of the media, would be to halt the journey out of Plato's cave after only having gotten a glimpse of the objects and fire behind the screen. A fuller understanding of how power is actually acquired and exercised in the U.S. political system (in contrast to the illusory narratives presented by the American mainstream media) requires a shift in focus to the structure of the Democratic Party, the DNC, and the forces exercising control over them. Only then might we begin to embark upon the journey out of the cave, and closer to the light of the sun.

ACT II
A Bankrupt Institution

WHAT EXACTLY ARE THE DNC AND DEMOCRATIC PARTY?

To answer the question, we might look first to what the law tells us. From a technical legal standpoint, the Democratic National Committee is the business name of a not-for-profit corporation known as DNC Services Corporation, with its principal place of business at 430 South Capitol Street Southeast in the District of Columbia. According to the Charter of the Democratic Party, "The Democratic National Committee shall have general responsibility for the affairs of the Democratic Party between National Conventions[.]"[245]

Together, the Charter and the Bylaws of the Democratic Party comprise a twenty-two page document. While it is freely available for download on the Democratic Party's website, I suspect the vast majority of registered Democrats and Democratic voters have never seen, let alone read it. A copy of the Charter and Bylaws is attached to this book as Appendix III.

In a lofty preamble, the Charter sets forth a rousing vision of an organization fully committed to the participatory essence of life in a democratic republic. It is worth quoting in full:

We, the Democrats of the United States of America, united in common purpose, hereby rededicate ourselves to the principles which have historically sustained our Party. Recognizing that the vitality of the Nation's political institutions has been the foundation of its enduring strength, we acknowledge that a political party which wishes to lead must listen to those it would lead, a party which asks for the people's trust must prove that it trusts the people and a party which hopes to call forth the best the Nation can achieve must embody the best of the Nation's heritage and traditions.

What we seek for our Nation, we hope for all people: individual freedom in the framework of a just society, political freedom in the framework of a meaningful participation by all citizens. Bound by the United States Constitution, aware that a party must be responsive to be worthy of responsibility, we pledge ourselves to open, honest endeavor and to the conduct of public affairs in a manner worthy of a society of free people.

Under God, and for these ends and upon these principles, we do establish and adopt the Charter of the Democratic Party of the United States.

The preamble paints a picture of a "responsive" and transparent organization, one that earns "the people's trust" by "listen[ing] to those it would lead," guided by the goal of facilitating "meaningful participation by all citizens" in the nation's political process. These values—which the preamble asserts to be paramount in shaping the Democratic Party's existence and operation—find their expression in various ways throughout the Charter and Bylaws. For instance, the Charter charges the Democratic Party with (1) enabling "all members of the Democratic Party full, timely and equal opportunities to participate in decisions concerning the selection of candidates, the formulation of policy, and the conduct of other Party affairs";[246] (2) developing "codes of political ethics" to guide public officials and employees;[247] (3) assuring "all Democratic voters full, timely and equal opportunity to participate" in the National Convention;[248] and (4) encouraging "full participation by all Democrats" in the affairs of the party.[249]

At the same time, the Bylaws direct the DNC, as the legal entity with managerial responsibility for the Democratic Party, to facilitate "Participation in All Party Affairs" by "all who desire to support the Party and who wish to be known as Democrats."[250] To accomplish the goal, the Bylaws command the DNC, along with other organizations affiliated with the Democratic Party, to undertake programs "designed to encourage the fullest participation of all Democrats in all Party affairs,"[251] including but not limited to those specifically designed "to facilitate and increase the participation of low and moderate income persons."[252]

The vision of the Democratic Party, as set forth in its governing documents, is inspiring: a robust and transparent organization built upon the ideals of broad-based participation in the public affairs of a democratic society. The problem, as we shall see, is that this vision exists only on paper. It is about as realistic a description of how the Democratic Party actually conducts its affairs as were Bernie Sanders's chances in the 2016 nominating process. Understanding what the Democratic Party really *is* (as opposed to what it *says* it is in the Charter and Bylaws) requires a realistic assessment of how this organization has come to dominate, along with the Republican Party, the institutions of government in the United States.

The concept of a democracy dominated by just two parties is, it turns out, a uniquely American phenomenon. In *The Tyranny of the Two-Party System*,[253] political scientist Lisa Jane Disch of the University of Michigan illustrates how the "doctrine of the two-party system" came to be enshrined as the very linchpin of the American system—despite the fact that political parties, much less the concept of a system dominated by two parties, are mentioned nowhere in the Constitution (much like there is no mention of democracy).[254] According to Disch, "the two-party system is the focal point of an American civil religion."[255] She identifies three core tenets underlying this doctrine: (1) the rise of two dominant, major political parties is an inevitable result given the manner in which the United States' electoral system is structured; (2) the two-party system is a "timeless and unchanging" feature of the U.S. political system; and (3) without the two-party system, there can be no democratic progress.[256] As we have seen, the language in the Charter and Bylaws of the Democratic Party reflects the notion that the two major parties are intertwined with the very concept of American democracy, perhaps best captured by the preamble's assertion that "the vitality of the Nation's political institutions has been the foundation of its enduring strength."

But as Disch demonstrates, the two-party doctrine—which has been deployed time and again to justify the primacy of the Democratic and Republican Parties to the exclusion of all others—is largely the stuff of myth. Not only that, and putting aside the question of number for a moment, the notion that political parties are inseparable from American democracy is sheer fallacy. As noted, parties are strangers to the Constitution, and they also did not exist in the colonies.[257] Indeed, the concept of popularly based political parties—*i.e.*, organizations that mobilize groups of voters with the aim of influencing policy and electing candidates to office—did not emerge until the early nineteenth century, at the state level, and as a means of challenging constitutional restrictions on popular sovereignty (such as the limitation of voting privileges to white male property owners).[258] The Founding Fathers expressed great skepticism about devices that promoted popular influence on government.[259] In Disch's words, "If the political party is an American tradition, it is . . . as an innovation contrary to the design of the Constitution."[260]

As it turns out, the concept that domination of the political system by just *two* parties is essential to American democracy—the core of the two-party system doctrine which has come to be virtually unquestioned as a prevailing feature of American political life—is even *less* of an American tradition. While two major, national party organizations did emerge by the late 1830s and early 1840s (the Democrats and the Whigs), they existed in vigorous competition with third parties—including the Know-Nothings, the Liberty and Free Soil Parties, the People's Party, and the Republican Party—throughout most of the nineteenth century.[261] At various junctures, third parties: (1) controlled various state legislatures and governorships; (2) regularly captured five percent or more of the popular vote in presidential elections; and (3) deployed electoral strategies, such as "fusion,"[262] to actually swing the balance of power in presidential, gubernatorial, and congressional elections. In 1860, a party which only six years earlier had been third party alongside the Democrats and the Whigs won the presidency when Lincoln was elected as a Republican.

Our politics came to be dominated by two major parties not due to any inherent feature of the system, but because at the dawn of the twentieth century, states began passing laws that effectively created and protected a two-party duopoly. Disch describes how the states seized control of the means of the nation's electoral system from the parties themselves. Whereas previously, "[e]lections were open to all parties that could afford to print and distribute a ticket,"[263] the adoption of the "Australian system" beginning in 1890 "gave the state the authority and responsibility for regulating nominations, campaign procedures, and other party activities."[264] This newfound authority meant, in the words of historian Peter H. Argersinger, that "those who controlled the state thus gained the power to structure the system in their own behalf, to frustrate or weaken their opponents, in a manner that would have astounded their predecessors and that was not only effective but by definition legal."[265] Such power was the genesis of ballot access laws and other onerous restrictions on the ability of third parties to meaningfully participate in the electoral process,[266] a framework that persists to this day. At the time, such laws, including those preventing third parties from "fusing" their ballot lines with the candidates of major parties, were decried as "providing for the extinction and effacement of all parties but the Democratic and Republican."[267]

This was prophetic. Over one hundred years later, an article in the *Harvard Law Record* would observe the "convoluted and discriminatory" nature of laws precluding ballot access for minor parties and independent candidates, that along with other factors including federal regulatory burdens and the complete control exercised by the Democratic and Republican parties over the Commission on Presidential Debates, serves to render American elections uniquely uncompetitive, predictable, and meaningless within the universe of so-called Western democracies.[268]

However one looks at the situation, and contrary to the historical and political theoretical mythologies proffered in support of the two-party duopoly, the two parties' dominance throughout the twentieth and twenty-first centuries has been anything *but* beneficial to the state of American democracy. Writing in 1965, political scientist Walter Dean Burnham observed that the construction of the two-party duopoly in the 1890s had also laid the groundwork for transforming a "thoroughly democratized" American political system into an "oligarchy."[269] From a purely participatory standpoint, the numbers are stark: the United States has consistently lagged in voter turnout behind almost every other developed democracy[270] and declining voter turnout has been a longstanding trend in American elections.[271] Turnout in the 2016 election marked a twenty-year low.[272]

The country's anemic voter participation rates are not the only evidence that the two-party duopoly has choked the democracy out of America's political institutions. Despite the lofty language in the Democratic Party's Charter and Bylaws, neither of the major parties has been the site of significant democratic participation by Americans in the twentieth and twenty-first centuries.[273] Viewed in relation to their counterparts in European democracies, both the Democrats and Republicans do remarkably little in the areas of political education or formulating actual policy; instead, they are practically singularly devoted to the task of filling offices such that the parties are typically "composed of an inner circle of office-holding and office-seeking cadres together with their personal supporters and a limited number of professional party workers."[274] Harvard political scientist Robert D. Putnam paints a dark and paradoxical picture of the nature of participation in the Democratic and Republican Parties through the twentieth century. While the finances and concomitant professionalization of political organizations skyrocketed to create a thriving "business of politics" in America, actual political engagement through such activities as volunteering in election campaigns and attending political meetings and campaign rallies has descended to measurable all-time lows.[275]

Notwithstanding the manifold indicia of increasing voter apathy and citizen disengagement that has characterized the era of two-party rule in the United States, the two parties have managed to embed themselves into the system's very fabric—not just via legislation that has made it virtually impossible for the duopoly to face serious challenges from third parties and independent candidates, but in the system's self-image as expressed in the Supreme Court's constitutional jurisprudence. In 1997, the Supreme Court, by a 6–3 majority, ruled that a state law prohibiting candidates from appearing on the ballot

on more than one party line—an example of "antifusion" legislation which has, in conjunction with other factors, effectively
precluded third parties from playing a meaningful role in the
electoral system—passed muster under the Constitution.[276] In
so doing, the Court adopted the two-party doctrine hook, line,
and sinker, finding that states may "favor the traditional two-
party system" because "American politics has been, for the most
part, organized around two parties since the time of Andrew
Jackson," and the two-party system promotes "political stability."[277] The Court's reasoning, which is as much conclusory[278]
as it is based on bad history,[279] thereby enshrines the duopoly
of parties as a function of constitutional law and, as a consequence, an irremovable feature of the political system—even
though political parties, much less the concept of an electoral
system dominated by two parties, have no textual basis in the
Constitution. But if the two-party system is an interloper in our
republic, it is one that has since achieved constitutionally protected status, thanks to the six Justices of the Supreme Court
comprising the *Timmons* majority.[280]

The Charter of the Democratic Party, with its emphasis on
"meaningful participation" by citizens in the life of the party
and polity, harkens back to a bygone era—the nineteenth century milieu where party politics was a "potent site of powers,"
where parties "governed the lives and livelihoods of their con-
stituents by providing social services and distributing patronage," and "created local identity and imbued local politics
with military intensity" through regular neighborhood rallies,
marches, and campaign clubs.[281] Ironically enough, however,
the Charter itself is not an artifact of this lost era, but a product
of mid-twentieth-century turmoil arising from the party's ongoing transformation into a vehicle for oligarchic interests.

The Charter is a child of the restless sixties—1968, to be precise. That year saw Hubert Humphrey, who declined to enter

a single primary, take the nomination at an epically raucous convention in Chicago in a deal brokered by Democratic Party insiders to defeat anti Vietnam War candidates Eugene McCarthy and George McGovern. The experience of 1968's bitter factionalism, alongside cries for reform by jilted party activists, gave rise to the McGovern-Fraser Commission. The twenty-eight-member body, convened after Richard Nixon's victory over Humphrey in the general election, was given the task of making the nominating process more inclusive. The McGovern-Fraser Commission introduced reforms responsible for shifting the focus of the nominating process from the brokering of deals by party elites at the convention, to primaries and caucuses in which candidates actively compete for the support of Democratic Party voters.[282]

In 1972, McGovern ran a vigorous grassroots progressive campaign for the nomination, making income inequality a centerpiece of his platform.[283] McGovern's campaign was the unmistakable archetype for Bernie Sanders's campaign over forty years later. Shunned by the big-donor Democratic establishment, McGovern utilized direct mail to raise over forty thousand individual donations averaging less than thirty dollars apiece.[284] Leveraging to his benefit the reforms introduced by the commission he had only recently chaired, McGovern succeeded in capturing the nomination—overcoming various attempts by party elites to derail his candidacy, including an "Anyone But McGovern" movement at the convention in Miami.[285]

But with establishment interests from both parties aligned against him, McGovern's loss to Nixon in the general election was historically lopsided, with Nixon winning the popular vote 60.7 percent to 37.5 percent, and the Electoral College 520 to 17. Two years later, the Democratic Party adopted the Charter—with its lofty appeals to inclusiveness, responsiveness, transparency, and a fair and evenhanded nominating process—after a year-long drafting process and in response to the question, "Can the Democratic party eliminate the squabbles that have caused us to lose?"[286]

McGovern's campaign seized a rare moment in the twentieth century when populist pressures on the Democratic party infrastructure had facilitated the possibility of nominating a progressive candidate for president. However, his loss to Nixon set in motion a series of events ensuring a progressive candidate would never be nominated again. Ideologically, McGovern's defeat became a justification for the Democrats' adoption of what would come to be known as neoliberalism. Centrists within the party successfully made the case that a McGovern-like candidate could never win the presidency, leading to the formation of the Democratic Leadership Council and an era of unprecedented patronage of the party by corporate donors, culminating in Bill Clinton's election in 1992.[287]

McGovern's overwhelming defeat, together with Jimmy Carter's loss in an Election Day blowout at the hands of Ronald Reagan, also led the party to adopt, in 1982, the system of what are now known as "superdelegates."[288] Under this system, approximately 14 percent of the total delegates to the Democratic national convention would be selected from party leaders/elites and free to vote for any candidate—unlike the remainder of delegates, who had to vote on the basis of state primary results.[289] The seventy-member Hunt Commission authored the rules introducing superdelegates on the premise that the McGovern-Fraser reforms were responsible for producing a string of losing nominees. As one member of the commission put it, party elites had to "regain control of the nomination."[290] In his address to the commission, the DNC chair at the time, Taylor Manatt, asserted that the body should be guided by the goal of "bring[ing] us victory in 1984," and "that's what we're all about."[291] And as the commission's chair, North Carolina governor James Hunt put it, "We're about the business of winning again."[292]

The introduction of superdelegates allowed the Democratic Party to accomplish two goals. First, by placing such a large chunk of the delegate count (which grew to approximately 15 percent of the total by 2016) in the hands of party elites, the DNC could ensure that no grassroots progressive candidate like McGovern would ever again have a realistic shot at capturing the nomination. At the same time, the Democrats were able to retain the system of primaries, which had given rise to the McGovern-Fraser reforms, thus securing the illusion of a participatory process, not to mention the reality of a burgeoning, lucrative political infotainment industry feeding off the primaries.

In truth, by adopting superdelegates, the DNC defied the core principles undergirding the Democratic Party's own Charter. Consider, for example, the provisions requiring the DNC and its officers and employees to "maintain impartiality and evenhandedness during the Democratic Party Presidential nominating process."[293] Because, by definition, the DNC is comprised of the very party leaders and elites constituting the class of people from whom the superdelegates are drawn, the superdelegate system undermines the ability of the DNC to function in an impartial or evenhanded manner. By granting the party leaders and elites the ability—indeed, the mandate—to tank a popular progressive candidate like McGovern by casting 15 percent of the delegate votes as superdelegates, the superdelegate system also rendered it impossible for the DNC to conduct itself as a fair and impartial arbiter of the nominating process. How could the DNC, on the one hand, maintain a neutral posture with respect to the candidates when, on the other hand, the party leaders also had a directive, in their role as superdelegates, to prevent certain types of candidates from obtaining the nomination?

By the same token, the very concept of superdelegates runs counter to the egalitarian core of the Charter, which strives to ensure "all members of the Democratic Party full, timely and equal opportunities to participate in decisions concerning the selection of candidates, the formulation of policy, and the conduct of other Party affairs."[294] What could be less "equal," vis-a-vis the participation of the Democratic Party membership, than allotting 15 percent of the delegates to party elites?

By the time Bernie Sanders announced his candidacy, the Charter of the Democratic Party was a dead letter, at least insofar as its guiding principles are concerned.[295] As an independent in a two-party duopoly, Sanders's progressive candidacy necessarily had to go through the Democratic nominating process to avoid being labeled a "wasted third party vote" (a la Ralph Nader in 2000) from the get-go. But upon entering the process, Sanders confronted a system that had been designed with the very goal of rejecting candidacies such as his.

In Act I, we explored how the DNC and Hillary Clinton campaign crafted a comprehensive media strategy to elevate Clinton to the nomination, even before Sanders had entered the race. This strategy assured Clinton of winning the crucial "invisible primary," so that Sanders's chances were effectively doomed even before the first voters cast their ballots in Iowa and New Hampshire.

It would be an oversimplification, however, to reduce those forces aligned against Sanders to the most visible phenomena—i.e., those which operate through the world of possibilities created by the mainstream media. The media's role is as much to present possibilities to the population as it is to justify what has already been decided. In the case of Sanders, the DNC had already negated the possibility of his campaign in 1982, when it adopted the superdelegate system—a system adopted precisely to preclude a progressive, grassroots candidate like McGovern from ever again capturing the nomination. From that point forward—and in direct conflict with its embrace of broad-based participation and role as neutral arbiter of the process under the terms of its own Charter—the DNC committed itself, above all, to "winning." And "winning," in the minds of the party leadership, meant excluding the possibility of nominating a grassroots progressive.

As such, when high-level DNC officials such as Donna Brazile and Debbie Wasserman Schultz repeatedly and blatantly transgressed their obligation to be "impartial and evenhanded" by advancing Hillary Clinton's campaign at every turn, they were acting in a manner fully consistent with the DNC's understanding of its own mission, at least as it has existed since the adoption of superdelegates in 1982. They were, in fact, marching in lockstep with the 571 superdelegates who, it was announced by the Associated Press late in the evening on June 6, 2016, had publicly committed their support to Clinton.[296] These superdelegate "commitments" permitted the Associated Press to announce that Clinton had taken the nomination[297] not only seven weeks prior to the convention, but before six states (including California and New Jersey) and the District of Columbia even held their primaries.[298] Taken together, these primaries accounted for over 17 percent of the unpledged delegates. As the *Washington Post* put it, the Associated Press was thereby empowered to "call[] the race for Hillary Clinton when nobody was looking."[299] One could say that the superdelegates had admirably performed their function of allowing the party elites[300] "to regain control of the nomination."

One might protest, as some have, that Sanders's plight cannot be laid at the feet of the superdelegates for the simple reason that because Clinton received more pledged delegates than Sanders, she would have taken the nomination even without the superdelegates' overwhelming support.[301] No doubt, such reasoning is tempting for those looking to salvage any shred of propriety from the results of the 2016 nominating process. It is a myopic point of view, however. Simply counting the delegate votes neglects to consider the role of superdelegates within the larger context of the nominating process. It fails to appreciate the critical role of superdelegates in allowing elites to maintain control over the process while perpetuating the myth of fair and inclusive primary elections.

Consider the fact that there is nothing preventing the DNC from setting the total number of superdelegates as any percentage of the total number of delegates it wishes. (The Hunt Commission originally proposed that 30 percent of the total delegates be superdelegates, before the DNC settled on 14 percent for the 1984 election.[302]) But making the number of superdelegates too great runs the risk of sapping vitality out of the primaries, thereby stripping out the legitimacy that these contests are supposed to confer upon the ultimate nominee. Recall that the twentieth-century movement to reform the nominating process began with Humphrey's loss to Nixon in 1968, and the view that the nominee had to emerge from a broadly participatory series of primaries and caucuses to facilitate success in the general election. Once it came into being through the McGovern-Fraser Commission and subsequent shift to primaries by most states, the modern primary system, to thrive, has required the participation of voters operating on the belief their votes actually make a difference in selecting the nominee. The fact that superdelegates are 15 percent of the total delegates (as opposed to 30 percent, 50 percent or even more) might best be explained as a balancing act for the Democratic Party: the number must be high enough to provide them with control over the nomination, but low enough to maximize voter participation in the primaries.

While attempting this balancing act, the superdelegate system proved to be potent in accomplishing its objective against Sanders in 2016. As we have seen, the DNC exercised control over the nomination, in no small part, when, in conjunction with the Clinton campaign, it implemented a media strategy that blacked out coverage of Sanders during the invisible primary, crippling Sanders with respect to the most salient indicator of which candidate ultimately wins the nomination.[303] When the mainstream media *did* mention Sanders, it was within the narrative of being the "likely loser."[304] The superdelegates played an integral role in framing the guiding trope of Clinton's invincibility. For example, *Newsweek* reported in October 2015—months before Iowa and New Hampshire—that Clinton had already received the support of more than half of the superdelegates.[305] The articles stated, *as fact*, that "[t]he backing gives her a commanding advantage over her two rivals."[306] Of course, *Newsweek* made no mention of Sanders's enormous rallies or extraordinary fundraising prowess—which by November 2015 were already on full display.[307] (As it was, the article barely distinguished between Sanders's and Martin O'Malley's standing vis-as-vis Clinton!) Moreover, whatever implications the public might have drawn from the visible manifestations of Sanders's bourgeoning support base would be nullified, in due course, by the rigidification of Clinton's inevitability as the chosen nominee in the prevailing media narrative. The role of the superdelegates in forging Clinton's inevitability cannot be understated, and reached its apex when, on June 6, 2016, the Associated Press announced Clinton as the nominee based on its internal survey of their "commitments" and, in so doing, effectively preempted the results of nine yet-to-be-decided primaries and caucuses (including the largest, California) representing some 781 pledged delegates.

The AP's announcement reflects an extraordinary moment in the history of the Democratic nominating process: a moment when the hitherto poorly understood power of the superdelegates revealed itself for all to see. For when the Associated Press bestowed the nomination on Clinton based on a survey of superdelegate "commitments," it is as if the superdelegates held their own primary for purposes of awarding Clinton the nomination in advance of the primaries still to be held, not to mention the Convention. It was a very public flex of muscle from a political body—the cadre of superdelegates—that had previously operated under a cloak of obscurity.

Of course, despite the DNC's resounding success in implementing its anti-McGovern strategy against Sanders, it did not result in producing a "winning" candidate. Hillary Clinton did not go on to win the general election, meaning that she suffered the same fate as Humphrey, McGovern, and Carter—whose so-called "weak" candidacies gave rise to the McGovern-Fraser and Hunt commissions, culminating in the introduction of superdelegates.

But from the perspective of its elite participants, the 2016 Democratic primaries were a success. In terms of voter participation, they engendered enough enthusiasm to produce the second-highest voter turnout in twenty-eight years, second only to 2008 and the primaries that Barack Obama ultimately won.[308] From a business standpoint, the primaries were undoubtedly wildly successful. According to one estimate, approximately $445 million was spent on the Democratic primaries alone. This includes money spent by the Clinton, Sanders, and O'Malley campaigns, as well as their allied Super PACs and other groups.[309] The flow of money meant ample funding for the world in which the political elites reside—the world of political consultants, lobbyists, strategists, media brokers, and the like. A not-insignificant chunk of this funding came from the $228 million raised by the Sanders campaign through small-donor donations. One company alone, Old Towne Media LLC, billed the Sanders campaign over $82 million to procure media advertising.[310] No doubt, the Sanders campaign resulted in significant paydays for numerous members of the political elite class.[311]

It is even fair to say that from a fiscal perspective, the DNC emerged from the 2016 election in a historically favorable position—with $10.8 million in cash on hand and just $3.7 million in debt at the close of January 2017.[312] One report attributed the DNC's financial health to a "deal" previously struck with the Clinton campaign, which had insisted that the DNC set aside $10 million for purposes of strengthening the party apparatus during her anticipated presidency.[313]

To appreciate the truth of the financial relationship between the Hillary Clinton campaign and the DNC, however, one needs to recognize that the word "deal" is something of a misnomer in this context. Owing to the Hillary Victory Fund, a species of election law entity known as a "joint fundraising committee," the finances of the DNC and Clinton campaign were intimately intertwined throughout the entire election season. Comprehending the nature of this arrangement is, in fact, critical to understanding what the DNC and Democratic Party truly embody—behind the lofty proclamations of the Charter and Bylaws, and even the not-so-lofty rules of the superdelegate system.

Per federal election law, a joint fundraising committee is a legal entity established to facilitate joint election-related fundraising efforts conducted among party organizations, non-party organizations, and candidates.[314] As a joint fundraising committee, the Hillary Victory Fund enabled the Clinton campaign, DNC, and thirty-eight state Democratic party committees to collectively raise over $529 million during the 2015-16 campaign cycle.[315] Its legal structure allowed the Hillary Victory Fund to solicit donations of up to $418,800 from the superwealthy by aggregating the limits on donations to political campaigns ($2700 per election), a national party committee such as the DNC ($33,400 per year) and state party committees ($10,000 per year).[316] Some of the Hillary Victory Fund's half-billion-dollar-plus haul came from parties hosted by the likes of actor George Clooney and media mogul Jeffrey Katzenberg. At one Clooney fundraiser, two seats at the head table with Hillary Clinton had a price tag of $353,000. Two Clooney-hosted fundraisers in California raised over $15 million on their own.[317]

The Hillary Victory Fund was pitched to the public as a fundraising tool for electing Democrats to Congress. Confronted with accusations of being a "corporate shill," Clooney replied that, "the overwhelming amount of the money that we're raising is not going to Hillary to run for president, it's going to the down-ticket."[318] But this was flatly untrue. While $112.4 million did go to state party accounts, 78.5 percent of that amount, or $88.3 million, was then transferred to the DNC.[319] This massive shift of dollars from the state parties to the DNC was made possible by the lack of any legal limitation on how much money may be transferred between and among state, local, and national party committees.[320]

Thus, at its essence, the Hillary Victory Fund was a vehicle for maximizing the flow of money from wealthy donors to the DNC—an organization which, we have seen, was fully committed to elevating Hillary Clinton to the nomination even before Bernie Sanders entered the race. The DNC's putative role as neutral arbiter of the primary process—supposedly bound by its own Charter to treat all candidates with "impartiality and even-handedness"—is, perhaps, nowhere more starkly exposed as fiction than through the dynamics of the Hillary Victory Fund. The very wherewithal of the DNC—to the tune of over $88 million—depended on Hillary Clinton's ability to raise funds through the Hillary Victory Fund. Given this dependency, the concept that the DNC would or could act neutrally in the primaries simply defies basic common sense.[321]

In critical respects, the Hillary Victory Fund, with its sharply drawn lines of fealty running from the DNC's coffers to the Clinton campaign's fundraising prowess, is the actual blueprint for the DNC's structure as it exists in the present day. This legal entity, through which the DNC's financial well-being was tethered to the ability of the Clinton campaign to attract outsized checks from ultrawealthy donors at lavish fundraisers, is much more revelatory of the DNC's institutional logic than the Charter or Bylaws, or, for that matter, even the system of superdelegates adopted in 1982. In fact, it is hardly a stretch to suggest that the Hillary Victory Fund explains, better than any other factor—including the historical mandate for superdelegates to protect against reincarnations of McGovern, such as Sanders—the unyielding loyalty of the vast majority of superdelegates to Clinton in 2016. To wit, once the DNC and the state parties partnered with the Clinton campaign on their half-billion-dollar-plus fundraising venture, the commitment of the party elites to vote for Clinton was at least "tacit," if not express.[322]

The intersection of the superdelegate system with the financial potentiality embodied in the Hillary Victory Fund represented a hitherto unseen alignment of forces in American politics that ensured the impossibility of Sanders obtaining the nomination. As we have seen, when the superdelegate system was adopted in 1982, it was in direct response to a series of perceived weak "candidacies" and with a pronounced desire to get the Democratic Party back into the "business" of "winning."[323] But those sentiments grew out of a different era in American politics, one which had not yet succumbed to the logic of virtually unrestricted campaign financing. As much (or perhaps even more) than any factor, the latter has molded the DNC's institutional logic, which manifested in a single-minded determination to elevate Clinton—whose campaign, it cannot be overemphasized, enriched the DNC to the tune of $88.3 million via the Hillary Victory Fund.

As we have seen, from a constitutional point of view, the two-party duopoly is an interloper to our system of government. The Founding Fathers would have viewed the concept of popularly based parties with great skepticism. Nonetheless, in decisions such as *Timmons*, the domination of electoral politics by the Democrats and Republicans has been afforded a constitutionally protected status by the Supreme Court. The Court has not only accorded recognition to this political duopoly but also played a vital role in perpetuating its existence—most significantly via the establishment and maintenance of an election law framework, within which constructs such as the Hillary Victory Fund are enabled and then encouraged to prosper.

Even before the DNC adopted the superdelegate system to squash the possibility of McGovern's reincarnation, the Supreme Court was already pouring the legal foundation for the Hillary Victory Fund. In 1976, just over three years after McGovern lost the general election to Nixon, the Court decided *Buckley v. Valeo*—a case that would pave the way for unlimited spending as a feature of U.S. political campaigns.[324] In *Buckley*, the Court struck down Congress's attempt to place caps on the amount of money that may be spent in support of a political campaign—by most individuals and groups outside of the candidate and political parties—as unconstitutional restrictions on the freedom of expression. In a "complex and at times impenetrable opinion,"[325] the Court held there could be no such limits on campaign spending—even though Congress had found them necessary as part of a comprehensive package of election reforms passed to prevent the kinds of egregious campaign finance abuses and corruption that had recently come to light with the events known as Watergate.[326] The Court found that the potential to limit the First Amendment rights of those who want to spend money on political campaigns was too important—and "the governmental interest in preventing corruption and the appearance of corruption"[327] too trivial—to justify any ceilings on how much they could spend.

Two features of this head-scratching but highly influential opinion are especially worth noting. First, the Court cites no real precedent for the proposition that *spending money* on a political campaign is equivalent to what we normally think of as speech or expression as protected by the First Amendment. Instead, it simply assumes they are one and the same thing based on the observation that "virtually every means of communicating ideas in today's mass society requires the expenditure of money."[328] In so doing, the Court posits a direct equivalence between the spending of money and the exercise of free expression—a bizarre proposition that would come to haunt our political system up through the present.

The *Buckley* Court's equivalence of money with speech rests on the assumption that the means of producing expression are equivalent to expression itself—in other words, because money buys the *means* of expression, money equals expression.[329] But only eight years earlier, in *United States v. O'Brien*,[330] the Supreme Court had rather forcefully rejected the thrust of this general proposition when it found no constitutional barrier to sentencing David Paul O'Brien to prison for the crime of burning his selective service registration certificate in protest of the Vietnam War and draft. The *O'Brien* Court was openly scornful of the idea that burning a draft card could be protected as speech, in and of itself, proclaiming that, "We cannot accept the view that an apparently limitless variety of conduct can be labeled 'speech' whenever the person engaging in the conduct intends thereby to express an idea."[331]

When, in *Buckley*, the Supreme Court embraced the notion that the means of expression are equivalent to expression itself, it did exactly what it said it would never do in *O'Brien*: The Court thereby adopted a point of view by which "an apparently limitless variety of conduct can be labeled as speech." The act of cutting a check constitutes speech, per *Buckley*, because the act causes speech to occur. But this is basically the same argument O'Brien had made to the Court about the burning of his draft card as a form of protest—the act of destroying a draft card should not be criminalized, he argued, because to do so is to punish an act that causes expression to occur, *i.e.*, a message of protest against Vietnam. The *O'Brien* Court derided this argument as "limitless" and rejected it out of hand. Unfortunately, *Buckley* is just one example of the Supreme Court's general tendency to ignore precedent—or even reverse itself—whenever there are entrenched corporate interests in need of protection, a tendency that has only gotten more acute in recent years.

Like the equivalence of money with speech, a second troubling aspect of *Buckley* would come to play a formative role in the structuring of campaign finance law down the road. This is the Supreme Court's discussion of what constitutes corruption sufficient for Congress to stanch the flow of money into politics. Whereas *Buckley* finds the government's interest in "preventing corruption and the appearance of corruption" to be "inadequate" for the purpose of supporting caps on independent expenditures on campaigns, in the same opinion, the Court states that "limit[ing] the actuality and appearance of corruption resulting from individual financial contributions" to campaigns is "sufficient" to justify imposing limitations on the size of donations to candidates.[332] In this portion of the opinion, the Court proclaims itself to be well aware of the "danger of actual quid pro quo arrangements" alongside "the impact of the appearance of corruption stemming from public awareness of the opportunities for abuse inherent in a regime of large individual financial contributions."[333] The "weighty interests" presented by the need to forestall corruption are served, according to *Buckley*, by limiting how much one can donate to a political campaign.[334] And yet when it comes to independent expenditures, the Court is unwilling to concede that the same "weighty interests" apply. Instead, the Court takes solace in the notion that because such expenditures are made "totally independently of the candidate and his campaign," there is little "danger" that "expenditures will be given as a quid pro quo for improper commitments from the candidates."[335]

Accordingly, *Buckley* exists within a framework where politicians may only be improperly influenced or "bought" via donations directly to their campaigns; but if the same money is spent "independently" on the same candidate and campaign, the potential for undue influence miraculously fades away. The distinction is hopelessly formalistic, naive, and out of touch with the commonsense reality of how influence is actually exerted on politicians outside of direct quid pro quo arrangements. As a consequence, *Buckley* also stands for a ludicrously narrow conception of what entails "corruption" necessary to justify regulating the transfer of money relating to political activity. Unfortunately, like the false equivalence between money and speech, the *Buckley* Court's simplistic reduction of corruption to quid pro quo arrangements ended up permanently infecting the body of American campaign finance jurisprudence.

By the time Bernie Sanders announced his candidacy, the seeds planted in *Buckley* had germinated into two distinct species of political fundraising juggernaut: (1) the Super PAC, capable of raising unlimited sums from corporations for independent expenditures; and (2) the joint fundraising committee, which, in the case of the Hillary Victory Fund, pumped hundreds of millions of dollars into the coffers of the Clinton campaign and the DNC. These formidable creatures owed their existence to Supreme Court decisions pushing the absurd and simplistic reasoning of *Buckley* to generate more outrageous conclusions.

In 2010, the Court decided *Citizens United v. Federal Election Commission*,[336] where it went out of its way[337] to rule that corporations cannot be stopped from making unlimited, independent expenditures on political campaigns.[338] In removing any limitations on what it referred to as "corporate speech,"[339] the Court hammered home *Buckley*'s cabining of corruption to quid pro quo arrangements, noting that "[t]he hallmark of corruption is the financial *quid pro quo*: dollars for political favors."[340] With *Citizens United*, the Supreme Court laid the vital groundwork for what has become known as the Super PAC: fundraising committees which can raise unlimited amounts of cash from corporations (as well as unions, associations, and individuals) for independent expenditures on campaigns.[341] Super PACs provided formidable support to Clinton's candidacy in 2016, with the largest, Priorities USA Action, taking in over $175 million and spending over $161 million to advance Clinton's candidacy.[342] By contrast, the largest Super PAC supporting Sanders (whose campaign repeatedly attacked the concept of Super PACs), National Nurses United for Patient Protection, raised $8.1 million.[343]

The same myopic view of what constitutes "corruption" found in *Buckley* and *Citizens United* animates *McCutcheon v. Federal Election Commission*,[344] the 2014 Supreme Court decision to which the Hillary Victory Fund owed its existence. In striking down aggregate limits on how much donors can contribute in total to all candidate or party committees in an election cycle, the Court reiterated its view that the government lacks authority to combat corruption defined as anything other than "actual quid pro quo arrangements."[345] In reaching the conclusion that aggregate limits can serve no role combating corruption, so narrowly defined, the Court specifically rejected an example,

presented by the lower court whose judgment *McCutcheon* overturned, whereby

> . . . a donor gives a $500,000 check to a joint fundraising com-
> mittee composed of a candidate, a national party committee,
> and "most of the party's state party committees[.]" The com-
> mittees divide up the money so that each one receives the max-
> imum contribution permissible under the base limits, but then
> each transfers its allocated portion to the same single commit-
> tee. That committee uses the money for coordinated expendi-
> tures on behalf of a particular candidate.[346]

This arrangement describes the Hillary Victory Fund practically
to the letter, and yet the Supreme Court—writing just seven-
teen months before the Fund filed its statement of organization
with the Federal Election Commission[347]—views its possibility
as "unlikely" and based on "speculation."[348] Either the justices
comprising the majority in *McCutcheon* lacked the most basic
understanding of the practical implications of their judicial decision making, or their words are disingenuous.

In a postelection public appearance, Hillary Clinton had
this to say about her relationship to the Democratic Party and
DNC during the campaign: "I inherit[ed] nothing from the
Democratic Party. I mean it was bankrupt, it was on the verge of
insolvency, its data was mediocre to poor, nonexistent, wrong.
I had to inject money into it . . . the DNC, to keep it going."[349]

It seems odd, laughable even, to characterize an organization which advanced Clinton's candidacy at every turn, including by raising over half a billion dollars through the Hillary
Victory Fund, as "bankrupt" and a source of "nothing." Some
might call her remarks ungracious. And yet, Clinton's cutting
view of the DNC, and its relationship to her campaign, reveal
painful truths about the state of our political system. The DNC

is, indeed, "bankrupt," though not in the sense of being unable to pay its debts. To be sure, the Supreme Court's campaign finance jurisprudence has virtually guaranteed the DNC's continued financial solvency as a potent fundraising arm for its chosen candidate.[350] Rather, the DNC is a *broken*[351] organization—broken away from its purpose as a site of democratic engagement and popular participation, as set forth in the Charter. The DNC is unable to perform the task to which it has committed itself because it exists within a political system that will not allow it to do so. Our laws, speaking through the Supreme Court, have endowed the payment of money by corporations—not individual citizen engagement, or even voting[352]—as the quintessential form of political participation in America.

Witness the Supreme Court's view (as expressed in *Citizens United*) that the "voices" of corporations "best represent the most significant segments of the economy."[353] According to the Court, corporations are the "best equipped" to influence the nation's policy.[354] And the fact that one who "spends large sums may garner influence over or access to elected officials or political parties" entails neither corruption nor the appearance of corruption.[355]

The system that confronted Bernie Sanders in 2016 is one constructed, over many years, to prevent candidates like Sanders from becoming president. The impossibility of Sanders's candidacy has become engrained in the law. From the two-party duopoly, to the DNC's superdelegate system, to campaign financing awash in unlimited corporate money, the law has embraced a view of governance based on the primacy of entrenched corporate interests. Thanks to Sanders's candidacy, the contours of that system have now become clear to anyone willing to open their eyes and look. However, the consequences of this knowledge—both positive and normative—have yet to be determined.

SUMMATION
Rule of Law Demands
Consequences

"Democracy demands the truth so people can make intelligent decisions."

Judge Zloch's parting words at the hearing held on April 25, 2017, ring in my ears from time to time. One of those times occurred on the day *Politico* released an excerpt from Donna Brazile's forthcoming memoir on the 2016 election, in which she acknowledges that the DNC "rigg[ed] the system to throw the primary to Hillary."[356] According to Brazile, the Clinton campaign had "control of the party before the voters had decided which one they wanted to lead."[357]

Brazile said this became apparent to her when she found a "funding arrangement" between the Hillary Clinton campaign and the DNC after she became interim DNC chair.[358] The "funding arrangement," which was not publicly available until Brazile's book excerpt was released,[359] specified that as of September 25, 2015, and in consideration for the Clinton campaign's fundraising efforts on behalf of the DNC, through the Hillary Victory Fund joint fundraising committee, the Clinton campaign would exercise control over all "strategic decisions" at the DNC as well as hiring and the money raised.[360] Prior to Brazile's revelation, publicly available information had already shown the dynamics of the Hillary Victory Fund to have destroyed any possible pretense of the DNC to being a neutral arbiter of the primaries. But now there is further direct, smoking-gun evidence that the primaries were rigged, and Bernie Sanders never had a shot. This latest information from Brazile connects the dots financially, from the Clinton campaign's coffers to the very identity of the DNC, in both its personnel and ability to make decisions. It is, in fact, just the kind of critical evidence we, as plaintiffs' lawyers, would hope to unearth in discovery and offer at trial, along with Brazile's statements that after assuming the reins of the DNC, she was told by the Clinton campaign's CFO that the DNC was "fully under the control of Hillary's campaign" and being deployed as little more than a tool to maximize donations to the Clinton campaign through the Hillary Victory Fund.[361]

Indeed, evidence such as the fundraising arrangement between the Clinton campaign and the DNC might make the centerpiece of our opening and closing statements to the jury, but for the fact that our lawsuit may never see a trial. On August 25, 2017, Judge Zloch dismissed the case, holding that none of the plaintiffs, including donors to the Sanders campaign, have standing to pursue legal action against the DNC or Wasserman Schultz based on claims that the primary was rigged.[362] It must be noted, his order went out of its way to reject the defendants' characterization of their duty to be impartial and evenhanded under the Charter as a "trivialization of the DNC's governing principles" and found that "the DNC, through its charter, has committed itself to a higher principle." At the same time, the order echoed Spiva's caution that the court not "wade into the political thicket," concluding that "the choice—and attendant consequences—between 'impartiality and evenhandedness' and Tammany Hall politics lies in the province of the DNC, not the judiciary."[363]

The case is now on appeal with the Eleventh Circuit Court of Appeals in Atlanta, Georgia.[364] As a lawyer, I have good reason to be pessimistic about our chances. In federal civil cases, appeals are successful only about 3 to 4 percent of the time.[365] While I am confident in the strength of the arguments we will be presenting in the appellate court, I have no illusions about the chances being slim of our legal complaint not turning out to be one of many that were germinated by the events of U.S. elections yet will ultimately fail to bear legal fruit.

Of course, our prosecution of the DNC fraud lawsuit was never about "legal fruit" to begin with. It started with our abiding faith in Bernie Sanders's candidacy—with our belief that Sanders could prevail in the Democratic primaries. It stemmed from our faith in the democratic character of America's electoral institutions.

From the standpoint of one who maintains this latter type of faith, perhaps the situation is not so bleak. Some have argued that in terms of the statements made by the DNC's counsel in a federal court, the lawsuit has already been substantially revelatory in terms of what it has disclosed about the Democratic Party, its self-image, and operational structure.[366] From this perspective, the lawsuit has already accomplished one of the legal system's aims, to bring truth into the light of day. The great justice, Louis D. Brandeis, who served on the nation's highest bench from 1916 to 1939, famously observed that "sunlight is said to be the best of disinfectants."[367] If you ascribe to this view, then you might agree that *Wilding* helped bring sunlight upon the workings of the DNC regarding the primary, which is what must happen to genuinely reform the Democratic Party. Per Justice Brandeis, knowledge by the general public of governmental corruption is a predicate to any movement for "remedial action."[368]

But I wonder about the relevance of Justice Brandeis's old quip. For one, sunlight is *not* actually the best disinfectant.[369] The natural disinfectant properties of sunshine are quite limited, in fact. Sunlight is most effective against water-borne pathogens only, has "no effect on chemical contaminants, like lead or toxic pollutants," and should be deployed only "where more complex forms of water purification are less accessible."[370] There is not sufficient ultraviolet light in the sun's rays to disinfect a cell phone left in the sun all afternoon.[371]

These concerns pose no mere rhetorical quibble with Justice Brandeis. What if the strain of corruption that has contaminated America's democratic institutions—which corruption produced the very forces that precluded Sanders from having a chance to gain the nomination—is so virulent that "sunlight," in the form of public knowledge, is incapable of providing meaningful decontamination? Justice Brandeis's formulation depends upon the view that the nation's democratic institutions are at a certain level of vitality, strong enough to translate the people's desire for change into governmental reform.

But are they?

Another quotation is frequently attributed to Justice Brandeis: "We can have a democratic society or we can have the concentration of great wealth in the hands of a few. We cannot have both."[372] Ralph Nader invoked these words at the outset of the 2000 presidential campaign, where he was on the Green Party ballot.[373] Perhaps the truth of Brandeis's latter observation negates any wisdom clinging to his aphorism regarding sunlight. If so, the enormous concentration of wealth in American society in so few hands—which was the very impetus for Bernie Sanders's candidacy *as well as* the genesis of those political forces which conspired to defeat his candidacy—means that Americans are not entitled to regard themselves as citizens of a "democratic society."

The signs have been in plain sight for a long time. In the first three chapters of this book alone, in seeking to explain why it was impossible for a candidate like Bernie Sanders to win the 2016 nomination, I have already cited the words of three prominent figures in American politics or political thought who have, at various times, characterized U.S. political institutions as essentially oligarchic: Walter Dean Burnham,[374] Richard Posner,[375] and Sanders himself.[376] They are not alone. In 2009, two professors of political science at Northwestern University, Jeffrey A. Winters and Benjamin I. Page, published a paper concluding that, "it is useful to think about the U.S. political system in terms of oligarchy."[377] Five years later, Page and another political scientist, Martin Gilens of Princeton, published an "exhaustive," data-driven analysis concluding that, "the wealthy few move policy, while the average American has little power."[378] In 2013, Harvard Law School professor Lawrence Lessig and, for a brief period, candidate for the 2016 Democratic Party nomination,[379] gave a TED Talk in which he described the United States as "Lesterland," where candidates for Congress are dependent on .05 percent of the population, *i.e.*, their campaign funders.[380] Ron Formisano, chair of the American history department at the University of Kentucky, puts it bluntly in the title of his latest book, released this past year: *American Oligarchy: The Permanent Political Class.*[381]

Isn't it time we faced the fact that the United States is an oligarchy or, as Winters and Page suggest, grapple with "the normative implications" of this truth?[382] In embarking on the task, however, let us not lose sight of the daring implications. Indeed, the Supreme Court has ruled the statement, "American democracy is a fraud" to be "not generally accepted" and "distasteful to most of us."[383] And the concept of American democracy is central not only to the nation's self-image, but its official orientation to the rest of the world, which purports to originate in an understanding that:

> Democracy and respect for human rights have long been central components of U.S. foreign policy. Supporting

democracy not only promotes such fundamental American values as religious freedom and worker rights, but also helps create a more secure, stable, and prosperous global arena in which the United States can advance its national interests. In addition, democracy is the one national interest that helps to secure all the others. Democratically governed nations are more likely to secure the peace, deter aggression, expand open markets, promote economic development, protect American citizens, combat international terrorism and crime, uphold human and worker rights, avoid humanitarian crises and refugee flows, improve the global environment, and protect human health.[384]

As Plato writes in the *Republic*, the acquisition of knowledge about the world can cause both agony and disorientation: the prisoner, freed from his chains in the Cave and turning toward the sunlight outside is "pained and dazzled and unable to see the things whose shadows he'd seen before."[385]

Plato and Aristotle had much to say about oligarchy and democracy. Greeks of their time were intimately familiar with both forms of government. The political understanding of their time was indelibly infused by the variety of regimes that could be supported through the vehicle of the emerging, independent Greek city-state."[386]

In Plato's famous ranking of political regimes, found in Book VIII of the *Republic*, oligarchy is third best, while democracy comes fourth. First is the kallipolis or "beautiful city" ruled by philosopher-kings, while the second-best regime is timocracy, rule by property owners. The worst regime, according to Plato, is tyranny.

In truth, however, oligarchies and democracies seem like equally bleak places to live in Plato's account. Oligarchies are characterized by the pursuit of wealth, above all else, while democracies value the pursuit of what Plato calls *eleutheria*—translated as "freedom" or "liberty"—to the point of threatening law and order. Of course, Plato was not so much concerned with painting a nuanced portrait of political life under any of the five regimes as seeking to distill certain core truths present in each of them.

Aristotle, who was more interested than his teacher in philosophizing about the world "as is," broadly defined "democracy" as "when the free and poor, being a majority, have authority to rule; oligarchy, when the wealthy and better born have authority and are few."[387] Within these broad categories, there are many varieties of democracy and oligarchy, depending on such factors as which segments of the population can hold office and whether the rule of law governs.[388]

The rule of law is especially significant for Aristotle because its absence is characteristic of the worst varieties of *both* democracy and oligarchy. "For in cities under a democracy that is based on law a popular leader does not arise, but the best of the citizens preside; but where the laws are without authority, there popular leaders arise."[389] The result is a kind of tyranny of the mob. At the same time, an oligarchy without law is an equally tyrannical regime—what Aristotle refers to as *dynasteia* ("dynasty").[390] The import of rule of law is of a piece with Aristotle's moral philosophy, in which he ascribes a critical role to the rule of law in cultivating individual virtue.[391] Perhaps Aristotle's reverence for law reflects his teacher, as Plato devoted a considerable amount of his own output to the subject.[392]

Before going any further into the normative implications of living under an oligarchy, it must be noted, then, that for Aristotle at least, there is an even more fundamental question:

whether or not rule of law is being enforced. As an attorney who (it should be apparent by now) has grown increasingly disenchanted with the functioning of the American legal system, this is not an altogether settling prospect. As counsel to the plaintiffs in the DNC Fraud Lawsuit, it is even less settling.

Recall that in open court, the DNC's lawyer, Bruce Spiva, compared his client's Charter obligation to be "impartial and evenhanded" as akin to a "mere political promise," unenforceable in a court of law.[393] Judge Zloch rejected this as a "trivialization of the DNC's governing principles," finding that "the DNC, through its charter, has committed itself to a higher principle." Nonetheless, he held that the plaintiffs lack standing to enforce the DNC's commitment. And more recently, the DNC's former chair, Donna Brazile, while acknowledging in one breath that the primaries were in fact rigged, has insisted that the rigging, although potentially "unethical," was "not illegal."[394]

Together, these propositions constitute more in a mounting pile of evidence that the rule of law is in serious jeopardy. Those of us who have closely followed the trials and tribulations of Bernie Sanders's ill-fated campaign have seen a whole raft of blatant election law violations go unpunished.[395] Meanwhile, those who have studied Hillary Clinton, either as a candidate or in her prior political life, cannot seriously have failed to detect a pattern of investigation upon investigation, all failing to bear legal fruit. Indeed, on July 5, 2016, the frailty of American rule of law was nakedly on public display. On that morning, the nation's top legal enforcement officer, director of the FBI James Comey, announced the conclusion of his agency's year-long investigation of Clinton's unauthorized use of a private email server while secretary of state, with the determination that while her conduct had been "extremely careless," no criminal prosecution was warranted. From a legal stand-point, the trouble with Comey's statement was that "extremely careless" behavior appears to be coextensive with the level of conduct required to support a violation of the relevant stat-ute, 18 U.S.C. 793(f) (a provision of the Espionage Act), which criminalizes "gross negligence" in connection with documents "relating to the national defense." While Comey pronounced that "no reasonable prosecutor would bring such a case," the proposition is contradicted by a history of Espionage Act pros-ecutions under the gross negligence standard successfully pur-sued in United States military courts.[396]

The fruitless email investigation was not the only criminal inquest into Clinton's dealings undertaken during the 2016 campaign season. A corruption investigation into the Clinton Foundation spanning multiple FBI offices failed to spur any legal process by the Department of Justice.[397] Investigators also dogged the DNC's former chair, Wasserman Schultz, in connec-tion with procurement and data transfer irregularities traced to a group of House IT network workers, which included one of her employees.[398] At a hearing of the House Appropriations sub-committee, Wasserman Schultz advised the chief of Capitol po-lice that there would be "consequences" if the police did not return her laptop taken as part of the investigation.[399] As of the writing of this book, the investigation has resulted in only rela-tively minor bank fraud charges being filed against two of the IT workers, both of whom have pled not guilty.[400]

Certainly, others have expressed alarm at the remarkable lack of will to bring public corruption prosecutions in pres-ent-day America.[401] But the sense of lawlessness is not just an abstract feature of political life in a twenty-first century pol-ity that is increasingly oligarchical in character if not official self-image. In her memoir, the former DNC chair conveys a creeping paranoia felt concurrently with the sense of lawlessness intruding her personal life:

> Brazile writes that she was haunted by the still-unsolved murder of DNC data staffer Seth Rich and feared for her own life, shutting the blinds to her office window so snipers could not see her and installing surveillance cameras at her home. She wonders whether Russians had placed a listening device in plants in the DNC executive suite.[402]

Elizabeth and I can surely relate to Brazile on this score. Seth Rich would have been a witness in *our* case. Seth, a data analyst at the DNC, was shot in the back in a supposed "botched robbery," but all his possessions, including a wallet, watch, and phone, were found on his body. Not only does *his* murder remain unsolved (with hundreds of thousands of dollars in outstanding reward money), but our process server, Shawn Lucas, dropped dead suddenly (before he was going to give us a sworn declaration on how he had fulfilled the service-of-process requirements) and we have never received a satisfactory explanation for this either. These are not the only disturbing events marring our prosecution of the lawsuit; we've received threats and other bizarre conduct directed at counsel and plaintiffs, including a voice-altered phone call received at our office that appeared to emanate from one of Wasserman Schultz's Florida offices. When things like this happen at your office, it does not help in the task of ensuring a pleasant place to work for your employees. Thankfully, our assistant Kimberly Diaz and associate attorney Beverly Virues have been rock solid, focused, and professional throughout.[403] But what is perhaps even more frightening than the strange and disturbing events that happened in the course of pursuing the case is the mainstream media's almost complete lack of attention to the lawsuit; and what little it has reported invariably has placed us, our clients, and our claims in a less-than-serious light.[404]

Perhaps oligarchies tend more to lawlessness than other types of regimes, and this is something we Americans should become more accustomed to as we become resigned to the true nature of our own government. Aristotle suggests as much, insofar as he notes that oligarchies are inherently less stable than democracies.[405] The governments of oligarchies are not only subject to attack from the mass of people who are not politically empowered, but they are vulnerable to assault from other oligarchs. In such an atmosphere of instability, it is not hard to see why adherence to the rule of law takes a back seat. In Plato's bleaker account of human imperfection and inevitable decay, "oligarchic man" comes into being through his very disregard of the law, which eventually comes to destroy law itself:

> The treasure house filled with gold, which each possesses, destroys the constitution. First, they find ways of spending money for themselves, then they stretch the laws relating to this, then they and their wives disobey the laws altogether.[406]

Even prior to the establishment of the Republic, America originated in a declaration of legal rights against tyranny. Given the nature of oligarchies, our modern-day regime presents unique challenges to this commitment. For those American citizens seeking to confront these challenges, what happened to Bernie Sanders suggests that we should not expect to be guided by conventional modes and manners of American citizenship. Being a passive consumer of the conventional press and regularly voting in elections as an "informed citizen" can no longer translate into being an informed or empowered citizen of the

United States—if it ever did to begin with. In contrast, the creation and deployment of new and effective modes of engagement with those who govern us may be the existential political task of our time.

Appendix I

UNITED STATES DISTRICT COURT
SOUTHERN DISTRICT OF FLORIDA
FORT LAUDERDALE DIVISION
CASE NO. 16-61511-CIV-WJZ
CAROL WILDING, ET AL.,
Plaintiffs,

v.

DNC SERVICES CORP, d/b/a,
DEMOCRATIC NATIONAL COMMITTEE, ET AL.,
Defendants.
Fort Lauderdale, Florida April 25, 2017 1:24 p.m.

Transcript of Motion Hearing had before the Honorable William J. Zloch, United States District Judge.
Proceedings recorded by mechanical stenography, transcript produced by computer.

APPEARANCES:

For the Plaintiffs: Jared H. Beck, Esq.
Beverly Virues, Esq.
Beck & Lee, P.A.
12485 SW 137th Avenue Suite 205
Miami, Florida 33186
and
Cullin O'Brien, Esq.
Cullin O'Brien Law, P.A.
6541 NE 21st Way Fort Lauderdale, Florida 33308
and
Antonino G. Hernandez, Esq.
Law Office of Antonino G. Hernandez
4 SE First Street
Second Floor
Miami, Florida 33131

For the Defendants: Bruce V. Spiva, Esq.
Mark R. Caramanica, Esq.
Thomas & LoCicero
601 South Boulevard
Tampa, Florida 33601

Court Reporter: Francine C. Salopek, RMR, CRR
Official Court Reporter
United States District Court
299 E. Broward Blvd., Room 205F
Fort Lauderdale, Florida 33301
(954)769-5657/mjsfcs@aol.com

TUESDAY, APRIL 25, 2017, 1:24 P.M.
(The Judge entered the courtroom)

THE COURT: Good afternoon. Please be seated.
　Calling Case Number 16-61511-Civil.
　Counsel, would you note your appearances?

, MR. BECK: Good morning, your Honor. Jared Beck on behalf of the plaintiffs.

MR. O'BRIEN: Your Honor, Cullin O'Brien on behalf of the plaintiffs.

MR. HERNANDEZ: Your Honor, Antonio Hernandez on behalf of the plaintiffs.

MS. VIRUES: Beverly Virues on behalf of the plaintiffs.

THE COURT: Good afternoon.

MR. SPIVA: Good afternoon, your Honor. Bruce Spiva on behalf of the defendants.

MR. CARAMANICA: And, your Honor, Mark Caramanica on behalf of the defendants.

THE COURT: Good afternoon.
　We're here this afternoon for—or upon the motion to dismiss filed by the defense.
　I have, obviously, questions for both sides. And what I'd like to do is, as we cover various technical issues, such as standing, the pleadings, class action allegations, and so forth, rather than hear from just one side, as we go through with individual questions, I'll hear from the defense, I'll hear from the plaintiff on that particular issue. All right. And, again, these are technical issues that we will be dealing with.
　But let me just give a brief description of the case at this point. The plaintiffs brought this suit as a putative class action against Defendants DNC Services Corp. and Deborah Wassermann Schultz. According to their first-amended complaint, that is, Docket Entry Number 8, the plaintiffs are,

quote, "residents of 45 states and the District of Columbia." They seek to represent three distinct classes:

One, all people or entities who contributed to the DNC from January 1, 2015, through July 13, 2016, referred to as the "DNC Donor Class."

Two, all people or entities who contributed to the Bernie Sanders campaign from January 1, 2015, through July 13, 2016, known as the "Sanders Donor Class."

And, three, all registered members of the Democratic Party, known as the "Democratic Party Class."

This case arises generally from the DNC's alleged bias in favor of Hillary Clinton during the 2015-2016 Democratic Presidential Primary, as well as the DNC's handling of donor information, which was attacked by an online hacker.

Plaintiffs bring six causes of action, each germane to particular proposed classes.

Count 1, fraud by the DNC Donor Class and the Sanders Donor Class.

Count 2, negligent misrepresentation by the DNC Donor Class and the Sanders Donor Class.

Three, violation of Section 28-3904 of the District of Columbia code by the DNC Donor Class and the Sanders Donor Class.

Count 4, unjust enrichment by the DNC Donor Class.

Count 5, breach of fiduciary duty by the Democratic Party Class.

And Count 6, negligence by the DNC Donor Class.

The defendants have moved to dismiss the first-amended complaint, Docket Entry Number 8. The defendants' arguments fall generally under three umbrellas.

First, the defendants argue that plaintiffs lack standing to bring their claims. Next, the defendants argue that the first-amended complaint fails to state a claim. And, third, the defendants argue that the class action allegations should be stricken.

Now, with that general description of the pleadings at this stage—well, let me do it this way. Are there any opening remarks that the defense would like to give? And then I'll hear from the plaintiff as well. And then I'll go into my questions.

MR. SPIVA: Your Honor, I was prepared to give some opening remarks, but if you would prefer to just ask questions, I'm also happy to do it that way.

THE COURT: Well, go ahead. You can give your—take your time. We have the whole afternoon.

MR. SPIVA: Okay.

And mindful of what your Honor said about wanting to take, you know, the issues kind of one at a time, maybe I'll cover the—I'll start with the issue of standing and whether the Court has subject-matter jurisdiction first. Because, of course, if we are correct that there is no subject—no standing and no subject-matter jurisdiction, then the entire complaint—all of the claims should be dismissed, your Honor.

THE COURT: So you were gonna go into your arguments.

MR. SPIVA: Yes. Well, why don't I do this. Why don't I—I'll give you just some very brief overview opening statement, and then I'll sit down, and the other side can do the same. And then we can—

THE COURT: Then I'll begin with my questions.

MR. SPIVA: Okay.

THE COURT: Because we'll cover all of these technical points.

MR. SPIVA: Sure. That makes sense, your Honor.

THE COURT: All right.

MR. SPIVA: Your Honor, just briefly, this is really an action that was brought as a political weapon against the DNC and its former chairperson, Congresswoman Debbie Wassermann Schultz. And it really threatens some serious First Amendment injury to the defendants, because the crux of the plaintiffs' claims here are that the DNC and Congresswoman Schultz purportedly breached an internal rule of the party in saying on the one hand that the party would remain neutral between the two candidates and on the other hand not doing that behind the scenes. That's the allegation.

And I think really what runs through all of these questions, your Honor, the questions that the Court would have to address to resolve that claim that really demonstrate why there is no subject-matter jurisdiction, why this can't be resolved as a class action, and why there's a failure to state a claim, and that is, your Honor, the Court would have to resolve such issues as what was the meaning of the Democratic Party's internal rule and how should it be enforced.

THE COURT: You're talking about the DNC's charter now.

MR. SPIVA: Yes, their bylaws, which is where this purported obligation arises to remain neutral as between the candidates.

THE COURT: Article V, Section 4.

MR. SPIVA: Correct, your Honor.

THE COURT: Go ahead.

MR. SPIVA: And the Court would have to basically tell the party that it couldn't change that rule, even though it's a discretionary rule that it didn't need to adopt to begin with.

The Court would have to find that these individuals were induced to give money to Representative Sanders—sorry—Senator Sanders on the basis that there would be this neutrality that there purportedly was not, and that they wouldn't have—they relied on that, and that they wouldn't have given that money otherwise.

And same with DNC members. The Court would have to define who is a member of the Democratic Party nationwide.

There is no national registration for either of the major parties. And so, this Court would have to determine what it means to be a Democrat and then determine whether the class that the Court defined was injured in some way by the allegations.

I think through each of these questions, your Honor—and there are more—they are not justiciable, because they are political questions that courts have repeatedly said they—that they are not the province of the civil courts.

It's not redressable, because if the Court were to seek to answer those questions and impose burdens upon the party, it would violate the First Amendment rights of the party for free association. And so it's not re-dressable.

And, really, I think there's an impossible showing of causation. I mean the Court would have to find that people who fervently supported Bernie Sanders and who purportedly didn't know that this favoritism was going on would have not given to Mr. Sanders, to Senator Sanders, if they had known that there was this purported favoritism.

And, of course, there are lots of other underlying factual determinations that this Court would have to make in terms of whether there was such favoritism, and how it affected the race, that also raise similar types of questions that really are without—it's outside the province of the Court.

I think this really runs through all of these issues, your Honor. I think it also shows why this can't be determined on a class basis, because every single person who was determined to be a member of one of these three subclasses would need to be deposed and would need to testify at trial about issues such as reliance.

And so, I think those questions really, your Honor, are at the heart of why this case should be dismissed for lack of subject-matter jurisdiction, why there's a failure to state a claim, and why the class action allegations should be stricken.

Thank you.

THE COURT: Thank you, Counsel.

MR. BECK: Thank you, your Honor.

THE COURT: Good afternoon.

MR. BECK: Good afternoon.

And thank you, Counsel.

Your Honor, we've been accused just now of wielding a political weapon. We've been accused of posing a threat to the First Amendment. But, in fact, the First Amendment is not absolute, and the Supreme Court recognizes that again and again. And, in fact, the First Amendment yields on many occasions to more ancient common-law rights that precede even the founding of this republic.

Freedom of speech and freedom of association are very, very important, but we also have a right not to be defrauded.

We also have a right not to be taken advantage of by a fiduciary. We have a right not to be deceived. There's no exception to those rights just because the fraudulent speech or the fraudulent conduct involved takes place in a political context. But that's what the defendants want you to conclude in this case. But if you concluded that, your Honor, you would be in direct contravention of what the Supreme Court has said time and again.

Virginia State Board of Pharmacy, quote:

"Untruthful speech, commercial or otherwise, has never been protected for its own sake."

The famous Gertz opinion, one of the seminal First Amendment cases, quote:

"There is no constitutional value in false statements of fact. Neither the intentional lie nor the careless error materially advances society's interest in uninhibited, robust, and wide-open debate on public issues."

And more recently in Madigan vs. Illinois, a 2006 opinion from the Supreme Court, the Court held:

"Consistent with our precedent and the First Amendment, states may maintain fraud actions when fundraisers make false or misleading representations designed to deceive donors about how their donations are used."

I think it's very clear that there is no real First Amendment issue involved here, simply because we are talking about speech which occurred in the political context. The First Amendment or the common-law admits no exception to the rights not to be defrauded, not to be deceived, just because speech was involved. That's very central to our system of justice.

And as to standing, which is the means by which a litigant enters court, standing here is a very, very basic question—or a very basic issue. And I think it's readily decided in this case, because we are talking primarily about the loss of money. And federal courts have recognized again and again that loss of money is a valid injury to confer Article III standing.

Just because that money was paid as part of a political process, again, we get back to the First Amendment, we get back to all those cases that the Supreme Court has decided. There's no protection of fraudulent speech that comes under the rubric of freedom of speech or freedom of association.

This is not a case about enforcing political promises. They want you to think that, I believe, because they want to paint this case in a line of cases that have been filed throughout the years where candidates may make political promises, and then disappointed voters bring lawsuits to enforce those promises or seek damages in one form or another. But that's not what this case is about. We're not talking about campaign rhetoric. We're not talking about a campaign platform of any kind.

What we're talking about here is the very core of what our democracy runs on, the very basis for our democracy, which is the conduct of free and fair elections. That's the basis, that's the bedrock on which the claims of this case take off, because the election—the elections—as American history has developed, the conduct of those elections, for better or worse, has come under the domain of the two major political parties in this country.

And in our case, in getting into the allegations of our case, what we are alleging and what we are very, I think, clearly alleging and specifically alleging in this complaint is that people paid money in reliance on the understanding that the primary elections for the Democratic nominee—nominating process in 2016 were fair and impartial. And that's not just a bedrock assumption that we would assume just by virtue of the fact that we live in a democracy, and we assume that our elections are run in a fair and impartial manner. But that's what the Democratic National Committee's own charter says. It says it in black and white. And they can't deny that.

THE COURT: Let me just interrupt you.

MR. BECK: Oh, sure.

THE COURT: And I apologize. This is not your problem.

MR. BECK: Okay.

THE COURT: But for those of you who are here as spectators—and there's at least one individual and maybe two—you are distracting the Court with your show of exuberance in support of counsel's arguments. You might as well be doing somersaults or backflips in support of counsel's argument. So, you are distracting me. So, if you want to help the side that you're here to support, let me listen to the lawyer, and please stop distracting me.

Counsel, go right ahead.

MR. BECK: Thank you, your Honor.

I was talking about the charter, because I was making the point that we're not just talking about a bedrock assumption of what it means to live in a democracy and what formed the bedrock understanding of the plaintiffs in this lawsuit, but it's also in the charter itself, which—

THE COURT: Article IV—or—excuse me—Article V, Section 4.

MR. BECK: Correct.

Which requires the DNC and its chairperson to act in an even and impartial manner with respect to the presidential nominating process.

THE COURT: Which is in paragraph 159 of your first-amended complaint.

MR. BECK: Correct.

And not only is it in the charter, but it was stated over and over again in the media by the Democratic National Committee's employees, including Congresswoman Wassermann Schultz, that they were, in fact, acting in compliance with the charter. And they said it again and again, and we've cited several instances of that in the case.

So, getting back to the question of standing, when you have money—in this case, it's in the form of political donations, but, again, I don't think the political context makes any difference—but when you have money that's paid in reliance on a false understanding and a false—or a false belief that is created by the defendant, then you have all of the elements of Article III satisfied.

You have an injury in fact. You have a causal connection, because the money, which is the injury in fact—and there's no denying the case law on that—the money was paid in reliance on the false understanding. And then in terms of judicial redress, the principal relief we're asking for in this case is damages.

So, I think—personally I think standing is—in spite of the defendants' efforts to muddy the waters and try to turn this into—and try to paint us with a political brush, like we're, you know, fighting some political battle, which is just totally not true, you know, I think standing's an easy question.

We may represent people that gave to Bernie Sanders, but that doesn't mean that this has—and—this lawsuit has any connection whatsoever to the political campaign that Bernie Sanders fought in 2016, which is now over. And in terms of the relief we're seeking, the principal relief we're seeking is damages.

Now, in terms of the complaint and in terms of the allegations of the complaint, and specifically what the DNC did wrong, I just think the context of when this complaint was drafted is important. We drafted this complaint and filed it in June of 2016, which was before the DNC primary—or the DNC convention occurred in July. And, at the time, the evidence that we had access to consisted of this set of documents that your Honor referenced in your prefatory remarks that were released by a figure named Guccifer 2.0.

And the core document that was released by that individual on that website purports to be an internal DNC memorandum, which outlines a strategy for advancing Hillary Clinton to the nomination of the Democratic Party before the primaries had even really gotten off the ground. And this was at a time—you know, Bernie Sanders I believe had announced for about a month before this particular memo came out. But we think that's clear evidence of what the DNC's intent was throughout the primary process. It was to leverage their connections with the media in order to advance Hillary Clinton's candidacy at the expense of everybody else.

Subsequent to this memorandum being released into the public by Guccifer 2.0, many more documents have come into the public domain. We have a wealth of information that was released by WikiLeaks that comes from e-mails from officials of the DNC, as well as the Hillary Clinton campaign, which really, I think, flesh out and fill in the detail of this really seminal internal document that Guccifer released and which is pled in our complaint.

These additional leaks have shown that DNC officials participated in creating and disseminating media narratives to undermine Bernie Sanders and advance Hillary Clinton.

It shows former DNC Chair Donna Brazile giving debate questions in advance to Hillary Clinton during the primaries.

It shows the DNC at one point changing its donor policies specifically to favor Hillary Clinton.

It shows the scheduling of debates to favor Hillary Clinton over Bernie Sanders.

It shows, in general, the DNC pouring its considerable resources and relationships into propelling Hillary Clinton to the nomination.

It shows the creation of an aura of inevitability of Hillary Clinton's candidacy that the DNC pushed into the media and, essentially, in our view, crushed the Bernie Sanders campaign.

It shows the DNC coordinating and taking direction from Hillary Clinton's campaign operatives, making hiring decisions based on what Hillary Clinton's campaign was telling them, picking sides in the disputes between the candidates.

I mean, there's one famous example of an alleged chair-throwing incident in Nevada, where instead of acting in an even and impartial manner,

Debbie Wassermann Schultz immediately sided with the Hillary Clinton campaign.

And all of this, you know, comes out of documents that have been released into the public domain subsequent to the drafting of this complaint, based on the Guccifer 2.0 leaks.

But we're not even getting into at this point—we're not even getting into the question of widespread reports of irregularities at polling locations in various states relating to the actual voting in the primary. There's widespread reports of voting machine irregularities, voter suppression, strange purging of the rolls.

I mean, your Honor, I think when all of this is seen together, it's really hard to deny that the DNC was not acting in accordance with its own charter and not acting in accordance with its role and, quite frankly, its duty as a custodian of this country's democracy. But, again, this is not a case about abstract political principles.

This is a case—and I have to make this point again and again, because I think this really gets back to the technical issues that your Honor identified at the outset, which is that we have standing here because there was payment of money in reliance on a false understanding that was created by these defendants.

And I do want to say that I think we have a second basis for standing that goes beyond money. And I don't want to forget this, but there's a whole line of cases which talks about the invasion of established common-law rights as a valid basis for standing. And I don't want to lose sight of that, because I don't think money is the only basis for standing. I think this especially—is of special relevance for the Democratic Party Class, and specifically the breach of fiduciary duty count, which doesn't necessarily rely on the payment of money.

Now, they've said in their opening remarks, essentially, that there's no such thing as the Democratic Party, or we can't ascertain who's in the Democratic Party. I mean, to me, you know, that's—that—I think that would be a surprising proposition to most people in this country. I think we can figure out who's a democrat and who's not. But I think those are factual issues anyway.

Perhaps those—you know, perhaps they have arguments that can be made at a summary judgment stage or something, but here we're talking about the pleadings, we're talking about what we've alleged, and I think we've pled enough to state a valid breach of fiduciary duty claim. The D.C.

law that we've cited I think is, uhm—recognizes a sufficiently flexible definition of what a fiduciary duty means in order to encompass the relationship between a party or the head of a party and its members.

In fact, there's a whole line of cases—and I know it's not the D.C. cases, it's New York cases—but under New York fiduciary law, a whole line of cases which recognize such a duty. So, I don't really think it's a stretch at all to say that, number one, there is a Democratic Party; and, number two, that the party owes a fiduciary duty to its members. And if the party's not—and if the party doesn't owe such a duty to its members, then who does it owe a duty to? Well, you know, I think in some ways that's what this case may be about.

I just want to finish up with a few points, and then I know your Honor has a number of questions, so I want to make sure to leave sufficient time for that.

I think the argument under Rule 12(g)(2) that the defendants have waived their right to bring a 12(b)(6) motion is a strong argument. I recognize that there's some tension in the case law on that. By no means does it seem to be a settled question. But the rule does specifically have an exemption for challenges to subject-matter jurisdiction, which I think makes sense, given what subject-matter jurisdiction entails. But it—I think it's [*sic*] very specifically says that if you bring a motion under 12(b), and then you bring a subsequent motion, unless you bring the arguments in the first motion, you've waived them.

And they filed a motion to dismiss based on service of process. They could have stated those arguments at that time. They chose not to. I think under the plain reading of Rule 12(g)(2), they've waived everything except their challenge to subject-matter jurisdiction.

I think they have—they take the position that we haven't pled enough in our complaint to—we haven't pled our claims for fraud and negligent misrepresentation with sufficient specificity. I think we've gone into very considerable detail about the public statements of the DNC, the content of its charter. And I think we very specifically pled that what the folks who are serving as plaintiffs in this case did in reliance on those representations, which is that they paid donations to a political campaign in some cases, or to the DNC in others, it's certainly been sufficient to put the DNC on notice of what the claims against them are. I don't think they have any mystery about what our theory of the case is. So, I think we've satisfied the pleading requirements.

We have specific allegations there related to Congresswoman Wasser-mann Schultz, specifically what she said in the media, what her role is in the organization, and, uhm, I think—and her title is referenced in the charter. So I don't think it's any mystery as to what the allegations are against her personally.

A couple final points. The CPPA, which is the D.C. consumer statute that we've pled as one of the claims, I do think that the statute is worded in a broad enough fashion to cover the claims in this case. Its whole purpose is to protect consumers of goods and services. And many of, if not the vast majority of the Bernie donor class (sic), are people that used an online or service or application called ActBlue, which charges a 3.95 percent processing fee in connection with every donation. So, that's a service.

Now, we haven't sued ActBlue. But I don't think we need privity under the D.C. cases that I've looked at and which we've cited to the Court. I think that the—well, a couple of those cases specifically say that anyone involved in the chain of supply is appropriate as a defendant in an action under that statute. And the DNC and its chairwoman were the entity and the person responsible that this election was going to be fair and even-handed—or the primary process was going to be fair and evenhanded, as they promise in their charters.

So, I think that under the statute, and bearing in mind that it's a broad consumer statute, I think we have a viable claim, and we've pled a claim there.

And, finally, I just want to close with a couple words on the negligence claim. Because the negligence claim specifically related to the data breach and the loss of the donors' data. Again, there is a difference of opinion in the case law specifically on this issue. We recognize that the Ninth Circuit and the Seventh Circuit have taken the position that the data doesn't actually have to be misused in order to have a valid claim based on a defendant's loss of private data. The Third Circuit has taken the other view.

I personally think that the Ninth Circuit and the Seventh Circuit have the issue right. And I think that the DNC's own donors were harmed the moment their sensitive personal data was released into the public domain, because the DNC failed to take sufficient steps to protect it.

So, I think that covers all the issues that I wanted to address in my opening statement. And I'll be happy to answer any questions the Court has.

THE COURT: All right. Thank you, Counsel.

Well, let me start with the defense. And I've got some questions regarding the operation of the DNC.

What does the DNC do as the head of the Democratic Party?

MR. SPIVA: I mean, the DNC coordinates with state and local parties. It supports the activities of candidates, democratic candidates. It has a role in the presidential primary process in terms of coordinating those elections. It is—essentially provides leadership for—in support of electing democratic candidates up and down the ballot nationwide.

THE COURT: What type of involvement does the DNC have in primaries at the state level?

MR. SPIVA: The—it—the DNC—those are primarily dealt with by state parties, state and local party committees, your Honor. There's some coordination between the DNC and those parties. The DNC also obviously runs the convention, the nominating convention, and there are certain rules about how delegates get seated and the like. But as a general matter, does not run the state-level primaries, if that gets to your Honor's question.

THE COURT: Does the DNC help to fund the state primaries?

MR. SPIVA: Uhm, you mean literally, the mechanics of the primaries, your Honor, the actual holding of the election, the primary election?

THE COURT: Does the DNC, with the money that it raises, use some of that money to help fund the states put on their individual state primaries?

MR. SPIVA: I don't believe so, your Honor. No.

THE COURT: But you don't know.

MR. SPIVA: I'm 90 percent on that, your Honor, but I don't believe that's the case. I believe that's generally state funded. In my experience—and I have had experience with a number of these—the funds for actually having the election is—they're state funds.

THE COURT: Well, you've said several times that the DNC helps coordinate. What do you mean by that?

MR. SPIVA: Well, the DNC sometimes works to sponsor debates and then get out a general democratic message, offers certain data services to candidates for the presidency, for instance, and for other offices as well. It collects data about voting behavior and other kinds of data. It obviously raises money. So, those are some of the activities that I was alluding to.

THE COURT: And what type of involvement does the DNC have with the state democratic parties?

MR. SPIVA: It coordinates with state democratic parties to try to help elect democratic candidates really up and down the ballot.

THE COURT: And does the DNC give its preference to the state democratic parties as to any particular candidate?

MR. SPIVA: No, not in—certainly not in the presidential elections, they don't set forth a preference, no.

THE COURT: What about the primaries, the democratic primaries?

MR. SPIVA: I'm sorry, I thought that was what you were referring to, your Honor.

No, the DNC does not take sides in the state primaries, presidential primaries.

THE COURT: What type of strategic support does the DNC provide to the state democratic parties?

MR. SPIVA: Well, I mean I actually—I don't know—I can't answer that in detail, your Honor, but, you know, certainly support in terms of issues, you know, addressing issues, I think funding support, and the like.

THE COURT: But I mean in light of the plaintiffs' allegations, you see the thrust of my questions.

MR. SPIVA: I—I'm actually—I see the thrust, your Honor, but I'm actually not sure where your Honor is going with this line, to be honest. I'm sorry, I may just be being—

THE COURT: Well, the plaintiff is alleging that the DNC, on its own—and I'm gonna paraphrase—but basically favored Hillary Clinton over Bernie Sanders. And so, I'm asking you, that preference that the plaintiff alleges about the DNC, did that work its way down to the democratic state primaries?

MR. SPIVA: Well, I mean our position, your Honor, is there was no such preference, and certainly there was no—the Democratic National Committee did not, you know, tell the state parties that it supported one candidate over the other.

So, if that answers your question. I mean, of course, stepping back and kind of going to our subject-matter jurisdiction issue, I mean, the litany of things that counsel referred to, to suggest that there was this favoritism, I think clearly illustrates the types of issues that the courts really don't wade into as an Article III matter. I mean these are what—I believe it was the Wymbs, the Republican State Executive Committee case in the Eleventh Circuit referred to as political squabbles that courts are—you know, really can't take a position on.

And so here you have a charter that says you have to be—where the party has adopted a principle of evenhandedness, and just to get the language exactly right, that they would be evenhanded and impartial, I believe, is the exact language. And, you know, that's not self-defining, your Honor. I mean that's kind of like, you know, saying, Who's a Baptist? You know, I mean, for your Honor to wade into that, you would really have to—whether the party was evenhanded or not, whether they gave each side equal debate time, and whether their hiring decisions reflected in some measure a bias towards Secretary Clinton, these are all issues that courts—really would drag this Court right into the political squabbles, and really there'd be no way constitutionally to offer redress for—even for what they are claiming.

THE COURT: So, are you suggesting that this is just part of the business, so to speak, that it's not unusual for, let's say, the DNC, the RNC to take sides with respect to any particular candidate and to support that candidate over another?

MR. SPIVA: Well, I'm not suggesting that that is par for the course, your Honor. But what I am suggesting is to have those kinds of allegations is the rough and tumble of politics. I mean, you know, certainly in the Wymbs case, if anything, that was a case which involved something that was maybe more concrete, where the issue was how the party decided who was gonna go to the convention as a delegate and who could speak for the party in the state, in Florida, in terms of how they selected delegates to the state party.

And, you know, there, there was a numeric component to it, because it was—the challenge was based on one person/one vote, and the district court in that case actually said, Well, you know, we should do this kind of like a Reynolds v. Sims, and it should be based on one republican/one vote. So, plausibly there, there's some kind of standard that maybe a Court could look to. And even there, the Eleventh Circuit said, No, that's internal party politics.

The party has the freedom of association to decide how it's gonna select its representatives to the convention and to the state party. And, as a matter of fact—and that case was decided in the early '80s, the Republican Party in Florida was a minority party. So they said, Well, it might not make sense to the party to have one republican/one vote as a matter of committee representation, because we have to attract the votes of democrats.

And so—but that's for the party to decide. The Court's not gonna get into that. Here, you have something far more inchoate, your Honor, which is this purported—this claim that the party acted without evenhandedness and impartiality. That—even to define what constitutes evenhandedness and impartiality really would already drag the Court well into a political question and a question of how the party runs its own affairs.

The party could have favored a candidate. I'll put it that way. Maybe that's a better way of answering your Honor's original question. Even if it were true, that's the business of the party, and it's not justiciable.

THE COURT: All right. Thank you, Counsel.

MR. SPIVA: Thank you. And I'm happy to answer—

THE COURT: Oh, no, I've got more questions.

MR. SPIVA: But on that issue—

THE COURT: I'm gonna give the plaintiff an opportunity.

MR. SPIVA: Okay. Great. Thanks, your Honor.

Yeah, people sometimes say that the lawyers will be more prepared than the judges they appear before. I think your Honor has disproved that today. But I do want to address whatever questions the Court has with respect to any of these issues.

THE COURT: Well, we're gonna go through standing, and the pleadings, and class actions allegations. Don't worry, we're going to cover the full breadth of it.

MR. SPIVA: Thank you, your Honor.

THE COURT: What does the plaintiff say on the operational aspect of the DNC?

MR. BECK: Well, your Honor, I'm shocked to hear that we can't define what it means to be evenhanded and impartial. If that were the case, we couldn't have courts. I mean, that's what courts do every day, is decide disputes in an evenhanded and impartial manner.

So, to me, it's not a difficult question at all what it means to be evenhanded and impartial. It doesn't mean having to wade in to a political dispute about how the party conducts its affairs, because that's what the party represented in its charter, that's what the party represented over and over again in the media, that's, frankly, what I think is at the bedrock of what it means to live in a democratic society. I think that's why the Democratic National Committee has it in its charter, because if you don't have the organization that is responsible for organizing in this very large sense the nominating process for president, which entails multiple elections in every state of the union, if you're not evenhanded and impartial, then you don't have a democratic process. I think it's that simple.

And I think what it means is the Democratic National Committee should not be putting any resources into one candidate at the expense of another.

I think it means that it should not be assisting the media in crafting narratives that hurt one candidate at the expense of another.

I think it means that when there's a dispute that comes up in one of the primaries, say, in Nevada, where there are allegations of misbehavior during a primary or an event, I think it means that the DNC should not be picking sides and should be adjudicating those disputes in a fair and even-handed manner.

I think this is not a difficult thing at all to decide. I think the language speaks for itself in many ways. And so, again—and I'll just say it again—they keep citing cases where plaintiffs have brought grievances that are political in nature. And now they're starting to use this defense of justiciability, which, interestingly, I don't think that particular defense, as phrased, appeared anywhere in their papers. I may be missing something, but I don't see how this is a political question.

We're not asking this Court to infringe on the province of another branch of this government or to get involved in the conduct of Congress or the conduct of the Office of President. We're asking this Court to determine whether representations and omissions were false and misleading, and whether money was paid on the basis of those representations, whether folks were injured in a financial sense as a result of those representations, and whether duties to the class members were breached, including fiduciary duties.

I think those—courts do those types of things all the time. There's nothing inherently political about those determinations. And I—again, I think this gets back to this theme that they keep putting in front of the Court that there's some type of immunity that comes out of the First Amendment, because we're talking about politics and sort of anything goes as far as political speech is concerned. I think that's kind of what their theory boils down to.

And I would just emphasize that, again, we are talking about the payment of money. And once money is involved, once people are paying money based on false understandings, clearly, there is standing, and I don't see the political question or a justiciability issue.

THE COURT: All right. Thank you, Counsel.

MR. BECK: Okay. Thank you.

THE COURT: All right. Let me ask the defense—we're going to go into the issue of standing now at this point.

Let me ask counsel. If a person is fraudulently induced to donate to a charitable organization, does he have standing to sue the person who induced the donation?

MR. SPIVA: I think, your Honor, if the circumstance were such that the organization promised that it was going to abide by some general principle, and the donee—or donor, rather, ultimately sued, because they said, Well, we don't think you're living up to that general principle, we don't think you're, you know, serving kids adequately, we think your program is—the way you're running your program is not adequate, you know, you're not doing it well enough, that that—that they would not have standing in that circumstance.

I think if somebody—a charitable organization were to solicit funds and say, Hey, we're gonna spend this money on after-school programs for kids, and the executive director actually put the money in their pocket and went down the street and bought a Mercedes-Benz, I think in that circumstance, they would have standing.

I think this circumstance is even one step further towards the no standing side of that, because here we're talking about a political party and political principles and debate. And that's an area where there's a wealth of doctrine and case law about how that—just simply giving money does not give one standing to direct how the party conducts its affairs, or to complain about the outcomes, or whether or not the party is abiding by its own internal rules.

And I should say, your Honor, I just want to be clear, because I know it may sometimes sound like I am somehow suggesting that I think the party did not—you know, the party's position is that it has not violated in the least this provision of its charter.

THE COURT: I understand.

MR. SPIVA: So I just want to get that out there. But to even determine—to make that determination would require the Court to wade into this political thicket. And—you know, which would invade its First Amendment interests, and also, I think, would raise issues—standing issues along all three prongs of the standing test.

Causation. Did—the thrust of plaintiffs' allegations appears to be that some—that one of the subclasses gave money to the Sanders campaign, because they thought the party was living up to this idea. They don't actually allege that any particular plaintiff, by the way, knew about this charter commitment or that they relied upon it in giving money to Sanders. But even if they had, showing the causation there, I think, is not something that can be done. And it's something that would require, again, the Court to wade into the political thicket.

Similarly, they purport to speak on behalf of this DNC Donor Class. Most, most of the class that they purport to speak on behalf of, you know, disagrees with them. And so, the Court would have to wade into that to establish causation. And it really can't—it can't be done.

The other part of their injury here appears to be that Mr. Sanders—Senator Sanders would have done better had the party supposedly been more evenhanded than it was. Well, that—there's all kinds of alternative factors for why Secretary Clinton actually got more votes in the end and won. And as everybody knows, Senator Sanders endorsed her and campaigned for her. And so, there's a causation problem. And there are other issues that we discuss in our brief—I won't repeat them—with causation.

There is certainly a redressability problem, which I think I've already covered in my previous remarks. I won't go over that, again unless your Honor has other questions.

And then in terms of concrete injury, which was really the first prong, that, again, is problematic, because—and this goes back to your Honor's question—there is no right to—just by virtue of making a donation, to enforce the parties' internal rules. And there's no right to not have your candidate disadvantaged or have another candidate advantaged. There's no contractual obligation here.

Nor is there a fiduciary obligation, although I know we're gonna get to that later. But there's—it's not a situation where a promise has been made that is an enforceable promise. And I think that goes both to the concrete injury prong and the redressability prong.

THE COURT: And then one other question on the issue of standing for the defense. Is there a difference between a campaign promise made by a political candidate and a promise that pertains to the integrity of the primary process itself?

In other words, President George H.W. Bush's—

MR. SPIVA: "Read my lips."

THE COURT:—promise—"read my lips, no new taxes," and then he raised taxes. Well, he could not be sued for raising taxes. But with respect to the DNC charter, Article V, Section 4, is there a difference between the two?

MR. SPIVA: Not one—there's obviously a difference in degree. I think your Honor—I'm not gonna—I don't want to overreach and say that there's no difference. But I don't think there's a difference that's material in terms of how the Court should decide the question before it in terms of standing, in that this, again, goes to how the party runs itself, how it decides who it's going to associate with, how it decides how it's going to choose its standard bearer ultimately. In case after case, from O'Brien, to Wymbs, to Wisconsin v. LaFollette, Cousins v. Wigoda, the Supreme Court and other courts have affirmed the party's right to make that determination. Those are internal issues that the party gets to decide basically without interference from the courts.

And the fact that money has—I know that my distinguished colleague on the other side has several times said that, Well, money makes this different, and it really doesn't in this context. You know, again, if you had a charity where somebody said, Hey, I'm gonna take this money and use it for a specific purpose, X, and they pocketed it and stole the money, of course that's different. But here, where you have a party that's saying, We're gonna, you know, choose our standard bearer, and we're gonna follow these general rules of the road, which we are voluntarily deciding, we could have—and we could have voluntarily decided that, Look, we're gonna go into back rooms like they used to and smoke cigars and pick the candidate that way. That's not the way it was done. But they could have. And that would have also been their right, and it would drag the Court well into party politics, internal party politics to answer those questions.

THE COURT: All right. Thank you, Counsel.

MR. SPIVA: Thank you, your Honor.

THE COURT: Let me have the plaintiff respond to those two questions of the defense. And then I have questions for the plaintiff regarding standing, and I'll let the defense respond to those—

MR. BECK: Okay.

THE COURT:—to those answers.

MR. BECK: Uhm—

THE COURT: First, your response to their answers.

MR. BECK: Yes. And I'll take the last part first, which was the question your Honor had posed, is there—and I'm paraphrasing it, but is there a material difference between a campaign promise, such as "read my lips, no new taxes," and representations that are made in the DNC's own charter?

And, quite frankly, if what defendant—or what the DNC has just said is true—and I really hope it's not true, but if what he said is true, then I think it's a really sad day for democracy in this country. Because what essentially the DNC has now stated in a court of law is that it believes that there is no enforceable obligation to run the primary elections of this country's democracy in a fair and impartial manner.

And if that's the case—and I think counsel just said it himself—then really, you know, the sky's the limit in terms of what the DNC and any party, for that matter, can do.

THE COURT: Can go around doing.

MR. BECK: And I'm—I hope that's not the case, but I don't think it is the case under the law. Because I think these are enforceable obligations. Because, again, money is involved, number one, payment of money based on false understandings that have been created by the defendants. That is textbook Article III standing, and the Supreme Court has settled that question. And it's settled that question in a context that's, I think, very close to the situation we have in the case pending before the Court.

And, specifically, I'm referring to Madigan vs. Illinois—or Illinois vs. Madigan, which was a case about charitable fundraising and the state's right to enforce laws against fraud and misrepresentation in the context of solicitations of charitable contributions.

And I think this gets back to the Court's first question that was posed to counsel, which is, is there standing in this situation where false representations are made, and those representations or omissions cause people to donate money to a cause? In this case, not a political cause but a charitable cause.

And—now, the Supreme Court says—and I'm reading from Illinois vs. Madigan at page—starting at page 623:

"Our decisions have repeatedly recognized the legitimacy of government efforts to enable donors to make informed choices about their charitable contributions."

And then it goes on further down:

"Just as government may seek to inform the public and prevent fraud through such disclosure requirements, so it may, quote, vigorously enforce antifraud laws to prohibit professional fundraisers from obtaining money on false pretenses or by making false statements."

Well, this is a case that involves political contributions as opposed to charitable contributions. But, again—and I think I've discussed the reasons I think this is so, but I don't think that the political context of the speech involved here or the money that was paid makes any difference to the Court's analysis, whether that analysis is cast in terms of First Amendment grounds, because the First Amendment has always recognized a right not to be defrauded or to be deceived, because those are common-law rights that precede the First Amendment, and the First Amendment is a very important right, but it by no means protects the rights of any organization to make false representations.

And in this case, I think that besides the First Amendment question, there's also implicit in Madigan and other cases that we've cited in the briefs, that, of course, there is standing when money is paid. That's the essence—one of the essences of Article III is that financial industry—injury gives rise to standing.

I submit that there's a second line of cases which also talks about invasion of common-law rights. I think that we have standing on behalf of all three of the classes based on both of those principles. And I know your Honor said—

THE COURT: I have questions.

MR. BECK:—you had questions.

THE COURT: All right. Thank you.

MR. BECK: So I'll be happy to take those.

THE COURT: With respect to the issue of standing on—you stated earlier that the plaintiff is seeking damages. Damages in the sense of return of the contributions or over and above that?

MR. BECK: Yes. The basis for the economic damages are the contributions themselves that were paid.

THE COURT: Okay. And what imminent future injury do the plaintiffs allege?

MR. BECK: Well, I think that the imminent future injury—and this has—sort of, I think, become apparent perhaps in the course of today's hearing, but the imminent future injury is that elections occur on a cyclical basis. And so, unless the Court—if we prove our claims, and unless the Court issues a remedy to prevent the—

THE COURT: DNC.

MR. BECK:—the DNC from engaging in this type of conduct in future elections, then there's nothing that's going to be stopping them.

THE COURT: Is it the donor plaintiffs' position that they would not have donated to the DNC or the Bernie Sanders campaign if they believed the statements described in paragraph number 160—1-6-0—of the first-amended complaint to be false?

MR. BECK: Oh, thank you.

THE COURT: And if so, which allegations support that position?

MR. BECK: Yes. That is our position. And the allegations that support that position can be found in paragraph 188, paragraph 195 . . . yes, those are the two paragraphs where we allege reliance.

THE COURT: All right. What injury have the DNC donor plaintiffs suffered as a result of the DNC's alleged negligence as set forth in Count 6?

MR. BECK: Yes. Our position as to Count 6, which is the data breach count, is that the release of the donor's sensitive data into the public domain itself constitutes the injury.

Now, we recognize that there's a circuit split on that issue. We think that the Ninth Circuit and Seventh Circuit cases that we cited in our brief, which agree that that's a sufficient allegation, we think that has the better reasoning. But there's also an opinion out of the Third Circuit, which takes the view that the—you actually have to allege that the data's been misused, which we haven't alleged.

So—and to my knowledge, the Eleventh Circuit has not come down on one side or the other on that issue.

THE COURT: All right. Then my last question for the plaintiff on the issue of standing is, how—excuse me—how have all registered members of the Democratic Party suffered a concrete and particularized injury as a result of the allegations in the first-amended complaint?

MR. BECK: Yes. So, this is, uhm, an issue that comes up specifically with respect to the breach of fiduciary duty count. And our—what we rely on with respect to that count specifically is that the breach of a fiduciary duty to folks that join the Democratic Party, were registered members of the Democratic Party, but saw the party that they chose to affiliate with, they saw that party violate the terms of its own internal charter, that breach is itself a breach of a common-law right, a recognized common-law right that itself is sufficiently concrete and particularized to satisfy Article III.

THE COURT: All right. Thank you, Counsel.

MR. BECK: Thank you.

THE COURT: Any other comments before I hear from the defense?

MR. BECK: Not at this time, your Honor. Thank you.

THE COURT: All right. Thank you.

All right. What does the defense say in response to those answers?

MR. SPIVA: Thank you, your Honor.

First, I just want to say—because in response to my hypothetical that the party could choose its nominees in a smoke-filled room, I want to just reiterate that the party ran the process fair and impartially, and does not do that and doesn't plan to do that. But these, again, are political choices that either party is free to make and are not enforceable in a court of law.

In terms of—I want to start from where the gentleman on the other side left off, the—

THE COURT: That was regarding the question of a concrete or particularized injury.

MR. SPIVA: Yes, your Honor. And I think the last question was, how have all members of the Democratic Party suffered a concrete injury?

And there really isn't an allegation in the complaint that explains that. You know, in terms of the donor class, you know, clearly many of the people who they purport to represent agree with the DNC and support—and continue to support it. With respect to the individuals who they are putative class representatives, they haven't actually alleged specific injury. They've just said that they donated money.

And although we are not relying on this for our standing argument, this kind of goes to plausibility. There are statements in the public by some of these class representatives that show that there was no reliance and no injury. Some of them even gave money in order to participate in this lawsuit.

And so, again, even if your Honor disregards that as being outside the pleadings, and your Honor can go outside the pleadings on a 12(b)(1) motion, but even if you disregard it, I think it just illustrates the implausibility that every single member of the Democratic Party has suffered a concrete injury.

In terms of the data breach, there is no allegation in the complaint, your Honor, that any of the named plaintiffs have actually even had their data breached, let alone that they've suffered an injury. And that is certainly required along with a plausible allegation of injury. And I would refer to the—I believe it was the Case v. Miami—your Honor's indulgence.

THE COURT: That's all right. Take your time. We have all afternoon.

MR. SPIVA: Okay.

Case v. Miami Beach Healthcare Group, a decision from this district, which we cite in our briefs, that you need to have not only an allegation that your data was actually breached, but that, you know, something was actually done with it.

And counsel referred to—in response to your Honor's questions about whether the donors' position was that they would not have donated to the Sanders campaign or the DNC campaign if they knew or believed that the charter statements and the other public statements regarding neutrality were false, and counsel referred to paragraphs 188 and 195 of the first-amended complaint. These are broad, general claims of reliance. There are no specific allegations with respect to the named plaintiffs of even knowledge of these statements, let alone reliance. And like I said, there are statements out in the public domain that show that that is not plausible. In fact, it's false. And, again, of course, I think illustrates that this can't be—A, this case shouldn't proceed in any procedural form, but it certainly couldn't proceed as a class action.

Reliance is really the third rail of class actions, because you can't prove predominance. And even in terms of ascertainability, who's in the class, who's in these subclasses, I think would pose an impossible task for the Court to do, and one that would require, really, in-depth inquiry into the parties', you know, files and membership and lists of voters, all these things that NAACP vs. Button and other cases have said the courts can't do that under the First Amendment. And it would require an invasion of Senator Sanders' campaign, frankly, to find out about how his supporters feel about this.

Counsel said that the plaintiffs are seeking an injunction to prevent the DNC from engaging in future conduct in future elections of this type. Again, very vague allegations of what the conduct at issue is. You know, no real answer to how a federal court can tell a party how it should conduct its affairs going forward.

And, by the way, your Honor asked whether the damages that were being sought were the return of the contributions. That is the case, but they also seek punitive damages, exemplary damages. And so it's—and the complaint actually says in order to make an example of them. And I would suggest, your Honor, that that is all the proof you need of the chilling of the First Amendment activities that this complaint seeks.

Just back to the—whether money makes it different. Does the fact that money was given create standing for the failure to live up to a promise by the party, an alleged failure in the primary? Someone said, We're gonna build a wall, and Mexico is gonna pay for it during the primaries. If their theory holds that money creates standing, the donation of money, that means that anybody could sue President Trump or the Trump campaign for statements that were made that—where the promise was not kept in the context of the primary.

I think I have covered everything that counsel covered in the last discussion. And so if your Honor has questions about any of the other claims or anything else, I'm happy to answer.

THE COURT: I have more questions, but not on that point.

MR. SPIVA: Okay.

THE COURT: We're gonna go into the pleadings and then into the class action allegations.

But I think what we'll do is, to give the court reporter a break, we'll take a short recess. And then we'll come back and conclude with my questions into those areas, and then any additional comments that either side wishes to bring to the Court's attention.

MR. SPIVA: Great. Thank you, your Honor.

THE COURT: All right. Let's have everyone back in here at, let's say, five after by the courtroom clock.

Court's in recess.

COURTROOM SECURITY OFFICER: All rise.

(The Judge exited the courtroom)
(Recess taken at 2:50 p.m. until 3:06 p.m.)
(The Judge entered the courtroom)

THE COURT: Please be seated.

We have two remaining areas to cover—the pleadings and then the class action allegations. And some of the comments that you've already made will have already touched upon some of the questions that I'm going to ask, but I want to ask them in any event so that we have a complete record.

And for the defense.

MR. SPIVA: Okay.

THE COURT: Having filed a previous Rule 12(b) motion, does Rule 12(g) bar the defense from filing a successive Rule 12(b) motion?

MR. SPIVA: No, your Honor, for a couple of reasons.

THE COURT: And take your time. There's no rush, there's no rush.

MR. SPIVA: Okay. Thank you.

First of all, 12(g)(2), your Honor, Rule 12(g)(2), which is the rule that plaintiffs cite for waiver here, doesn't apply to a 12(b)(1) motion. I think they concede that, the subject-matter jurisdiction.

With respect to the 12(b)(6) motion, it actually doesn't apply to that either. It—you know, it refers to 12(b)(2) through (5).

And here, we asked for more time to raise 12(b)(6) issues in the motion to quash that we filed, and the plaintiffs raised no objection at that time that we would have waived the 12(b)(6) motion based on a failure to state a claim. And there's really, I think, no question that we could raise the same arguments in a 12(c) motion for judgment after the answer. And so, I think this would—even if the rule did apply here, this would be one of those cases—and I think one of the cases we cited was Carelogistics and some other cases in our brief—where it really wouldn't make any sense. I mean it kind of cuts against the purpose of the rule, which is where you're trying to prevent piecemeal litigation of defenses. After the defendant loses one, they bring another.

That's not what has happened here, your Honor. You know, we weren't properly served. We offered to accept service of process. The plaintiffs refused to do that. And so we were forced to file the motion. We actually won the motion. They refiled. And here, you know, really, this is the first kind of, I think, first time at bat, if you will, your Honor, in terms of the 12(b)(6) merits-type issues.

And given that we could raise those in a 12(c) motion, it really doesn't seem like it would serve any kind of judicial efficiency interests to not consider those arguments if the Court gets to them. I mean, of course, our position is that because there's no subject-matter jurisdiction, the Court won't need to reach those issues.

THE COURT: If the Court concludes that Rule 12(g) prevents the defense from making their failure to state a claim arguments in the motion to dismiss, does the defense anticipate that they will file a Rule 12(c) motion?

MR. SPIVA: Yes, your Honor. I mean assuming that the Court didn't dismiss everything based on the 12(1)—12(b)(1) portion of the motion.

THE COURT: All right. Thank you.

Any comments from the plaintiff? Take your time.

MR. BECK: Thank you, your Honor.

I think in response to the Court's questions on the effect of Rule 12(g)(2), I think for us it's really a simple question of what the rule states. And when you look at 12(g)(2), it—the Court—it clearly permits them to raise subject-matter jurisdiction in a successive motion under Rule 12, but it states that you may not raise other issues, including Rule 12(b)(6) issues, if you fail to raise those in your original motion.

I'm not sure why the defendant making a request for additional time to raise such issues in connection with its original motion would do anything to alter the plain language and the plain effect of the rule. I think the rule makes a lot of sense, and it gives the defendant an option, which it's already said it's planning to take—avail itself of, should the Court—were the Court find the rule to preclude them from raising these issues now, but it gives them an option to file a motion for judgment on the pleadings, which is I think—I think makes perfect sense.

These are very significant issues that have been placed in front of the Court. The law surrounding these issues is not uncomplex. And so, I think when you put so many big picture arguments in one motion at one time, and you're trying to argue subject-matter jurisdiction, and at the same time you're arguing failure to state a cause of action, at the same time you're arguing motion to strike class certification, you know, it makes—it perhaps doesn't crystallize the issues as well as they could be.

So, if the defendants had wanted to bring these issues with the Rule 12 motion, they had every opportunity when they filed their motion to dismiss based on service of process. They failed to do so. The rule is very clear what happens in that circumstance. It allows them to raise subject-matter jurisdiction issues, but it doesn't allow them to raise 12(b)(6) issues. And it gives them an option to do so in the context of a motion for judgment on the pleadings. And based on what the rule says, we think that's what ought to happen.

Thank you.

THE COURT: All right. Let me ask the plaintiff, with respect to questions regarding the pleadings, as you've just stated, the plaintiffs contend that the defendants' failure to state a claim arguments are barred by Rule 12(g)'s consolidation requirements.

If the defendants may simply raise these arguments again in a Rule 12(c) motion, what is the expedience of avoiding those issues now?

MR. BECK: Well, I don't think it's just a matter—I don't know that expedience is the only consideration behind that rule. Certainly that's always a value and a consideration that ought to be taken into account in judicial labor. And we understand that.

But a motion for judgment on the pleadings is predicated on them answering to the allegations in the complaint. And so, should they go ahead and file a motion for judgment on the pleadings, as the rule specifically directs that they do, the Court will have a fundamentally different record in front of it. It will have not just the first-amended complaint, but it will also have, presumably, an answer and affirmative defenses.

And without knowing how the DNC and the congresswoman are going to answer the allegations in the complaint, I think it may be a little difficult to foresee how the issues might come up, differently in a judgment on the pleadings, but they certainly could. And because that's what the rule specifically refers to, I have to think that there's some intent behind how that rule's written to promote a value that's not just expediency, but having a fuller record in front of the Court, when, in fact, the defendants could have raised those arguments on their first motion, and they chose not to.

THE COURT: If the Court proceeds to consider the defense's failure to state a claim arguments, how would the plaintiff be prejudiced at this time?

MR. BECK: Well, I don't think that we would be specifically prejudiced at this time. I think the only issue would be that the rule states what it states. But as to—I think we've—I feel comfortable that we've briefed the issues in a way that doesn't prejudice us and that we've had certainly a hearing today on the issues. So, I don't think we would take the position that we're prejudiced.

THE COURT: All right.

With respect to paragraph numbers 188 and 195 of your first-amended complaint—and, again, take your time—

MR. BECK: Yeah. Yes, I've got them in front of me.

THE COURT:—what factual allegations support the legal conclusions set forth in those paragraphs—

MR. BECK: Right.

THE COURT:—that the plaintiffs relied on various statements made by the defendants?

MR. BECK: All right. So, in terms of the factual allegations that are incorporated into each of those counts—

THE COURT: And, again—and I apologize for interrupting you—but without reading them into the record.

We are all mindful of the Rule 9(b) pleading requirements.

MR. BECK: Understood.

THE COURT: Go ahead, Counsel.

MR. BECK: Understood, your Honor.

I think that the allegations that support reliance in this case are the only allegations in the complaint, which pertain to the plaintiffs, really the only activities in the complaint that they're alleged to have done, which is to have contributed money to a presidential campaign.

So, my first—the first part of my response would be to direct the Court to paragraphs 2 through 109, which in each of those paragraphs, the plaintiff is named, their residence is given, and then the only activity that any of these plaintiffs is alleged to have done is stated, which is the contribution of a specified amount of money either to the Bernie Sanders campaign or to the DNC.

So, that can only be the activity that the plaintiffs undertook as part of the reliance element in those two counts, because it's their only activity in the complaint. And I think the only fair reading of the complaint is that those—that is the activity.

In terms of what the plaintiffs relied on in paying those sums of money, I would direct the Court to the paragraphs starting with paragraph 159, which describes the DNC's charter and quotes it, and then goes on to describe the various specific statements in the media that were made by various officials of the DNC, including the congresswoman, which repeat what the charter says in terms of the DNC's commitment by its own charter to running the process in a fair and evenhanded manner.

And, again, there are no other—there is no other category of misrepresentations that's alleged in the complaint. And we've also alleged that the deception occurred by way of omission.

So, we don't believe that we have to prove that any particular plaintiff relied on the specific statements cited, but because this was conduct occurring behind the scenes, not publicly disclosed by the DNC until their computers were accessed or information leaked out into the public domain, and it became known how the DNC was actually running the nominating process contrary to its charter, contrary to its public statements, that is a— what we believe is an adequate—to be an adequately alleged omission that the plaintiffs relied on.

In other words, the failure to state that the democratic process was not, in fact, democratic, but biased and predetermined from the beginning for Hillary Clinton over Bernie Sanders.

THE COURT: Where does the complaint allege that the defendants intended to gain as a result of their alleged fraud?

MR. BECK: I think the first paragraph which alleges that is paragraph 187, which is that the defendants intended that the false statements and omissions would induce the DNC Donor Class plaintiffs and Sanders Donor Class plaintiffs to rely on them. And that allegation is substantially repeated in paragraph 194 under the negligent misrepresentation count.

I think we've also alleged that in connection with other counts what we've alleged in paragraph 204, that the conduct was intentional, willful, wanton, and malicious.

We've done the same in paragraph 210 of the complaint under the unjust enrichment count.

We've also alleged substantially the same in paragraph 216 for the breach of fiduciary duty count.

THE COURT: You're saying that those paragraphs that you have just referenced to the Court support the legal conclusions in paragraphs 187 and 194.

MR. BECK: I think they do support those.

I would also direct the Court back into the factual corpus of the complaint.

THE COURT: Because that was gonna be my next question. Well, let me just ask—

MR. BECK: Yes.

THE COURT:—the question.

What factual allegations support the legal conclusions in paragraph numbers 187 and 194 of the first-amended complaint that the defendants intentionally induced plaintiffs to donate to the Sanders campaign and to the DNC?

MR. BECK: Right. I think that those allegations are supported starting at paragraph 161 and going on through paragraph 171. And these are getting to the issues and the allegations of what exactly the DNC did in violation of the charter and the commitment to neutrality.

And, essentially, these paragraphs set forth that the DNC was biased in favor of one candidate, that the DNC was devoted to supporting Clinton's candidacy over everybody else's candidacy, including Senator Sanders, and that the DNC actively concealed its bias from its own donors, as well as the donors to the Sanders campaign.

And I think the concealment comes from the public statements that were made by the congresswoman and other officials of the DNC, which created a media narrative that the DNC was following the terms of its charter, when, in fact, this was not the case.

And so, in terms of the allegations of, you know, whether—the intentionality here, I think the intentionality is an inference from the fact of the support for Senator Clinton.

In other words, that the DNC was going to do . . . I'm sorry. The DNC was going to do whatever it could to advance and predetermine the nomination for Hillary Clinton, while at the same time maintaining the fiction that it was operating in a fair and evenhanded manner.

If I could just take one moment and confer with counsel?

THE COURT: Go right ahead.

MR. BECK: Okay. Thank you.

THE COURT: Take your time. Feel free to do so.

MR. BECK: Thank you.

(Discussion had off the record between counsel)

THE COURT: Take your time.

MR. BECK: So, I think those allegations going to what exactly the DNC was doing for the Hillary Clinton campaign behind the scenes, how it was working with the Hillary Clinton campaign, this was all part of a preset strategy that was set down in various internal documents that have come to light through Guccifer, which, obviously, that's the basis for our complaint. There have been leaks that have come out since the complaint was put on file. But I think they all show the same thing, which is an intentional, predetermined strategy to advance Hillary Clinton's candidacy to the nomination.

And in terms of satisfying the element of intent for these claims, I think those allegations support that.

THE COURT: All right. Thank you.

My next question is: How is donating to a political campaign considered a consumer transaction under the District of Columbia law?

MR. BECK: Your Honor, the District of Columbia law in question is a broad consumer statute, which defines its terms in a very broad manner to protect individuals in the purchase of goods and services.

To quote one recent case from the D.C. Superior Court:

"The purpose of the D.C. Consumer Protection Procedures Act is to protect consumers from a broad spectrum of unscrupulous practices by merchant. Therefore, the statute should be read broadly to assure that the purposes are carried out."

Now, in terms of who may file suit under the CPPA, that is specified in the D.C. code at Section 28-3905, Sub (k), which defines "consumer" to include any person who, quote, "would purchase or receive consumer goods or services." And "goods or services" is defined to mean, quote, "any and all parts of the economic output of society at any stage or related or necessary point in the economic process." And it includes consumer credit, franchises, business opportunities, real estate transactions, and consumer services of all types. All types.

And that's found in Sections 28-3901, Sub (a)(2), and Section 28-3091, Sub (a), Sub (7) of the D.C. code.

So, the plaintiffs who made their donation payments through this company called ActBlue, which we've specifically described in the complaint, those plaintiffs are—do qualify as consumers, we believe, and we believe they're entitled to bring suit under the CPPA. Because, as we've alleged, ActBlue charges a 3.95 percent fee for processing services on each donation. So, in essence, when somebody donates through ActBlue, maybe they do it on their iPhone or their computer or what have you, they are paying this percentage fee for processing. And under the terms of the statute, that makes them consumers.

So, then the next question becomes, if the plaintiffs are consumers, who do they have a cause of action against? And I think that in their papers, the defendants take the position that you need to have privity—some sort of privity of contract between the plaintiff and the defendant in order to support a cause of action under the statute. And I don't think the statute, in fact, has that requirement.

Obviously, we're not suing ActBlue. We're suing the DNC and Congressman Wassermann Schultz (sic), because those are the—that's the entity and the person that were responsible for running these primary elections, leading the process from the top.

And when you look into the D.C. law on this issue—and I'm specifically referring to the case we've cited in our brief—Calvetti vs. Antcliff out of the District of Columbia Circuit, 2004, which states that:

"The CPPA liability extends to, quote, any person connected with the supply side of a consumer transaction."

That's really quite broad language—"any person connected." I would say that if the transaction is deemed to be the moment when the plaintiff donates a specified sum through ActBlue, either to the Sanders campaign or the DNC, and gets charged that 3.95 percent fee, making them a consumer, the entity that's running the election, which encompasses the candidate to which they're donating to, is a person connected with the supply side of the consumer transaction. Because they're essentially responsible for the ultimate—it's not a product, it's not a commercial transaction, but it is the end result of the money that people are paying.

The supply is the political campaign. And the political campaign is ultimately under the auspices of this organization that purports to be fair and impartial.

So, I know that's sort of a long answer to a short question, but I think a fair reading of the statute allows us to plead a claim for those reasons.

THE COURT: And you may have just answered my next question, but what services have the DNC donors purchased from the DNC?

MR. BECK: Right. I wouldn't—I would not say that they've purchased don—services from the DNC. I would say that the service that's being purchased is the processing fee that is being offered by ActBlue to consummate this political contribution transaction. So, there is—I would not go so far as to say that there's a purchasing of services in the way that the statute means. But the fact that they haven't purchased services doesn't mean that the DNC and Debbie Wassermann Schultz are not persons connected with the supply side of the transaction. And for that reason, we think there's a valid cause of action under the statute.

THE COURT: My next question for the plaintiff is:

What is the DNC's "special relationship" with registered members of the Democratic Party?

MR. BECK: Well, I think the "special relationship" comes down to the fact that this organization is the face of the leadership of the political party that these particular proposed plaintiffs, the Democratic Party Class have joined. That's the special relationship.

I think that the New York cases that we cited show that courts have no hesitation, at least in those cases, of finding that there's a responsibility owed from a party to its members, and it finds that this duty is sufficient to form a fiduciary duty. Admittedly, those are New York cases. They're decided under New York law.

I think it's premature to engage in choice of law analysis at this stage. I'm not sure that the record is fully complete. But I do think that on the face of it, this is a D.C. corporation that's based in D.C. It would seem to me that D.C. law would apply to the question of whether a—of what, if any, fiduciary duty is owed by the DNC to its members—the leadership of the party to the party's members.

And the D.C. law on this question is, as just to quote Kemp vs. Eiland, which is a 2015 case from the District of Columbia circuit:

"District of Columbia law has deliberately left the definition of fiduciary relationship flexible so that the relationship may change to fit new circumstances in which a special relationship of trust may be properly implied."

In a situation like this, the trust, I think, is that folks have joined the Democratic Party believing that the Democratic Party is a custodian of a fair and impartial election process, as it states in the DNC's own charter and as the DNC has repeatedly—or did repeatedly state in public, according to our complaint.

And I think pursuant to this particular definition of D.C. law, which I think applies here, because we're talking about a D.C. organization. This is the organization that's entrusted with the process. This is the organization that folks have registered based on the assumption that this is a democratic process that's being carried out. So, I mean, at least at the pleading stage, it seems to me to be a clear case—that we've alleged enough, just based on who the DNC is, who the members of the class are, to support the existence of a fiduciary relationship given the case law that we've cited.

THE COURT: And maybe you've already answered my next question, at least to a certain extent. But how is it that an entity can owe the same fiduciary duty to millions of people at the same time?

MR. BECK: Well, I think that actually—it's perhaps not as unusual as it first sounds, when you think that in the context—when you consider that in the context of private corporations in the commercial world, companies have duties to their shareholders, and that's a rather uncontroversial proposition. And there's a concept that when you become a shareholder of a company, you become part of an enterprise, and the folks at the top have a duty to you when they—in terms of running the company.

And I mean in this case, I don't think it's that much of a stretch of an analogy. I mean this may be a different market we're talking about. We're not talking about economics, we're talking about politics. But, again, I think as the discussion has developed today, we strenuously take the position that just because we're talking about politics doesn't mean that the rights that exist at common law and under the D.C. statute are vitiated.

And so I would say that, in answer to your question, in this case, we are talking about the political realm. But if the members of the Democratic Party are considered to be shareholders in that entity, in that political enterprise, then it seems perfectly reasonable that there would be a fiduciary duty to run the party according to what the charter itself says. That would not be unlike a situation one finds all the time with public corporations in the economic domain.

THE COURT: If registered democrats are actually members of state Democratic parties, not the DNC itself, how is it that the DNC owes those registered democrats a fiduciary duty?

MR. BECK: Again, I think this gets into some—perhaps some factual issues that aren't quite encompassed by the complaint at this stage. But—in terms of how the DNC exercises its command over the party, and that command trickles down through all the state parties.

It seems to me that exactly how that happens, I think we—there was some discussion of it earlier between counsel for the DNC and your Honor relating to funding. But I think the DNC does much more than that. I think it—at the end of the day, I don't think anyone is really under any illusion that the DNC runs the show in terms of the overall policy that the Democratic Party pursues at a national level. I mean in this case, we're talking about a national election.

In terms of—perhaps the best analogy is that a board of directors of a corporation owes a duty to the shareholders. The shareholders are members of a company. They're not members of the board of directors. But it's the board of directors that's running the show, so the duty does run down, because that's who's calling the shots. And I think we've pled enough in this complaint to—for one to reasonably infer that the DNC is, in fact, calling the shots when it comes to the Democratic Party, if that is defined to mean all of the constituent state Democratic parties.

THE COURT: And then my last question for the plaintiff is: What is Deborah Wassermann Schultz's connection with the data breach described in the first-amended complaint?

MR. BECK: With respect to that specific allegation and the claim associated with that allegation, our position is that the congresswoman is the—at the time of the events alleged, was the leader of the DNC. It was up to her ultimately to implement policies that reasonably protected the information of the DNC's own donors. And by virtue of the data breaches occurring, she clearly failed in that responsibility.

THE COURT: All right, Counsel. Thank you very much.

MR. BECK: Thank you.

THE COURT: And I'll hear from the defense with respect to those questions and answers.

MR. SPIVA: All rightee.

THE COURT: Take your time.

MR. SPIVA: Thank you, your Honor. I'm just trying to find my place.

So, I'll start back at the beginning of your Honor's last line of questions. And I think the first one, your Honor asked what the factual support was for paragraphs 188 and 195 of the first-amended complaint, which set forth fraud and negligent misrepresentation allegations. And I think, quite rightly, your Honor noted that Rule 9(b) applies here, which is—you know, requires a detailed pleading, particular pleading specificity. As one of the cases says, the who, the how, the what, the where, the when of the alleged fraud. And there's no allegation, really, with respect to any of these individual plaintiffs, your Honor, about, you know, who made a statement to them, how it defrauded them.

If you look through the paragraphs that counsel directed your Honor to, paragraphs 2 through 109, all it says is that these individual plaintiffs gave money and where they live. And it doesn't say that they received these statements, knew about these statements, relied upon these statements. And we know that with respect to many of them, it couldn't, consistent with Rule 11.

And that's a big deal, your Honor. It's not just a simple minor pleading defect. This is a fraud allegation. And, as your Honor noted, there's a reason why Rule 9(b) requires specificity—excuse me—specificity.

And opposing counsel said that he didn't believe that they had to prove that a particular plaintiff relied on a specific statement. But that, in fact, is exactly what they would have to prove and I think, again, shows why this certainly couldn't work as a class action.

Your Honor asked where in the complaint did they allege—did the plaintiffs allege that the defendants intended to gain as a result of the alleged fraud? And my response would be really nowhere, your Honor. The vague and generalized allegations in paragraphs 187 and 194 don't say that, that the defendants intended to gain by doing this.

And in terms of plausibility, your Honor, under the Iqbal and Twombly standards, some of this, frankly, just doesn't really make logical sense, I mean that the party tried to induce—was—favored Secretary Clinton and so induced many members of the party to give to Senator Sanders. It just doesn't—that just doesn't make logical sense, your Honor. And there really isn't any allegation that defendants intended to gain as a result of the alleged fraud.

I think your Honor's next question was: How is donating to a political campaign a consumer transaction under the D.C. Consumer Procedure Protection Act (sic), an act which I have some familiarity with.

First of all, you know, as—we quoted the language in our brief that the D.C. CPPA defines a consumer as "a person who, other than for purposes of resale, does or would purchase, lease, or receive consumer goods or services, including as a co-obligor or surety, or does or would otherwise provide the economic demand for a trade practice," clearly doesn't apply to donating money to a political campaign.

The act goes on to define a consumer good or service as something that "is used primarily for personal or household use." Clearly, donating, again, to a political campaign is not—first of all, there is no service or good that is being purchased; and, second of all, certainly, even if one could somehow characterize it as a service being purchased, it's certainly not for household—primarily for household or personal use.

In addition, plaintiffs tried to link this to ActBlue's commission on donations. That also doesn't really make any sense, your Honor. You know, ActBlue is not a defendant here. Certainly the DNC and certainly Congresswoman Wassermann Schultz is not a merchant under the definitions of the act. And the fact that ActBlue charges a commission doesn't convert either of them to a merchant, and certainly you can't sue the defendants that are present in this case for something that ActBlue—it's unclear what—but ActBlue allegedly has done wrong.

And keeping in mind, of course, that the plaintiffs are seeking the return of all of the donations. They're not just asking for the commission that ActBlue charges. They're asking for a complete return of all of the donations.

So, this act just does not apply to the donations at issue here.

The other issue, your Honor—and this kind of goes back to class certification—is they're trying to apply this D.C. statute nationwide to anybody in the country, no matter what state they reside in. And that also is not proper to do.

It wouldn't take a complicated choice of law analysis to say you can't apply a local state law, even if there were a consumer transaction here or a merchant involved under the act, to consumers all over the country. We don't have consumers here, but if we did, that—there's no basis to do that.

Your Honor asked: What services have the DNC donors purchased from the DNC? I think I just addressed that.

And then moving on to the fiduciary duty, your Honor asked: What is DNC's special relationship with the members of the party? And I would just note that the plaintiffs' position on what law applies here has kind of shifted. I mean at first, we—the complaint doesn't really apprise the defendants of what law is being asserted here. I think we thought it was Florida law, and we addressed that in their briefing, and then in their response, I think they said it was D.C. law. And now counsel said it's too early to do that kind of a choice of law analysis.

But, regardless, the—it would not be appropriate to find a fiduciary duty here. You know, it's kind of a misnomer even to speak in terms of members of the DNC. There is no national registration. Some states don't even have party registration. Many states, in fact. I mean Virginia, when you register to vote, you don't register as a democrat or a republican or whatever. So, as far as the party's concerned, they are trying to encourage people to vote for democratic candidates and to support democratic policies and values. But that's not a class of people that can be defined by the Court. And that changes with every election and possibly, and probably, more frequently than that.

That's not a situation that's akin to a shareholder of a corporation. It certainly can't, I think under, really, any state's law, be the basis of some kind of a special relationship of the type that would create a fiduciary obligation.

Counsel cited a D.C. Circuit case. I'll just briefly note that the D.C. Circuit actually is not the authoritative source for D.C. state law. D.C. is not a state, obviously, but there are local D.C. courts that actually are the authoritative source for what a fiduciary relationship would be under D.C. law, and the same would apply to the D.C. Consumer Procedure Protection Act.

Your Honor asked: How can one entity owe fiduciary duty to millions at the same time? And I think—you know, my earlier comments, I think, went to that. I really don't think it is possible, your Honor, with such a nebulous, changing relationship, to say that there's a fiduciary duty created between the party and people who believe in democratic—you know, the values of the Democratic Party or who vote for democratic candidates.

And I would note, because counsel for the plaintiffs said many times,

Well, it should be reasonable, I think this or that about the DNC, and I just want to note that it is the plaintiffs' burden here to establish that there is a fiduciary duty, and what the basis of that fiduciary duty would apply, and what law would the Court look to, to determine that. And if they can't do that, then they can't state a claim. And they haven't.

In all, I think what I just said would apply even more strongly to Congresswoman Deborah Wassermann Schultz. I keep forgetting to say each time that I'm speaking for both, your Honor, but I certainly am. And what reminded me of that is your Honor's next question is: What is Congresswoman Wassermann Schultz's connection to the data breach described in the complaint? And really there's no allegation of her connection to that data breach. She is mentioned in three paragraphs of the complaint, none of which address a data breach, frankly, none of which could support any of the claims that have been brought against her.

Counsel said that as the leader of the DNC, she's essentially responsible for what happened on her watch. But that would be a strict liability standard, your Honor, and that's certainly not the case with respect to a data breach or these types of tort claims, or contract claims, for that matter, that you could say that the head of an organization, or the CEO of a corporation, for that matter, is—can be held liable for everything that happens within that organization or allegedly due to the actions of the organization, without specific allegations of what that person actually did to cause the alleged harm.

Thank you, your Honor.

THE COURT: All right. Thank you.

I have some questions for the defense.

MR. SPIVA: Okay.

THE COURT: We'll go into the class action allegations at this point.

With respect to the class action allegations, we'll keep in mind, obviously without reading them into the record, the threshold requirement that is required for the plaintiff to meet, and then assuming that the threshold is met, then Rule 23(a) and 23(b) come into play.

But with those requirements in mind, assuming that the Court rejects the defendants' standing arguments, why should the Court address the class issues now rather than waiting for a motion for class certification?

MR. SPIVA: Well, I think this is the appropriate time in this case, your Honor, for a few reasons. First, even to define really any of the three classes, but particular—subclasses, but particularly with respect to the Democratic Party Class, your Honor, the Court would have to invade the party's associational rights and define what it means to actually be a member of the Democratic Party.

And that would also entail discovery that would invade the party's rights and the rights of the Sanders and the Clinton campaigns. Of course, the campaigns aren't themselves corporations, they're third parties. They're not parties to this litigation, but there would be discovery of both of those campaigns.

And all of this would invade the First Amendment. And I think it really highlights that the class really is not ascertainable, your Honor. And so, the Court should strike the allegations at this stage to save a huge amount of resources on behalf of both the parties and the Court in terms of fighting those motions and the discovery that would come with that.

In addition, there are problems with standing with respect to individual members of the putative class. And so, even if your Honor rejects our overarching standing argument, we would still have the right, your Honor, to challenge each class member's standing. Did they rely on statements of the DNC? Did they even know about them? Would they have not given if they had known? Same with the Sanders subclass. Same with the third subclass.

And so, millions of people have no injury. And it would require both invasive, expensive, you know, thousands, if not millions, of essentially depositions and, of course, a minitrial on each individual standing alone. The same issues, I think, come up with respect to predominance and typicality and probably several other of the requirements under 23(b).

And so, we submit, your Honor, that now is the appropriate time to avoid that thicket, which would, I think, enmesh the Court in a lot of political issues, would invade the First Amendment interests of certainly the defendants here.

And at the end of the day, your Honor, this is a class that is not certifiable. It—you know, the reliance—and that's not the only problem, but reliance, again, is the third rail of class certification. And they can't prove that on a class-wide basis without individualized proof from every single class member, which destroys any usefulness of the class device here.

THE COURT: All right. And, again, understanding that if—or assuming arguendo that the Court were to reject the defendants' standing arguments, if the Court strikes the class allegations, will the Court have jurisdiction over the claims in the first-amended complaint?

MR. SPIVA: So I'm assuming the Court has rejected our standing arguments, but struck the class allegations.

THE COURT: Allegations.

MR. SPIVA: I mean, there's—

THE COURT: Let's do it this way.

MR. SPIVA: Okay.

THE COURT: If I did what I suggested—

MR. SPIVA: Right.

THE COURT:—the jurisdiction for the remaining claims would be based on what?

MR. SPIVA: Well, I would submit, your Honor, that there would be no jurisdiction for all the reasons that there is no standing. The reason I'm having difficulty is, if I assume you're rejecting the standing arguments with respect to—

THE COURT: Well, would it be based on diversity?

MR. SPIVA: Oh, that is what plaintiffs have alleged, that there's diversity jurisdiction here.

THE COURT: So the question is: If I struck the class allegations, would I still have jurisdiction over the claims in the first-amended complaint?

MR. SPIVA: And, again, I'm putting standing to one side.

THE COURT: Sure.

MR. SPIVA: My first answer would be no because of standing. But—but I—I'm not sure, your Honor, and this is the reason. I believe that what gets them into diversity with the class allegations is CAFA. And I'm not positive, standing here at this moment—I can check—whether every single one of those putative class representatives lives outside of Florida—I'm sorry— lives outside of D.C. Because, of course, if one of the plaintiffs—

THE COURT: Well, the DNC is registered in the district.

MR. SPIVA: Right. Right. The District of Columbia.

THE COURT: And has its principal place of business in the district.

MR. SPIVA: Right. To be clear, whether every single one of the named plaintiffs—putative named plaintiffs lives outside of the District of Columbia. Because I believe that if there is one—and I believe there is at least one—that lives in the District of Columbia, that would destroy complete diversity, and the Court would not have jurisdiction.

THE COURT: All right. Go ahead. That's all right.

MR. SPIVA: Okay.

THE COURT: I've got a chart here somewhere.

MR. SPIVA: And I can take a quick look when I next—

THE COURT: No, that's all right. That's all right.
    Your argument is that if one lives in the district, the Court would not have diversity jurisdiction. That's all right.

MR. SPIVA: That's right.

THE COURT: Okay.

MR. SPIVA: That's right, your Honor.

The other thing that I—I'm not sure they could meet the amount in controversy, but I—but I'm—yeah, I'm not sure that they could meet it even collectively. I mean there are a lot of—maybe they could, because there are about a hundred-some people on the list. But I'm—but if one lives in the District of Columbia, that would destroy complete diversity.

THE COURT: All right. Thank you.

MR. SPIVA: Thank you, your Honor.

THE COURT: I'll hear from the plaintiff.

MR. BECK: Your Honor, on the issue of their motion as it pertains to the class action allegations, this is alternative relief that they sought by way of their—what they styled their motion to dismiss. And the last sentence of the defendants'—the first paragraph in their motion states, quote:

"In the alternative, to the extent any portion of the complaint survives, the Court should strike the allegations which are facially unsustainable."

They don't cite a specific provision of Rule 12 in making that request to the Court. But the one provision of Rule 12 that deals with anything relating to a motion to strike or a request to strike allegations is 12(f).

And because of that, I think my first point on this line of questions from the Court is that I do believe we get back to 12(g)(2) and the argument that they've waived these arguments, for the same reason that we discussed in connection with their 12(b)(6) motion or the aspect of their motion relating to whether we state a cause of action. But I would add a proviso, and getting back to the Court's previous question when we were addressing 12(b)(6), the Court asked how would it prejudice us to decide those issues now, and our answer was, with respect to 12(b)(6), we don't suggest there is any prejudice.

I think the situation is somewhat different with respect to the class act allegations. I think that the 12(g)(2) still applies, but with the addition that there is prejudice to entertaining a motion to strike class action allegations at this stage, and that this prejudice has been articulated in the case law.

And we cited some cases, including cases from this district, Martorella vs. Deutsch Bank, which is a Southern District case from 2013, which states that the question of class certification is generally not addressed on a motion to dismiss.

There's also Gill Samuel (phonetic) from 2014—again, appearing on page 2—page 18 of our brief—which holds that "an order on a motion to strike class action allegations would, by its very nature, carry more finality and less prospective flexibility than the typical order on a class—on motion for class certification."

And for that reason, the Court deemed that these types of motions are contrary to the spirit of Rule 23, which allows for some flexibility, and also contemplates that there would have been an opportunity to conduct some discovery in connection with the class certification determination.

So, we would submit that based on—again, based on 12(g)(2), based on the cases from this district, which disfavor ruling on a class certification motion—or defer ruling on a motion to strike class certification allegations outside of a formal motion for class certification, we submit, then, in view of those two sources of authority, that it's premature to even consider the defendants' arguments at this time.

That said, just to quickly address some of the points they've made. They suggest that it's impossible for us to maintain a class action in this case, because we've pled reliance, and we've pled reliance on false statements. There's a whole line of cases that certify class actions in the context of uniform omissions. And I think that ultimately this is a case that's more about omissions than specific statements of fact. Because as I think we've addressed more than a couple times throughout this hearing, the essence of the claims in this case is that folks made contributions to a political candidate and a political party's governing body, based on the assumption that the primary process was fair and evenhanded, and the true facts were concealed from them, because behind the scenes, the DNC was being anything but fair and evenhanded in connection with the primary.

So, in that sense, I think we have more than enough material for a uniform omissions theory of class certification. But, again, I submit that it's premature to even be discussing those issues at these stages.

And the Court asked the question about jurisdiction.

I recently dealt with that issue, but it was in the Ninth Circuit. And if my recollection serves me well, the question of jurisdiction is determined at the time that the complaint is filed and makes the allegations that invoke CAFA jurisdiction, which is what we've done in this case. So—and this was in the context of a Court then subsequently denying class certification in a written order, and at the same time recognizing that the case still had jurisdiction under CAFA in that court, notwithstanding the class certification motion having been denied.

So, if that principle also holds in the Eleventh Circuit, and I haven't looked at that issue, then I would submit that the Court still would have jurisdiction, regardless of where the particular plaintiffs live, because CAFA jurisdiction was properly invoked in the original complaint.

And, finally, there's a thread that runs throughout the defendants' arguments, which suggests that by conducting this as a class action, there will be rampant violations of people's rights to association, because they—by virtue of how the classes are defined, they will be swept into a lawsuit that alleges claims which either they disagree with or for whatever reason, they may not want to have any part of it.

Rule 23, as this Court knows well, is a very—it has—is a very flexible rule that contains mechanisms for addressing just those types of issues that someone doesn't have to be dragged into a lawsuit that they want no part of. There are opt-out mechanisms. There are notification mechanisms. There are issues relating to how the class could be defined. There are issues relating to the formation of subclasses. In connection with some of the choice of law issues that we've discussed, those can be handled through those Rule 23 mechanisms. So I just don't think those are valid concerns that the defendant has raised.

But, again, I would stress that I really think that the Court would—and the parties would benefit most by having a chance to conduct discovery and fully brief a formal motion for class certification before any of the issues that have been raised by defendant in connection with this aspect of their motion are decided by the Court.

THE COURT: All right. Thank you, Counsel.

Now, I have some questions for the plaintiffs regarding the class action allegations. And you've answered one of them already, regarding what were to happen if the Court were to strike the class allegations.

My next question—well, actually, my first question for the plaintiff is: Are each of the plaintiffs diverse in citizenship from each of the defendants?

MR. BECK: Your Honor, I'm just going to grab a copy of the complaint.

THE COURT: No, no, take your time. Take your time. And consult if you need to.

MR. BECK: If I may.

THE COURT: We're not going anywhere.
(Discussion had off the record between counsel)

MR. SPIVA: I definitely don't mean to interrupt, your Honor, but I actually have the answer to this now, if—

THE COURT: Well, you can step over and talk with counsel. I mean that's . . .

MR. BECK: Sure.
(Discussion had off the record between counsel)

MR. BECK: Yes. Counsel has informed me—and it is, indeed, the case—that paragraphs 55 and 87 are—they're related to plaintiffs who live in the district. So, those plaintiffs would not be diverse, because I—because the DNC is a member—or a resident of the district.

THE COURT: And where might the Court find the allegation of citizenship for Deborah Wassermann Schultz?
(Discussion had off the record between counsel)

MR. BECK: Paragraph 154 is the paragraph which speaks to the congresswoman and specifies that she maintains offices in Pembroke Pines and the District of Columbia. However, I'm looking at this now, and it doesn't appear to contain an allegation relating to her.

THE COURT: Citizenship.

MR. BECK: Correct. I would agree with that.

THE COURT: That's fine. That's all right.
My next question for the plaintiff is: Are there Bernie Sanders donors who would not have standing to participate in this lawsuit?

MR. BECK: I can't think, as I sit here now, why any Bernie Sanders donor would not have standing to participate.

THE COURT: All right. Would a Bernie Sanders supporter who donated to Senator Sanders' campaign because of the DNC's alleged bias have standing?

MR. BECK: A Bernie Sanders donor who donated to the Bernie Sanders campaign.

THE COURT: Campaign.

MR. BECK: Yes, they would have standing—to the Bernie Sanders campaign, yes, they would have standing—oh, the question is, because of the DNC's alleged bias.

I think this gets into some issues in terms of how the defendant has framed our allegations, and, of course, they have this footnote in—first of all, I don't see how a donor to the Bernie Sanders campaign could—would be in a position to have the knowledge that the DNC was predetermining the outcome for Hillary Clinton in the way that the complaint alleges.

I think that certainly there was campaign rhetoric throughout the campaign. And I would not deny this, that there was a sense and a feeling, through the process, that it was unfair and that it was slanted.

That said, I think there were orders of magnitude at issue in this case, which take this out of the realm of—you know, I just don't see how a Bernie Sanders campaign—a Bernie Sanders donor would have the knowledge to know that the DNC had predetermined the result for Hillary Clinton, number one.

And, number two, it just doesn't make sense to me why somebody would participate in a political process by paying money into the process, when they knew that that process was rigged from the start, which is what we're alleging. I mean that's what we're alleging in this complaint.

THE COURT: Sure.

MR. BECK: It just doesn't seem like a plausible position to be in at the same time we're having this exchange in the context of not having conducted discovery and just on the basis of the four corners of a complaint, as I think is called for given the motion that the defendants have filed.

So, it—I just don't know that—I guess it's hard to imagine that situation given the state of the record at this point.

(Discussion had off the record between counsel)

THE COURT: Are there DNC donors who would not have standing to participate in this lawsuit?

MR. BECK: Again, I think that—I think, fundamentally, people give money to candidates and can—and political parties, because they believe that we have a fair democratic process. And I think that that's a baseline assumption whenever a donation is made.

I think if it's proven that the process is not what people believe it to be, then I think we've alleged standing on the basis of a false understanding that's been created by the defendants.

And so, again, I would think that all DNC donors have standing, because I believe that people—when people participate in the process in this way, and they actually write a check to a party or to a candidate, they believe that the process is fundamentally fair and democratic.

THE COURT: Would a person who donated to the DNC without reading the DNC's charter or hearing the statements described in paragraph 160 of the first-amended complaint have standing?

MR. BECK: Yes. I think that a person in that situation would have standing. I think—again, I think that this is a case that ultimately and probably for many and many people in the classes, as we've defined them in this complaint, this is a case of omission and concealment of what was actually going on behind the scenes at the DNC. And so, I don't think a person necessarily has to read a news article where the DNC is specifically proclaiming its neutrality, or I don't think a person has to read the charter itself.

I think that there's a fundamental understanding in this country that's taught from a very early age, certainly I remember it, that we live in a democracy. And I think a fundamental part of what a democracy means is that elections are not conducted in this biased and predetermined way. And I think that everybody who seeks to participate in the political process, especially when they're going to the trouble of cutting a check to a candidate that they support or a party that they support, they believe that those candidates and entities are taking place in a process that is fair and impartial, because they believe in a process that's democratic.

So, I don't think someone necessarily needs to read the articles we've cited or the charter to be in the class of people that have been defrauded or deceived or unjustly treated in terms of the unjust enrichment claim by the DNC's conduct.

THE COURT: Are there registered members of the Democratic Party who would not have standing to participate in this lawsuit? And maybe your last answer would be the same.

MR. BECK: Yeah, I think that's a similar answer to the previous question. I think, again, if there is, indeed, a fiduciary duty owed from the leadership of a party to the party's members, as we maintain in this case, then the DNC doesn't just abuse that relationship when it favors—it doesn't just abuse its relationship with its members who are Bernie Sanders supporters, it abuses the relationship with all of its members, because it's ultimately not acting according to what its charter requires it to do and, I would submit, according to what its position in this society as a trustee of our democratic institutions requires it to do.

And so, I think in the long run, it hurts everybody in the party. And, you know, that may involve some factual issues that are not appropriately at issue before the Court right now. But I do think it's something that can be demonstrated.

THE COURT: If there are persons who meet the plaintiffs' proposed class definitions who would not have standing, how could this Court certify the class?

MR. BECK: Well, I think—again, I think that the definitions as we've set them forth in our complaint describe people who do have standing for the reasons discussed.

That said—and, again, this is why I think in some ways these issues merit a full class certification process and discovery and briefing and so forth, as opposed to an alternative relief sought in a Rule 12 motion.

But that aside, I think that the rule, Rule 23 specifically, is flexible enough for courts to change class definitions, certify subclasses, and so forth. So, I think it's—I don't think it would be the first time that a class—you know, if that were to happen, if that determination were made, I don't think it would be the first time that a Court had determined that perhaps a class was overbroad or whatnot and needed to be refined. But, again, I think those determinations are best made in the course of a Rule 23 motion for class certification.

THE COURT: Is it possible to narrow the class definitions in such a way that class members are readily ascertainable by objective criteria while persons who do not have standing are excluded?

MR. BECK: Well, again, I don't think I'm—I would concede the point that, as defined in the context of our allegations and claims, that anybody—that any of these plaintiffs don't have standing, or any of the people who would be compassed within the class definitions don't have standing. That said, if it's just a matter that—of people—I mean there are mechanisms by which people can opt out of class actions. And class definitions can also be revised throughout the course of a litigation and frequently are.

So, it seems to me that that could be a possibility as well. But, again, I don't think that there's anything about this particular class action that makes it any less susceptible to being managed by the flexible tools that are available under Rule 23 and at the Court's disposal. And, again, just because it happens to deal with politics as opposed to a securities class action or something that's more commonly seen in lawsuits.

THE COURT: Given the nature of plaintiffs' claims, will individualized issues predominate over common issues?

MR. BECK: I don't think that's the case—I don't think that would be the case, your Honor. Again, and I think this gets back to the point that the predominant rung here is the defendants' acting behind the scenes to rig a primary process and not disclosing that to the public. And, in fact, making—taking actions to conceal that from the public.

So because it's more an issue of what was concealed as opposed to what was specifically stated, to me, that has the badge of a uniform omissions case. And my understanding of the law in this district and the Eleventh Circuit is that cases, even fraud cases, can be certified when a pattern of uniform omissions is established. And that analysis I would think would apply to the fraud and negligent misrepresentation claims that we've asserted.

THE COURT: What law will the Court be applying with respect to Counts 1, 2, 4, 5, and 6?

MR. BECK: Let me confer with counsel.

THE COURT: Go right ahead. Take your time. Take your time.
   (Discussion had off the record between counsel)

THE COURT: Take your time.
   (Discussion had off the record between counsel)

MR. BECK: My cocounsel wanted me to correct something that I stated to the Court earlier—

THE COURT: That's all right. Go right ahead.
   MR. BECK:—in regards to the residence of Debbie Wassermann Schultz.

THE COURT: Citizenship.

MR. BECK: Yes, the citizenship. My impression is that we had—that was the only paragraph that we had referenced her. But my counsel's alerted me to the fact that in paragraph 1, we specifically state that Deborah Wassermann Schultz resides in and is as congresswoman representing portions of this district, meaning the Southern District of Florida. So, I think that is probably sufficient to establish her as a citizen of Florida.

But to get to the question posed by the Court just now, which is what law should the Court apply to those specified counts? You know, our brief assumed Florida law or D.C. law. Again, I just—I don't know that the record is well-developed enough to make a choice of law now. So certainly I don't think it was fully briefed in the papers.

And my understanding is that in the course of a class action, oftentimes subclasses are created which correspond to the various laws invoked specifically to the various plaintiffs based on their citizenship, if, in fact, that's a factor that determines the choice of law analysis. And I'm not sure, again, that that issue is really before the Court now.

We cited, I think, one case in our brief which suggested that courts ought to await a more fully developed factual record before engaging in those determinations. So, I guess at this stage, we would rest on the position in our briefs to assume that Florida or D.C. law applies to those counts, but without waiving any argument that other laws may not apply to those class members as well.

THE COURT: If my count is accurate, taking it—that count coming from the first-amended complaint, assuming arguendo that the Court must apply 46 different jurisdictions' laws to this case, would a class action be manageable?

MR. BECK: I think there are cases that address that issue in the class certification analysis. And oftentimes it depends on the—whether or not there are material differences in the various laws being applied such that manageability becomes a problem.

I guess without delving into the—what may be the material differences for those counts—and I don't know that there are any—but, again, that's a—you know, I think that's an issue that comes up on Rule 23—in the context of a Rule 23 motion. And I think, you know, in making that determination, the Court is probably best—would benefit most from having full briefing and discovery on those specific issues as they relate to class certification.

THE COURT: And, again, assuming arguendo that the Court must apply 46 different jurisdictions' laws to this case, are there questions of law common to all members of each class?

MR. BECK: Yes, I do think that regardless of whether—how many states' laws would ultimately apply, the issues of law—I mean, it would surprise me that there is—that if the law of fraud, the law of negligent misrepresentation, the law of unjust enrichment, the law of negligence as it applies to the data breach claim—I mean it would surprise me if the elements of those laws varied so considerably from state to state that they presented issues that threatened commonality in a Rule 23 analysis.

But, again, I would state that I think we can—I think that question would probably benefit most from a class certification brief that directly addressed those issues and analyzed whatever differences there are between the state laws at issue, because I don't know that there are material enough differences to create a manageability issue in this case.

THE COURT: And then, finally, what evidence do the plaintiffs anticipate discovery would yield regarding certification of each of the proposed classes?

MR. BECK: Well, I think that discovery in terms of the class certification issues would proceed—I mean I think it would address each of the class 23 elements that we'd need to prove to prevail on a motion for class certification. So, I think we would be addressing issues of commonality, typicality, predominance, superiority, manageability, all of the standards issues. I think that we would be creating a—obviously, I mean I wouldn't be surprised if the defendants would be conducting discovery of our class representatives—usually they do something like that from their end. So I think that would be part of the process.

But from our end, we would be taking document discovery that we at this point anticipate would fill in the details of what we've already alleged in the complaint, which is that there was a systematic, unified, and overarching effort to work behind the scenes to advance Hillary Clinton's candidacy to the nomination. And so, from the perspective of commonality, from the perspective of whether any of those common issues predominate in the analysis, which ultimately we would have to show on a Rule 23, those would be the issues that would be addressed in the discovery process.

THE COURT: All right, Counsel. Thank you very much.

I appreciate your answers.

MR. BECK: Thank you, your Honor.

THE COURT: All right. Let me hear from the defense.

MR. SPIVA: All rightee.

Thank you, your Honor.

I'll just kind of quickly go through the questions.

THE COURT: Take your time.

MR. SPIVA: All right.

THE COURT: We're not going anywhere.

MR. SPIVA: So, I think you already got an answer to the question about whether all the plaintiffs are diverse from each defendant; they are not.

And then, are there Bernie Sanders donors who would not have standing, was I think the first question after that your Honor asked. And clearly there are. I mean—and clearly the only way to find out would be to do an individualized inquiry of each of them. Because here, where we're talking about reliance, we're talking about knowledge, we're talking about motive, not only the defendants' alleged motive, but the motive of these individuals. I mean, Bernie Sanders himself endorsed, voted for, campaigned for Hillary Clinton. And so, presumably, he donated to his own campaign, and I assume he wouldn't—would not consider himself to be a member of this class. And there are other donors. There are millions of Bernie Sanders donors and voters who voted for Hillary Clinton. And so, those people would not have standing to bring this suit. They would have no injury.

There are many Bernie Sanders donors who gave because they thought the system was rigged, to use Donald Trump's phrase, or that it was an unfair system and they wouldn't have standing.

So, I think clearly there would. And the greater problem, your Honor, is that the only way to find out would be to invade—you know, to query each one of them and invade their privacy and First Amendment rights and, on the other hand, invade the privacy—rather, the First Amendment rights of the party. And we heard again and again—

THE COURT: Just slow down a little bit for the—

MR. SPIVA: Sure.

We heard again and again that certain questions could be potentially resolved through discovery, and one can only imagine how burdensome this discovery would be. Counsel didn't actually specify what types of information that counsel thought he would discover. But, clearly, there's a contemplation of going through the files of the DNC and trying to explore what the strategy and internal workings of the party was. Clearly, protected by the First Amendment.

And, of course, we would need to seek discovery of the Sanders campaign and the individuals who gave to Senator Sanders and individuals who gave to the DNC, and they have a First Amendment right not to be questioned in that way.

So, to answer your Honor's second question, a Bernie Sanders supporter who donated to the campaign because of a perceived bias also would not have standing.

There was also a phrase that kind of pervaded counsel's last presentation about—it's kind of shifted from the allegations in the complaint, which is that the DNC and Congresswoman Wassermann Schultz deviated from the bylaws in showing impartiality and evenhandedness to a focus on the results being predetermined.

There's really no allegation in the complaint that the results were predetermined, nor could there be. I mean millions more people voted for Secretary Clinton than voted for Senator Sanders. And those individuals certainly wouldn't have standing, even though they would fall within one of the subclasses that have been articulated.

And one of the answers to that question that your Honor was given, was that it's not plausible that someone would give to the Sanders campaign if they viewed the system as rigged. But I think actually the opposite conclusion is more logical and certainly apparent, that you would to try to beat the system, if you viewed it as rigged.

Your Honor asked whether there are DNC donors who would not have standing. And, clearly, there would be. I mean, clearly, there are millions of people who voted for Secretary Clinton and gave to the DNC in both the primary and the general, and they would not have standing, because they haven't been injured. And they don't agree with the point of view of the plaintiffs in the lawsuit.

You asked whether a person who gave to the DNC without having read the DNC's charter were—any of the allegations where the DNC was alleged to have made statements about neutrality, would that person have standing? Well, there couldn't be reliance if they didn't have any knowledge of the statement. So that person would also not have standing.

And then your Honor asked that if there are members of the plaintiffs' proposed classes that would not have standing, how can the Court certify the class? And, again, the answer was discovery, your Honor. But I think the answer is actually that really wouldn't be proper to certify a class where certain members of the proposed class don't have standing, and where the only way to determine whether they do is to actually, you know, take discovery from each individual.

And that's not gonna change. That's the thing. If they're allowed to amend again, that is always going to be the case, that there are gonna be some people in these classes as proposed who do not have standing, and the only way to determine that is to ask them individually.

And that goes to the next question your Honor asked, which is potentially changing the class definitions. And I think counsel had said that it's not infrequent that class definitions get narrowed or defined, and that is not—it's not that it doesn't ever happen, for sure, but at the same time, it's still the plaintiffs' burden to identify an ascertainable class, one that's manageable, that—where common issues predominate. And none of that's the case here, your Honor.

And answering your Honor's next question, it really isn't possible to narrow these class definitions so that the class is ascertainable by objective criteria. All of the allegations in the complaint, and certainly all the statements made today, are shot through with subjective determinations, which can only be resolved through individualized discovery and trial.

There was an analogy to securities class actions, which I'd submit, your Honor, is wildly different from the political realm here with the First Amendment issues that we've—that I talked about, where it's potentially the only place where you have a notion of fraud on the market, you know, such that reliance can, in certain circumstances, be presumed totally different and inapplicable and an inapt analogy to this situation.

Your Honor asked whether individual issues would predominate over common issues. I think the answer is clearly yes. I've kind of covered that, so I won't go over that again.

Your Honor asked about choice of law, and what law the Court would apply to Counts 1, 2, 4, and 6.

THE COURT: Five.

MR. SPIVA: And five, thank you.

And—that's the breach of fiduciary duty count, yes. I think that's not clear at this point.

And I think the answer that I heard, your Honor, was basically that the plaintiffs sued the defendants, but they're not gonna tell the defendants until later what law they're alleged to have violated. Because, of course, if you're not saying what state's fiduciary duty law they've alleged to have violated, or what state's unjust enrichment law, et cetera, then you're not even meeting the basic requirements under Rule 8. And, certainly, class certification is not the stage at which to decide what law applies to the claims that they're asserting. It destroys commonality; it destroys predominance.

And I don't think there's a case that I've ever seen—and none has been cited—where a Court has said that through the discovery process, a class with 46 states represented could—you know, through the discovery process, we could discover what law applies. That would be totally unmanageable, your Honor. And I submit it would have to be a violation of due process for the defendant to have to respond to that and the types of massive discovery that that would entail.

And it's really their burden to figure this out in advance and put it in their complaint. It's not something to be resolved either through class certification or through discovery.

Your Honor asked, assuming that the Court must apply the laws of 46 states, would the class action be manageable? And I submit, your Honor, the question almost answers itself.

I mean, you know, no. It would be, I think, an impossible management problem. It would—there'd be no commonality, no predominance.

And one of the answers was, it would surprise me if elements of these various causes of action varied so considerably as among states. But, again, this is the plaintiffs' burden to figure out at the outset. I mean that's very rare where a federal court is going to say, Well, we're gonna apply a nation-wide standard of contract, breach of contract, for instance—I'm just using that as an example—because a breach is a breach wherever you are. That's very rare. But, certainly, at the very least, the plaintiffs have to identify those causes of action for which the law doesn't vary significantly, and why they could meet the class certification standards, and why it would be manageable. It's not for the Court to assume or for the plaintiffs to assume and we get to it later. That's just not proper.

Your Honor asked what evidence did the plaintiffs anticipate discovery would yield regarding certification of each of the proposed classes. And I didn't really hear a definite answer other than anything going to the various Rule 23 elements, document discovery, which would fill in the details. And, again, that—the only kind of document discovery that could even conceivably be relevant to the types of claims being made here would totally invade the province of the party's strategizing, their internal workings, and, similarly, Congresswoman Wassermann Schultz's First Amendment rights as well.

And so—and I think, frankly, your Honor, even if that weren't an issue, there really isn't discovery that can fix these problems other than individualized discovery of every single plaintiff. And so, I don't think that that's an adequate answer to your Honor's question. I don't think there's discovery that can fix the problems with the complaint.

THE COURT: All right. Thank you.

Hold on for one second.

MR. SPIVA: Thank you.

(Discussion had off the record between the Court and court reporter)

THE COURT: I'm gonna give the defense five minutes for any additional comments, any clarification of any previous answer or response, and then I'll give five minutes to the plaintiff for the same.

MR. SPIVA: Thank you, your Honor.

I will endeavor and I will not repeat what I've said. But I think, starting with standing, this is a case where plaintiffs have not met their burden to show causation of harm here, that—a particularized injury that is redressable by the Court, and that that really should end the lawsuit right there.

I think their state law claims, I guess I'll group them—the ones that focus on issues such as fiduciary duty and the like, first, all suffer from the same problem, but also are defective on the pleadings and would be totally unmanageable in terms of a class certification.

And then I think what I would do, so as not to repeat, because I have made these arguments, but I just want to emphasize that there really is a body of case law here, I think, that supports the notion that this is really not the province of the courts. This is the rough—what we've heard is the kind of thing—you certainly heard on the Republican side, you know, President Trump alleged that the Republican primary was rigged. He ended up getting more votes than the other primary members and ultimately at least got more electoral college votes and that's how our system works.

And so this is very common to have these kind of inter/intraparty squabbles about doctrine, about policy, about rules, about selection of delegates. And the courts have said from the O'Brien case to the LaFollette case, the Berg v. Obama case, which I think is very—has some very close similarities to this one in terms of people saying they were duped by certain statements about what the party stood for, the Wymbs case in this circuit vs. the Republican State Executive Committee, all of these cases I think come down to the same thing, that really these are matters for the parties. They are private associations. Yes, they play a big role in the election of the president of the United States. But they are still private associations. They still have a right to order their own affairs.

If someone's not happy with the party that they've been aligned with, their choice is to start another party, or to give to the other party, or to give to a candidate that they think will shake things up within the party.

But giving a donation gives no one the right to succeed, to have their candidate win an election. It doesn't give them the right to tell the party how to conduct its affairs or to, you know, rifle through the strategizing of the party.

And I want to be clear, I know I've said this, but I, you know—because this has become somewhat of a public case, that the defendants absolutely deny that there was any unfairness here or impartiality. But the allegations that have been made are very common in terms of political process. And the courts have been clear that that is a matter for the parties and for private associations, not for the courts.

And I think really that runs through—that premise, that precedent really runs through all of our arguments, and that's the reason why there's no standing here, why there's a failure to state a claim, and so why this case should be dismissed with prejudice.

Thank you, your Honor.

THE COURT: Thank you, Counsel.

MR. BECK: Thank you, your Honor. And I want to thank the Court for hearing us today.

Counsel mentioned a concept that's familiar in the context of securities actions known as fraud on the market.

And his suggestion was that this—to paraphrase him—that this case is—invokes principles that are wildly different to fraud on the market cases that make that analogy inappropriate.

Well, I think that it's an extraordinarily appropriate analogy. We're talking about the political market here. This is fraud on the political market. The DNC, by virtue of how the democracy of this country has developed over history, is one of two parties in a two-party democratic system that essentially has custody over the market for how candidates are chosen and elected and nominated and ultimately run in general elections.

And the shareholders in this case are not people that have purchased stock or purchased shares in a company, but they've bought into this political process, because at bottom, they believe in American democracy and that we live in a democratic system. And they bought into the process how? By donating their money to candidates. In this case, they've donated to Bernie Sanders' campaign. But this is how people participate in the political process these days aside from voting. And they've also registered as democrats, because that was the party that they chose to align themselves.

And in making those decisions and undertaking those actions, I submit that they're no different than people that purchase shares of stock believing that the company is a good investment. I see no reason that somebody would take their hard-earned money and throw it at a candidate in a democratic primary knowing full well that the outcome was predetermined.

And I know my friend on the other side takes issue with my use of the word "predetermined" to describe this election, but I think it's entirely inappropriate (sic) , because it captures the state of where we are as a country today, which is to say that when you have one of the two major political parties working hand in glove with all of the arrayed media outlets that are in the position of disseminating information to the American public, and they are engaged in a concerted effort to advance one candidate at the expense of the other candidates in the field, I submit that that outcome is nothing other than predetermined. And to say anything less is to undersell the power of politics and media in this country.

It may be that we've reached a dire state of affairs in this country politically. When I heard counsel state that it would be more likely for somebody to donate to a candidate if they thought the process was rigged, that made me really sad, actually. I mean I'm somebody that's donated to political campaigns. I know a lot of people who have donated to political campaigns. And when I made those donations, I never suspected or believed that the process was rigged in the way that we allege that this process was rigged in the complaint.

If it's the case that an entity, the DNC, its chairperson can rig an election, and there's no remedy at law for people who've made financial contributions on the basis of what they've omitted to tell the public, well, I submit that that's a really dire road for this country to be on. But what gives me hope is that we have an ancient tradition of common law in this country that goes back even well before the founding of this republic and protects against fraud and protects against deceit. And it makes no exception for people who are in the political realm. And it doesn't offer blanket immunity for people to make misrepresentations simply because those representations are made in the context of a political campaign.

THE COURT: One minute.

MR. BECK: And they've said that—and, again, I think all of their arguments as to why—against us having the right to conduct discovery fall back on this First Amendment argument, which I submit to the Court is a fiction.

And I just want to close with this. We're not seeking to undo the results of an election. We're not seeking—we're not sitting here saying that Bernie Sanders should be the nominee, and there should be a do-over. We're not asking for relief like that. Our relief is confined to remedying the injuries that we've identified in this complaint, which are very concrete and tied to the payment of money and membership in a political party, and are not tied to any of these voter standing-type theories, which you see in all the cases, or many of the cases that they've cited, where a person tries to enforce a political promise or—for instance, I think an example was given of a promise made by President Trump. None of that is remotely at issue here.

We're talking specifically about people who bought in to the political process by donating money, by registering as democrats. If there is no possibility of judicial or legal relief for those individuals, then I submit that the prospects for democracy in this country are dark indeed.

Thank you, your Honor.

THE COURT: All right. Thank you very much.

Well, I want to thank counsel for your responses to the Court's questions. They've been very helpful. This is a very interesting case, to say the least. And counsel for the plaintiffs spoke about whether or not our society—these are the Court's words, not his words, he did not use the word "society"—but whether society is in a dire situation. And so I leave the lawyers with this. Democracy demands the truth so people can make intelligent decisions.

Everyone have a safe trip back and I'll be putting together an order based on the arguments presented here today.

I'll be candid with you, that's gonna take some time. The legal issues are complex for the Court to consider and to rule upon.

So everyone have a safe trip back and everyone have a great week.

There being no further business, this session of the court is adjourned.

MR. SPIVA: Thank you, your Honor.

THE COURT: Take care.

MR. BECK: Thank you, your Honor.

MR. O'BRIEN: Thank you, Judge.

THE COURT: Go ahead. Court's in recess.

(The Judge exited the courtroom)
(Proceedings concluded at 5:20 p.m.)

CERTIFICATE

I certify that the foregoing is a correct transcript from the record of proceedings in the above-entitled matter.

/S/Francine C. Salopek
Francine C. Salopek, RMR-CRR
Official Court Reporter

4-28-17

Appendix II

UNITED STATES DISTRICT COURT
SOUTHERN DISTRICT OF FLORIDA
CASE NO. 16-61511-CV-ZLOCH
CAROL WILDING, et al.,
Plaintiff(s),
vs.
DNC SERVICES CORPORATION, d/b/a, DEMOCRATIC
NATIONAL COMMITTEE, et al.,
Defendant(s).

Fort Lauderdale, Florida
August 23, 2016

MOTION HEARING BEFORE THE HONORABLE WILLIAM J.
ZLOCH UNITED STATES DISTRICT JUDGE

APPEARANCES:
FOR THE PLAINTIFF(S)

Cullin A. O'Brien, Esquire
Cullin O'Brien Law, PA
6541 Northeast 21st Way
Fort Lauderdale, Florida 33308

Antonino G. Hernandez, Esquire
Law Office of Antonino G. Hernandez
4 Southeast First Street
Second Floor
Miami, Florida 33131

Elizabeth L. Beck, Esquire
Jared H. Beck, Esquire
Beck & Lee Trial Lawyers
12485 Southwest 137th Avenue
Suite 205
Miami, Florida 33186

FOR THE DEFENDANT(S):

Bruce V. Spiva, Esquire
Perkins, Coie, LLP
700 13th Street, Northwest
Suite 600
Washington, D.C. 20005

Gregg D. Thomas, Esquire
Thomas & LoCicero, PL
601 South Boulevard
Tampa, Florida 33606

REPORTED BY:

Tammy Nestor, RMR, CRR
Official Court Reporter
299 East Broward Boulevard
Fort Lauderdale, Florida 33301
tammy_nestor@flsd.uscourts.gov

INDEX

WITNESS	DIRECT RECROSS	CROSS	REDIRECT
RICARDO VILLALBA CABRAL			
BY MR. O'BRIEN	22		30
BY MR. SPIVA		25	

PLAINTIFFS' EXHIBITS	PAGE
1	6
2	7
3	7
5	43

DEFENDANTS' EXHIBITS	PAGE
1 and 2	40

Thereupon, the following proceedings began at 10:59 a.m.:

THE COURT: Good morning. Please be seated.

Calling case No. 16-61511-Civil. Counsel, would you note your appearances.

MR. O'BRIEN: Good morning, Your Honor. Cullin O'Brien for the plaintiffs.

MR. HERNANDEZ: Antonio Hernandez for the plaintiffs, Judge.

MS. BECK: Elizabeth Beck for the plaintiffs.

MR. BECK: Jared Beck for the plaintiffs.

THE COURT: Good morning.

MR. SPIVA: Good morning, Your Honor. Bruce Spiva from Perkins, Coie for the DNC and Congresswoman Debbie Wasserman Schultz.

THE COURT: Good morning.

MR. THOMAS: Gregg Thomas on behalf of both the defendants.

THE COURT: Good morning. Please be seated.

MR. O'BRIEN: Thank you, Your Honor.

THE COURT: We are here this morning pursuant to the defendants' motion which the Court—the defendants' motion to dismiss which the Court has considered a motion to quash service of process. The Court has set an evidentiary hearing on the motion to quash. Is the plaintiff ready?

MR. O'BRIEN: Yes, Your Honor. I apologize for being late. We were outside getting some stipulations to try to move this along.

THE COURT: That is fine.

MR. O'BRIEN: May I present some of the stipulations to Your Honor?

THE COURT: Sure. Go right ahead.

MR. O'BRIEN: Thank you, Your Honor.
So we plan to show Your Honor a video of the service of process event. The defendants stipulate to it coming in, admissibility, except there are some statements that are made by the people on the video that the defendants want not considered by this Court. We would have no objection to that.

THE COURT: That is fine.

MR. O'BRIEN: And then we have a witness—I'm sorry.

THE COURT: Just a moment. Has the video been marked as a plaintiffs' exhibit? Is it a CD or DVD?

MR. O'BRIEN: It's on a jump drive.

THE COURT: Okay. And that is going to have to be marked as Plaintiffs' No. 1.

MR. O'BRIEN: Yes, Your Honor, Plaintiffs' 1.

THE COURT: Any objection?

MR. SPIVA: No objection, Your Honor, assuming this is the YouTube video because there are some other video exhibits that I understand the plaintiffs are intending to—

MR. O'BRIEN: I think you mean Facebook. I think you may have it reversed.

MR. SPIVA: I thought you were talking about the YouTube. Assuming we are talking about the Facebook Live stream, we don't have objection to that with the exception of—

THE COURT: The statements.

MR. SPIVA: There's some verbiage about the DNC has accepted service. That is our objection to that.

THE COURT: You can point that out to the Court during the video.

MR. SPIVA: Will do, Your Honor.

THE COURT: That's fine. Plaintiffs' 1, being a thumb drive, is in evidence.
    (Thereupon, Plaintiffs' 1 received in evidence.)

MR. O'BRIEN: Thank you, Your Honor. The second stipulation, Your Honor, would be a police report regarding the death of the process server as well as an email confirming same to plaintiffs' counsel. The defendants do not object to that coming into evidence.

THE COURT: All right. And what exhibit number is that?

MR. O'BRIEN: May we make that, Your Honor, Exhibits 2 and 3?

MR. O'BRIEN: Thank you, Your Honor.

THE COURT: For the record, Plaintiffs' 2 is?

MR. O'BRIEN: The police report that was attached to our response. I don't want to mischaracterize it, but we would say it's a police report of the death of the process server.

THE COURT: All right. That is Plaintiffs' 2. Is there any objection?

MR. SPIVA: No objection, Your Honor. My understanding is it's being offered to show his availability.

THE COURT: Plaintiffs' 2 is in evidence.
    (Thereupon, Plaintiffs' 2 received in evidence.)

THE COURT: And Plaintiffs' 3?

MR. O'BRIEN: Your Honor, it would be an email from the D.C. police attaching the police report to plaintiffs' counsel confirming that the death report is a person by the name of Shawn Lucas.

THE COURT: Any objection?

MR. SPIVA: No objection, Your Honor.

THE COURT: Plaintiffs' 3 is in evidence.
    (Thereupon, Plaintiffs' 3 received in evidence.)

MR. O'BRIEN: With respect to what is going—what we ask Your Honor to consider on the video, the defendants have stipulated that the woman towards the end of the video is Ms. Rebcca Herries. And they have also stipulated that the gentleman who is bald is the Shawn Lucas that is in the police report.

THE COURT: Okay.

MR. O'BRIEN: So that takes care of a bunch of exhibits.

THE COURT: Fine.

MR. O'BRIEN: And then we do have a dispute, Your Honor, on the last exhibit. It would be an email that was obtained on Wikileaks. I believe the defendant—I'll let the defendants state their position, but the nature of the dispute, as I understand it, the defendants—

THE COURT: Would you be offering this email?

MR. O'BRIEN: I want to offer it. And I don't want to just offer it just to show that Rebecca Herries was the special assistant to the then CEO. The purpose that I want to offer it for is that we believe the email speaks for itself. It shows Ms. Herries organizing a staff-wide meeting.

And our argument would be, based on that, that Ms. Herries is someone who would have that sort of authority to accept service. That would be the purpose for which we would want to issue the—have the email into evidence.

But there is a dispute. They object to it coming into evidence. They would stipulate that Ms. Herries is the special assistant—was the special assistant to the then CEO of the DNC, but beyond that—

THE COURT: Just slow down a little bit. Take a deep breath.

MR. O'BRIEN: Sorry, Your Honor, Too much coffee.

THE COURT: That's all right. Slow down for the court reporter. Finish your statement though.

MR. O'BRIEN: Thank you, Your Honor. The defendants would at least stipulate that Ms. Herries at the time of the disputed service of process event was the special assistant to the then CEO. But beyond that, they object to anything else.

So we may ask Your Honor to rule in advance about the email or however Your Honor wants to handle that.

THE COURT: All right. Do you want to have that marked as an exhibit? You would intend to offer it if allowed?

MR. O'BRIEN: Yes, Your Honor.

THE COURT: And that would be Plaintiffs' 4?

MR. O'BRIEN: 4, Your Honor.

THE COURT: And this is an email from?

MR. O'BRIEN: Ms. Herries.

THE COURT: To?

MR. O'BRIEN: Staff at the DNC.

THE COURT: First of all, let me see the email.

MR. O'BRIEN: Yes, Your Honor. May I approach?

THE COURT: Yes.

MR. O'BRIEN: Okay. This is—

THE COURT: Show it to counsel.

MR. O'BRIEN: Is this okay?

MR. SPIVA: It's the one that you gave us? Yes.

MR. O'BRIEN: Okay. Thank you.
     Your Honor, the demarcation is when we had submitted our exhibit list, it was a different exhibit.

THE COURT: That's all right. First of all, you will need to remark this. Do you have stickers?

MR. O'BRIEN: We do, Your Honor. We have a clean copy.

THE COURT: What would be the objection?

MR. SPIVA: Well, Your Honor, there are at least two that I just note, first of all, that we would stipulate that she was the special assistant to the then CEO, and that's the only real purpose that I think this email could serve. Our objections are as follows:

One, this email was stolen, and there is case law that even if—you know, counsel, obviously we are not suggesting that they stole the email, but Wikileaks obtained it from a stolen source, that it is still a confidential email, and it shouldn't be permitted to be used. There is an ACLU case out of the District of Colombia that holds that and—

THE COURT: Do you have that cite?

MR. SPIVA: Yes, Your Honor. Can I get it to you in just a minute? I think I might need to consult an electronic device, Your Honor. I apologize.

Second basis, Your Honor, there is really no way to authenticate this, I don't think, with any of the people that are on their witness list. And also it's hearsay. So we would have those objections as well.

Mainly I don't see why they need it. We are willing to stipulate that that was, in fact, her title, special assistant to Ms. Dacey.

THE COURT: Any reply to those objections?

MR. O'BRIEN: Yes, Your Honor. I will start with the caveat that I have not seen the D.C. case or in West Law. I searched Wikileaks and I couldn't find a case on this. So I don't know—I think this may be a first impression as to whether something like this could come in based on the allegation that it's stolen; although, we don't have proof it's stolen. But we wanted Ms. Herries here.

THE COURT: I understand.

MR. O'BRIEN: We asked them to bring Ms. Herries here so we can cross-examine her or take her testimony. We don't have her.

THE COURT: But they were not required to do that.

MR. O'BRIEN: They were not required and she's outside the subpoena power. We wanted to establish, because it's our burden, that Ms. Herries had the authority. This email, not only shows that she was the special assistant which they stipulated to in their motion to quash, but she's organizing—

THE COURT: Well, they stipulated to it here today.

MR. O'BRIEN: Here today, yes, Your Honor, they stipulated to it here today. In this email, we would be offering it, not just for that purpose, but because it appears that she's organizing a DNC-wide meeting in the Wasserman conference room.

So our argument would be, based on that, that she is the kind of person, if she's organizing a meeting for the entire DNC in the Wasserman conference room, then she's someone with authority to come down and get service on Debbie Wasserman Schultz and the DNC. That would be the argument we would make.

As far as hearsay, I think it would be non-hearsay because it would be an admission. We cited in our exhibit list Rule 801(d)(2). Alternatively, it's a hearsay exception under Rule 803, subsection 6. I think it's a business record. I think it's self-authenticating. And the only way we could think to try to get it in would be to have our two witnesses say they went to Wikileaks which they did, typed in Becca Herries which they did, and saw this exhibit on Wikileaks. I mean, I don't know how else to get it in other than to say that someone went to the internet which is what happened. That would be our way to try to get it in.

THE COURT: I am going to reserve on Plaintiffs' 4 at this point. I am going to reserve ruling on it.

MR. O'BRIEN: Thank you, Your Honor.

THE COURT: Let me just ask for a clarification so that the record is clear. Do you have an extra copy of Plaintiffs' 4?

MR. O'BRIEN: May I give you a clean copy, Your Honor?

THE COURT: You hold on to the clean copy because this is not marked other than the exhibit number that is not pertinent right now. So you hold on to the plain copy.

MR. O'BRIEN: Thank you, Your Honor.

THE COURT: Just make sure you mark them with the appropriate exhibit sticker, all the exhibits.
    I have reviewed the complaint and the first amended complaint.
    Counsel, go ahead and be seated.

MR. SPIVA: Thank you, Your Honor.

THE COURT: I have reviewed the complaint and the first amended complaint. Is it the plaintiffs' position that Congresswoman Schultz is being sued individually and not in her capacity as then the chair of the DNC?

MR. O'BRIEN: May I consult with my colleagues? I think—I need to make sure that I get this answer right, Your Honor.

THE COURT: Because if you read the complaint and the first amended complaint and in particular page 20 of the first amended complaint—but go ahead, consult with your counsel.

MR. O'BRIEN: Thank you, Your Honor.

MR. SPIVA: Would it be all right if I consult my electronic device to get you that cite while they are conferring?

THE COURT: Go right ahead.

MR. SPIVA: Thank you.

MR. O'BRIEN: Your Honor, thank you. I think Your Honor is referring to paragraph 154 on page 20.

THE COURT: Well, paragraph 154 in particular.

MR. O'BRIEN: I think we would take the position that our complaint is suing Ms. Wasserman Schultz in her individual capacity.

THE COURT: Okay.

MR. O'BRIEN: She happened to be a chairperson, but this is in her individual capacity, Your Honor.

THE COURT: All right. Because obviously that capacity would affect the service of process analysis.

MR. O'BRIEN: I think Your Honor could reasonably state that because it's in her individual capacity, maybe we had to treat her—go to her house or something like that.

But we would be taking the argument that, because she was DNC chair at the time, that that was a good place to serve her.

And beyond that, based on what Ms. Herries said, she accepted service on behalf of—

THE COURT: No, I understand. We will get to the argument at a later point. But for the purposes of the record, just so the record is clear, Congresswoman Schultz is being sued in her individual capacity?

MR. O'BRIEN: Yes, Your Honor, in the first amended complaint, Your Honor.

MR. SPIVA: May I be heard on that briefly, Your Honor?

THE COURT: Yes.

MR. SPIVA: Our understanding up until now is that she was being sued in her corporate capacity.

THE COURT: That is why I asked for the clarification.

MR. SPIVA: So this is kind of the first time we are learning this as well, so I just wanted to make that point—

THE COURT: Counsel, go ahead.

MR. O'BRIEN: —with the argument.

THE COURT: Are we finished with exhibits?

MR. O'BRIEN: We are finished with exhibits, Your Honor. May I discuss the witnesses?

THE COURT: Go right ahead.

MR. O'BRIEN: Thank you, Your Honor.

MR. SPIVA: Your Honor, sorry to interrupt. I did find the cite that I was looking for. One of the reasons we didn't have this in our reply brief is we didn't know this was going to be one of their exhibits until after we had filed it.

THE COURT: That's fine.

MR. SPIVA: But the case that I was citing was ACLU versus Department of State, 879 F. Supp. 2d 215, and that's out of the DDC 2012. And that's one of the cases that suggests that—

THE COURT: That is out of the D.C. circuit?

MR. SPIVA: Yes. Well, it's the district court in D.C., yeah.

THE COURT: District court case?

MR. SPIVA: Correct, Your Honor.

THE COURT: Okay.

MR. SPIVA: And the case where the ACLU sought to obtain some documents that had been published on Wikileaks that the government contended had been stolen or leaked, and the court said, you know, that you couldn't—that the ACLU couldn't obtain those documents or use those documents despite that they were public.

THE COURT: I will take a look at that. Thank you.

MR. O'BRIEN: Your Honor, may we on our side be able to respond to this case?

THE COURT: Sure.

MR. O'BRIEN: I don't want to give Your Honor an impression that we are trying to make Your Honor rule inconsistent with the case, but I want to see this case and—

THE COURT: That's fine.

MR. O'BRIEN: Thank you.

THE COURT: All right. Are you ready to proceed with the evidentiary phase of the trial?

MR. O'BRIEN: Yes, Your Honor. One stipulation on witnesses and then one manner of disagreement on witnesses.

THE COURT: Go right ahead.

MR. O'BRIEN: Our first witness we would like to call is Ricardo Villalba, and he was the videographer. I don't believe there is any objection to him testifying by the defendants.

THE COURT: Any objection?

MR. SPIVA: No blanket objection to his testifying, Your Honor. I mean, obviously we would have to see what he says. But, yes, we don't have an objection, a blanket objection.

THE COURT: Let me just ask you this for a convenience of time standpoint. If there is no objection to the video, do you think you still need the witness?

MR. O'BRIEN: We wanted to be very careful. Because it's our burden, we wanted as many witnesses as we could possibly have. We wanted the security guards. We wanted Ms. Herries. We brought him in the abundance of caution.

I do agree with Your Honor that much of what the witness will say will be apparent on the video. But in case Your Honor had any questions or in case there's just context we wanted to give Your Honor for why he was there but, yeah, since the video is now in evidence, there is very little that would be helpful. However, in an abundance of caution, he flew down from D.C. for this hearing, so we wanted to make him available and we intended to call him.

THE COURT: If you wish to, go right ahead, or you can have him—obviously he will be here throughout the hearing.

If anyone has any questions regarding the video, he could be called to the witness stand. But proceed in whatever fashion you would like to.

MR. O'BRIEN: Thank you, Your Honor. The second witness would be the first named plaintiff, Ms. Carol Wilding, who is here. The defendants object to her testifying. We would want her to testify in case it was needed to show that she watched the live stream. The video of service of process event was on live stream on Facebook, and she watched it in case—because it's our burden to give a different perspective of what was happening and to testify she didn't hear anything inconsistent with what's on the video. This is in an abundance of caution. I understand that we don't want to duplicate or take up Your Honor's time unnecessarily, but we wanted to make sure we had as many witnesses as possible here.

THE COURT: The video obviously speaks for itself, correct?

MR. O'BRIEN: Yes, Your Honor.

THE COURT: And what is on the video is on the video.

MR. O'BRIEN: Yes, Your Honor.

THE COURT: And Ms. Wilding would not testify as to anything different, correct?

MR. O'BRIEN: Yes, Your Honor.

THE COURT: So do you think that you still need her as a witness?

MR. O'BRIEN: No, Your Honor. Now that there is a stipulation of the video into evidence, I—oh, the other thing would be to bring in that Wikileaks either through the first witness or the second witness. We were prepared to have them say, because it's true, they went to Wikileaks, and that's how we would get the exhibit in.

THE COURT: Regarding Plaintiffs' 4—

MR. O'BRIEN: Correct, Your Honor.
   THE COURT:—the email?

MR. O'BRIEN: Yes, Your Honor.

MR. SPIVA: Your Honor, we don't think she's a competent witness to testify to either of those things. I mean, she didn't take the video. At least Mr.—and I don't want to butcher his name, Mr. Villalba.

MR. O'BRIEN: Villalba.

MR. SPIVA: Villalba, thank you. You know, he apparently took the video and I assume was going to testify to that. But she didn't take the video. They are just saying she watched it which means that if she's a competent witness to testify to what's in the video, anyone in America really who saw the video would be a competent witness. So we would object to that, Your Honor.

And as far as the Wikileaks document, again, she didn't create the document. She didn't receive the document. She's just saying she pulled it up on Wikileaks. And so we don't think she's competent to testify to that either.

THE COURT: Well, if you want to call the witness with respect to whatever she did at Wikileaks, feel free to do that. You can call that witness whenever you wish to. If you want to go forward with the video first, that is up to you.

MR. O'BRIEN: Thank you, Your Honor. We would like to go forward with the video first. And my colleague Ms. Beck is going to play the video if Your Honor would allow it.

THE COURT: Fine.

MR. O'BRIEN: Thank you, Your Honor.

THE COURT: This is Plaintiffs' 1. Take your time.
 If you need assistance, we have our technical assistant here.
 (Thereupon, the videotape was played.)

MR. O'BRIEN: Your Honor, for the record, that was Plaintiffs' Exhibit 1.
 And now Ms. Beck will be playing Plaintiffs' Exhibit 2 if Your Honor would allow it.

THE COURT: Which is a continuation of the video?

MR. O'BRIEN: Yes, Your Honor. There is a couple-minute gap in it.

THE COURT: All right. But we are still on Plaintiffs' 1, for the record.

MR. O'BRIEN: It's a composite 1. I apologize, Your Honor.

THE COURT: That's all right, because Plaintiffs' 2 is a police report.

MR. O'BRIEN: I apologize, Your Honor.

THE COURT: That's all right. Don't worry about it.

MR. O'BRIEN: Yes, Your Honor.
 (Thereupon, the videotape was played.)

MR. O'BRIEN: Your Honor, that completes Exhibit 1.
 And we have offered that into evidence. I would like to offer into evidence as well Plaintiffs' Exhibits 2 and 3.

THE COURT: All right. Now, already in evidence is Plaintiffs' 1, composite 1, being the thumb drive.

Plaintiffs' 2 and Plaintiffs' 3 are in evidence. The Court has reserved on Plaintiffs' 4.

MR. O'BRIEN: Thank you, Your Honor. I would like to call Mr. Villalba, Ricardo Villalba.

THE COURT: Fine. Please step up to the witness stand.

THE WITNESS: Good morning, Your Honor—or good afternoon.

THE COURT: Please remain standing and raise your right hand.

RICARDO VILLALBA CABRAL: Having been first duly sworn on oath, was examined and testified as follows:

THE COURT: Thank you. Please be seated. You can adjust that microphone. Please speak directly into it. Please state your full legal name for the record and spell your last name for the reporter.

THE WITNESS: My first name is Ricardo, R-I-C-A-R-D-O. Do I have to give my middle name too or—

THE COURT: No, just your last name.

THE WITNESS: My last name, I have two last names, Villalba Cabral. The first last name is spelled V-I-L-L-A-L-B-A, and my second last name is C-A-B-R-A-L.

THE COURT: Thank you. You may proceed.

MR. O'BRIEN: Thank you, Your Honor.

DIRECT EXAMINATION

BY MR. O'BRIEN:

Q Good morning, sir.

A Good morning.

Q Sir, where do you live?

A I live in Washington, D.C.

Q How long have you lived there?

A For about 20-plus years.

Q What is your profession?

A I am a substance abuse case manager for youth. I'm also filmmaker, you know.

Q You saw the video that was played here in court, sir?

A Yes, I did.

Q Was that you recording on the video, sir?

A Yes.

Q Was that you recording both the first video that stopped and the second video?

A Yes, it was me.

Q Sir, what day of the week, if you recall, and year was that video taken?

A It was Friday, July 1st of 2016, of this year.

MR. O'BRIEN: Your Honor, I would like to show the witness what has been marked for identification purposes only Plaintiffs' Exhibit 4.

   May I approach the witness?

THE COURT: Fine. Go ahead.

MR. O'BRIEN: Thank you.

THE COURT: That is the email?

MR. O'BRIEN: Yes, Your Honor.

BY MR. O'BRIEN:

Q Sir, I have handed you what has been marked for identification purposes only as Plaintiffs' Exhibit 4. Do you see that document?

A Yes, I do.

Q   Do you recognize the document?

A   Yes, I do recognize it.

Q   What is the document?

MR. SPIVA: Objection, Your Honor. He hasn't laid any foundation that he would have a basis to answer that question.

THE COURT: He is allowed to try to identify the document.

What is the document that you are looking at, sir?

THE WITNESS: It is an email from Becca Herries to the staff at the DNC headquarters.

BY MR. O'BRIEN:

Q   Sir, how do you know that?

A   I went into Wikileaks and I searched Becca Herries, and this is what came up. And I read it, and it seems that it's an email.

MR. SPIVA: I don't want to keep interrupting, Your Honor. I'll just say objection, lack of foundation, hearsay.

THE COURT: It hasn't been offered yet.

MR. SPIVA: Okay.

BY MR. O'BRIEN:

Q   The exhibit that is in your hand, are you testifying that you saw that by doing a search under Becca Herries at the Wikileaks database?

A   Yes.

MR. O'BRIEN: Your Honor, I would like to offer Plaintiffs' Exhibit 4 into evidence.

MR. SPIVA: Same objections, Your Honor.

THE COURT: I am going to reserve on Plaintiffs' 4 at this point.

MR. O'BRIEN: Your Honor, may I consult with my co-counsel to see if we have further questions from the witness?

THE COURT: Yes, sir. Take your time.

MR. O'BRIEN: Thank you.
Your Honor, for the purposes of direct, I have no further questions.

THE COURT: Cross-examination?

MR. SPIVA: Yes, Your Honor. Thank you.

CROSS EXAMINATION

BY MR. SPIVA:

Q Good morning. It's still good morning, Mr. Villalba—sorry, Villalba
   Cabral. Did I get that right?
A You're close.
Q All right. Thank you, sir. So on the video that you took, one of the
   things that you said was that you didn't expect to find many people at
   the DNC that day, is that correct?
A That is correct.
Q And that was because it was the Friday before the July 4 holiday week-
   end, correct?
A That is correct.
Q And you, in fact, noticed, I think you noted on the video, that there
   weren't a lot of people around, fair?
A That is correct.
Q Okay. And, sir, you didn't fill out either of the affidavits of service in
   this case, did you?
A No, I didn't.
Q And you weren't there that day serving as a process server, were you?
A No, I wasn't.
Q Okay. You were there and you saw when the woman who identified her-
   self as Becca came down from upstairs, correct?
A That's correct.
Q And you didn't ask her her last name, did you?
A No, I didn't.
Q And you didn't hear Mr. Lucas ask her her last name, correct?
A Correct.
Q And she didn't provide her last name to either of you, correct?

A   No, she didn't.

Q   And she didn't provide her title either, did she?

A   No, she didn't.

Q   She didn't say that she had authority to accept service of process, did she?

MR. O'BRIEN: Objection, Your Honor, calls for a legal conclusion.

MR. SPIVA: I asked what she said.

THE COURT: I'll overrule the objection.

THE WITNESS: No.

BY MR. SPIVA:

Q   Okay. And she didn't say that she was an officer of the DNC, did she?

A   No.

Q   And Mr. Lucas didn't ask her if she was an officer of the DNC, did he?

A   No.

Q   And she didn't say that she was a managing agent of the DNC, I take it?

A   No.

Q   And, likewise, she didn't say that she was a general agent of the DNC, correct?

A   Correct.

Q   And she didn't say that she was the treasurer of the DNC, did she?

A   No.

Q   Or the cashier of the DNC?

A   No.

Q   Or the secretary of the DNC?

A   No.

Q   Or the general manager of the DNC?

A   No.

Q   And she didn't say she was a director of the DNC?

A   No.

Q   And Mr. Lucas didn't ask her whether she was any of those things, did he?

A   No.

Q   Now, she also didn't say that she had authority to accept service of process on behalf of Ms. Wasserman Schultz, did she?

MR. O'BRIEN: Objection, Your Honor. The evidence speaks for itself. What she said is what she said, and we would disagree with the characterization, the legal conclusion.

MR. SPIVA: I'm just asking what she said.

THE COURT: I will overrule the objection.

BY MR. SPIVA:
Q   She didn't say that she had the authority to accept service on behalf of Ms. Wasserman Schultz, did she?
A   No, she didn't.
Q   Okay. At some point while you were there—you were there about 14 minutes, is that fair?
A   A little bit longer. There was a time lapse between that recording, so yeah, between 14, 16 minutes.
Q   All told, from the time you went in the building, you kind of came out for a while and went back in, about 16 minutes?
A   I would say 15 minutes all together.
Q   And there was a time kind of in the middle there where the security guard, several of the security guards specifically asked you to stop videoing, is that right?
A   That is correct.
Q   And you ultimately agreed to stop videotaping, correct?
A   That's correct.
Q   In fact, you and Mr. Lucas stepped outside for a short time at that point?
A   That's correct.
Q   And you told the individuals who were watching on live stream that you were going to have to stop videotaping because you had been asked by the security guard, correct?
A   That is correct.
Q   But then you went back into the DNC a short time later, correct?
A   Yes.
Q   And you started videotaping again, did you not?

A   Yes, I did.

Q   But you didn't tell the security guards that you had started videotaping again, did you?

A   That is correct.

Q   In fact, on the live stream video, there was an update that says we are not going to tell them this time that we are videotaping, we are not going to tell security that we are videotaping, correct?

A   I believe so.

Q   And you did that because you knew that they would ask you to leave if you made them aware that you were videotaping again?

A   That is correct.

Q   And Mr. Lucas said to you at one point during the encounter at the DNC that anybody in the building can accept the service, the documents, correct?

A   I believe he said something like that, yes.

Q   Okay. And he said he had volunteered for the assignment?

A   Yes.

Q   Okay. And the reason you were there making the video is because you wanted to be able to tell people—you wanted to be able to tell people at the DNC, quote, you have been served, correct?

A   Not me in particular. I know that's what Mr. Lucas wanted to do. I was just commenting to someone. Someone put a comment on the Facebook Live, and I just comment to that. But me in particular, I wasn't there to say any of that.

Q   Okay.

MR. SPIVA: No further questions, Your Honor.

THE COURT: Redirect?

MR. O'BRIEN: Yes, Your Honor. Thank you.

REDIRECT EXAMINATION

BY MR. O'BRIEN:

Q   Why did you continue videotaping after the security guards told you to stop?

A   As a filmmaker, I believe that it was necessary to document this event, not just for me, but also for the audience that we have. Prior to tuning out the live streaming, we had over 300 viewers, and I needed to bring closures to them.

At the same time, Mr. Lucas and I had a conversation. The building, the DNC building, has several cameras. They videotape us going into the building. They videotape us approaching the building. So there's a lot of cameras in the building as well. So I felt that it was necessary for us to continue videotaping. I didn't see any signs saying that I couldn't videotape.

When I first walked in, none of the officers—the first security officer saw me videotaping. They didn't say nothing. This happened after the other supervisors came out.

The reason why I couldn't videotape, I felt it wasn't reading law or reading rule. I felt they were just making things up, and that's the reason why they asked me to stop.

Q   How many security officers did you and Mr. Lucas interface with when you entered the building?

A   When we first entered the building, we talked to one security officer. It looked like he made several attempts to reach someone. Eventually three other officers came. Mr. Lucas spoke to a female security officer explaining what we were there to do. The female security officer said, let me bring my supervisor. An officer with a white shirt that made us believe—you know, we believe he was a supervisor also approach Mr. Lucas.

Mr. Lucas once again explained to him what we were there to do. I would say in total we spoke to three officers about what we were there to do.

Q   At any point in time, did any one of those officers say today is not a good day to serve the DNC, no one here is able to accept service for the DNC?

A   No.

Q   At any point in time, did any of those officers say today's not a good day to serve Debbie Wasserman Schultz, there is no one here to accept service for Debbie Wasserman Schultz?

A   No.

Q   When Ms. Herries came down, at any point in time did she say I'm not able to accept service for the DNC?

A   No.

Q   At any point in time, did Ms. Herries say I'm not able to accept service for Debbie Wasserman Schultz?

A   No.

Q   At any point in time did Ms. Herries say today's not a day to serve the DNC—

MR. SPIVA: Objection, Your Honor. He's leading the witness.

THE COURT: Refrain from leading.

MR. O'BRIEN: Thank you, Your Honor.

BY MR. O'BRIEN:

Q   Were you given any indication by Ms. Herries that she was not authorized to accept service on behalf of the DNC?

A   No.

Q   Same question with respect to Debbie Wasserman Schultz.

A   No.

Q   Did you hear Ms. Herries say, Shawn, hi, Becca?

A   Yes.

Q   Did you hear Ms. Herries say, I'm just with the DNC upstairs?

A   Yes.

Q   Did you hear Shawn respond, you are with the DNC?

A   Yes.

Q   Did you hear Ms. Herries respond, yes?

A   Yes.

Q   Did you hear the—did you hear Shawn say, all right. Well, this is going to be a service to the DNC?

A   Yes.

Q   Did you hear Ms. Herries say to the DNC, okay?

A   Yes.

Q   Did you hear Shawn respond, and this is for Debbie Wasserman Schultz?

A   Yes.

Q   Did you hear Ms. Herries respond, perfect?

A   Yes.

Q   Did you hear Shawn say, you guys have been served?

A   Yes.

Q Did you hear Ms. Herries respond, okay?

A Yes.

Q Did you hear Shawn respond, thank you so much. We'll see you in court?

A Yes.

Q And before Shawn—you heard Shawn say, all right, well, this is going to be service to the DNC, did you see Shawn hand Ms. Herries the service of process packet?

A Yes.

Q And before Shawn said and this is for Debbie Wasserman Schultz, did you see Shawn hand Ms. Herries the service of process packet?

A Yes.

Q How far away from you were—during this interaction?

A Maybe one or two feets. I was right next to him, right behind him.

Q At any point in time, were you given the indication that you needed to come back, that Shawn Lucas needed to come back to effect service on the DNC or Ms. Wasserman Schultz?

A No.

Q Did you hear Shawn indicate to the security officers that he was there to serve the DNC with legal papers?

A Yes.

Q Did you hear Shawn say to the security officers he was there to serve Debbie Wasserman Schultz with legal papers?

MR. SPIVA: Objection, Your Honor, leading and also calling for hearsay now.

MR. O'BRIEN: I want to know—it's not hearsay, not offered for the truth, just as the defendant said, just want to know what was said.

THE COURT: Well, you are asking the witness to repeat what is on the video, correct?

MR. O'BRIEN: You're right, it's duplicative in that sense. I just want to cover my bases, Your Honor.

THE COURT: That's fine. You can ask the question. I will overrule the question. He is simply testifying about what is on the video.

THE WITNESS: Yes.

MR. O'BRIEN: May I ask the question again, Your Honor?

THE COURT: Sure.

BY MR. O'BRIEN:
Q Did you hear Shawn say to the security guards, I'm here to serve legal process on Debbie Wasserman Schultz?
A Yes.

MR. O'BRIEN: Your Honor, may I consult with my colleagues to see if we have further questions?

THE COURT: Take your time.

MR. O'BRIEN: Thank you, Your Honor.

BY MR. O'BRIEN:
Q When you were in the lobby of the DNC headquarters, did it appear that the offices were closed?
A No.
Q Did you see people walking in and out to the elevator bank?
A Yes.

MR. O'BRIEN: Your Honor, I have no further questions.

THE COURT: Recross?

MR. O'BRIEN: Thank you.

MR. SPIVA: No, Your Honor, no further questions.

THE COURT: All right. Thank you, sir. You may step down. Watch your step, please.

THE WITNESS: Thank you, sir. Take the evidence?

THE COURT: Just give that to counsel.

MR. O'BRIEN: Thank you, sir. Your Honor, may we confer to see whether we would like to try to call Mrs. Wilding?

THE COURT: Sure. Take your time.

MR. O'BRIEN: Thank you, Your Honor.

Your Honor, may I tell—consult with Mrs. Wilding, the first named plaintiff, about our thought process?

THE COURT: Go right ahead.

MR. O'BRIEN: Thank you, Your Honor.

THE COURT: You can step out of the courtroom if you need to.

MR. THOMAS: Your Honor, would it be possible for us to have a comfort break, five minutes?

THE COURT: We will take a short recess. Let's have everyone back in the courtroom at five after. Court is in recess for ten minutes.

MR. THOMAS: Thank you, Your Honor.

(Thereupon, a recess was taken at 11:56 a.m.)

THE COURT: Please be seated. All right. The plaintiff may call its next witness.

MR. HERNANDEZ: Your Honor, after discussing the matter with our colleagues and the plaintiff, we have decided not to call Ms. Wilding today. We wanted to provide the Court with the widest net possible, but in light of the testimony and the evidence we have proffered, we respectfully retract calling her.

THE COURT: All right. That's fine.

MR. HERNANDEZ: Thank you, Judge.

THE COURT: The plaintiff rests?

MR. O'BRIEN: For the evidence, yes, Your Honor.

THE COURT: All right. Thank you.
    Any testimony or evidence on behalf of the defense?

MR. SPIVA: I think the answer is no, Your Honor. I just wanted one clarification. The plaintiffs had filed the two affidavits of service on the record, ECF No. 7 and ECF No. 6. And I am assuming that I don't need to introduce those into evidence. I know the Court has already considered them, I think you've mentioned in your recent order. And that's the only thing that we would rely upon in our argument that hasn't been introduced by the plaintiffs here today.

THE COURT: I am not considering them for the purposes of this hearing.

MR. SPIVA: Well, these are the affidavits of service from Mr. Lucas—

THE COURT: Oh, I'm sorry.

MR. SPIVA: Yeah—that the plaintiffs submitted.

THE COURT: You said affidavits, and I thought that you were talking about—

MR. SPIVA: I apologize, affidavit of service. The plaintiffs had submitted earlier affidavits of service, one—both are signed, I think, by Mr. Lucas. And one is at ECF—

THE COURT: Docket entry—

MR. SPIVA: No. 7.

THE COURT:—6 and 7?

MR. SPIVA: Yes, Your Honor.

THE COURT: Any objection from the plaintiff?

MR. O'BRIEN: Your Honor, I believe that the burden was on the defendants to bring in any testimony or witnesses. We wanted Ms. Herries here. We wanted the security guards here to sort of double back on the original affidavits. We would just—we would object on the basis that it's hearsay. But it's in the court file, so I don't know how Your Honor could not take it into account.

But with respect to the affidavit of service, we have an affidavit from Mr. Lucas that's dated—oh, it's July 7th that has—appears to have corrections. We did not file it. And I don't know if Your Honor would accept this in lieu of accepting the ones that—this would sort of be a rebuttal exhibit to that.

MR. SPIVA: I have never seen that, Your Honor. And these were filed by the plaintiffs themselves, you know, purporting to show how they accomplished service. I don't think it's hearsay. It's clearly statement by an agent of the plaintiff. And they filed it for the purpose of showing—of meeting their burden of showing that they had effectuated service. I can move them formally as exhibits if need be, Your Honor, but they are on the ECF record.

THE COURT: Well, for the purposes of the hearing, you should move them in as defense exhibits if that's what you wish to do.

MR. SPIVA: Yes, Your Honor.

THE COURT: Take a look at the exhibits that plaintiff is showing you.

MR. SPIVA: Okay. So if I might, Your Honor, may I go ahead and move in the two affidavits of service?

THE COURT: Do you want to mark them separately or as a composite exhibit?

MR. SPIVA: I think I should mark them separately, Your Honor.

THE COURT: All right. Defendants' 1 and 2?

MR. SPIVA: Yes, Your Honor. So the one that appears at ECF docket No. 6 we would mark as Defendants' Exhibit 1, and the affidavit of service that appears at ECF document No. 7 we would mark as Defendants' Exhibit 2.

THE COURT: Any objection from the plaintiff?

MR. O'BRIEN: Your Honor, it's part of the court record. I don't know how I could make an objection that Your Honor wouldn't consider it other than technically it's hearsay, and we would ask to be able to submit this rebuttal exhibit if that's allowed.

THE COURT: I will overrule the objection.

Defendants' 1 and 2 are in evidence.

(Thereupon, Defendants' 1 and 2 received in evidence.)

MR. SPIVA: Your Honor, I believe this is the first time I have seen this revised affidavit of service, so I would object if they are intending to, I guess, introduce this in their rebuttal case, but maybe I should wait until their rebuttal.

Your Honor, we are not going to introduce any further evidence. At some point I don't know if Your Honor is going to entertain argument today, but based on evidence that the plaintiffs have submitted, the previous—

THE COURT: I'm not going entertain argument right now.

MR. SPIVA: Okay.

THE COURT: Any additional evidence or any testimony from the defendant?

MR. SPIVA: I don't think so, Your Honor. Let me just confer with my co-counsel just briefly.

No, Your Honor. With the exception of those two exhibits, that's it. Thank you.

THE COURT: So the defendants rest?

MR. SPIVA: Yes, Your Honor.

THE COURT: Any rebuttal testimony or evidence from the plaintiff?

MR. O'BRIEN: Yes, Your Honor. I would like to offer rebuttal evidence. It's an affidavit of service signed by Mr. Lucas. The purpose of this is to show that Mr. Lucas tried to correct who he thought he served. And on the exhibit, it has a Rebecca Christopher which is who he thought he was serving, one of the people on the list that he gave the security guard as seen on the video. I know the defendants—we didn't know that they were going to produce rebuttal exhibits, so this would be our counter to the other affidavits that are already in the court file.

MR. SPIVA: Your Honor, I may be missing something, but this looks exactly the same to me as what we have marked as Defendants' Exhibit 2, which was document No. 7. I just went through it kind of line by line, and I can't find what the difference is.

THE COURT: Well, I haven't seen them, so . . .

MR. O'BRIEN: The difference is, Your Honor, when it says I, Brandon Yoshimura, it looks like the form was filled out with the wrong name and—

THE COURT: That is the only change?

MR. O'BRIEN: Is that the only change?

MS. BECK: Yes, Your Honor.

MR. O'BRIEN: Yes, Your Honor.

MR. SPIVA: In that case, Your Honor, with the stipulation that that is the only change here, I would not object to the admission of this. I'm not withdrawing the exhibit that I entered.

THE COURT: I understand.

MR. SPIVA: Because I want to show that there was an inaccuracy there. But I don't object to this also being—

THE COURT: That will be Plaintiffs' Exhibit No. 5?

MR. O'BRIEN: Yes, Your Honor.

THE COURT: All right. There being no objection, Plaintiffs' 5 is in evidence being an affidavit of service.
(Thereupon, Plaintiffs' 5 received in evidence.)

MR. O'BRIEN: Your Honor, we have no further evidence.

THE COURT: All right. The plaintiff rests?

MR. O'BRIEN: Thank you, Your Honor.

THE COURT: All right. I will hear argument from counsel.

MR. SPIVA: Since this is our motion, do you want to hear from us first, Your Honor?

THE COURT: Yes.

MR. SPIVA: Thank you, Your Honor. First I must say we first offered to accept a waiver of service form over a month ago, and so I'm a little bit, you know, kind of taken aback or confused as to why we are really here.

Clearly service was not provided in the proper manner. I think the videotape only confirms that. You know, this was done on the weekend before July 4th when they knew that nobody would be there, and they didn't make any attempt to really to get a proper person. They didn't even ask the person that they got what her last name was, what her title was, whether she fit any of the categories under either the D.C. statute or the Florida statute or any of the federal rules. So frankly, usually—

THE COURT: When you say the federal rules, you are talking about Rule 4—

MR. SPIVA: Yes, Your Honor.

THE COURT:—of the federal rules?

MR. SPIVA: Yes, Your Honor. And with respect to either Ms. Wasserman Schultz or the DNC itself, you know, frankly, when this has happened in the past, you know, when counsel offers to accept waiver, you know, the waiver form, the opposing counsel goes ahead and does that. And we certainly would have been willing to negotiate over the time frame to respond. I know that would have given us more time.

But we can't waive this type of service because it would just open the floodgates to anybody kind of, you know, as a matter of political theater, you know, coming into the DNC offices and, you know, kind of grabbing the first person they can get ahold of.

On their face, if you look at either the revised or the original affidavits of service by the process server, they are deficient. He doesn't even state in there that the person he talked to said that they were authorized to have service because, as the tape shows, she clearly didn't. He has the wrong person in the affidavit of service which only confirms what the tape shows which he didn't even ask what her last name was. He must have looked it up on the internet.

The person he thought he was serving, Rebecca Christopher, also isn't authorized to accept service.

THE COURT: Is or is not?

MR. SPIVA: Sorry, Your Honor?

THE COURT: Is or is not?

MR. SPIVA: Is not, Your Honor. She's a creative strategist. She's not an agent, a managing agent, all of the other—treasurer, the other things that you would need to be.

When it's not a holiday weekend and someone comes and asks for that type of a person, in the past they have come down and accepted service.

There were other options available. They could have served by registered mail under certain conditions in D.C.

They didn't avail themselves of that. And then, of course, you know, as I mentioned at the beginning, they could—and even know, Your Honor, we would be willing to fill out the waiver of service form and accept service that way.

We have now been put to considerable expense, you know, trying to uphold this principle that you can't just kind of serve people by dropping paper on a Friday afternoon on the first person you come across. And, you know, so that's unfortunate, Your Honor, but we would still—you know, we are not trying to evade service, as has been suggested in the papers of the plaintiffs. We are still willing to figure out a waiver of service form. I would be willing to do it today.

And, you know, the only thing we would ask is for an extension, Your Honor, in terms of our time to respond. We have had to spend so much time on this that we haven't yet been able to get to responding on the merits.

THE COURT: But the parties have stipulated that Ms. Herries was then the special assistant to the CEO of the DNC on July 1, 2016, correct?

MR. SPIVA: That is correct. But she was not, and there's certainly no evidence in the record that she had any authority to accept service on behalf of the DNC or on behalf of Ms. Dacey or anyone else and she didn't. And certainly the plaintiffs have not come forward with any evidence that she had such authority. I mean—

THE COURT: How is it that she ended up in the lobby then?

MR. SPIVA: They refused to leave until they spoke to someone. It's not clear from anything that we have heard today what she was told before she came down.

But what is clear, though, is that the process server thought that he could give the papers to anybody in the building, that basically all she said was, hi, my name is Becca. And, you know, Your Honor has seen the video, so I won't repeat it but, you know, there was no question, are you authorized to accept service of legal papers for the DNC for Ms. Wasserman Schultz, and she clearly was not.

THE COURT: Why did she accept them then?

MR. SPIVA: I don't even know that she knew—I'm sure that she didn't know she was accepting service of the process. I think she thought she was taking—

THE COURT: Why did she take the papers?

MR. SPIVA: Because they handed them to her. Somebody said to her that, according to her declaration, that there were people in the lobby who wouldn't go away until they got to speak to somebody from the DNC. She tried to get ahold of her superiors and couldn't.

THE COURT: Well, according to the video, Ms. Herries says, quote, Shawn, hi, Becca.

Ms. Herries says, I'm just with the DNC upstairs.

The process server, Mr. Lucas says you're with the DNC.

Ms. Herries, yes.

The process server, all right. Well, this is going to be a service to the DNC.

Ms. Herries, to the DNC? Okay.

The process server, and this is for Debbie Wasserman Schultz.

Ms. Herries, perfect.

The process server, you guys have been served.

What did Ms. Herries think was going on?

MR. SPIVA: I don't know, Your Honor, but I think from the face of that, from the video that Your Honor just read, he didn't say service of process. He didn't say service of a lawsuit. At the end he said, see you in court, but I think it was entirely ambiguous what he was saying. Service to the DNC could mean anything. This is a low level employee who simply went downstairs—

THE COURT: Well, that's difficult to say, that she's a low level employee at the time if she's the special assistant to the CEO, the chief executive officer of the DNC.

MR. SPIVA: Well, the special assistant, Your Honor, is an administrative—you know, it's a pretty entry level position. I mean, it's not—this is not a policy making—

THE COURT: I'm not saying that, but I am saying that it is the right-hand man, if you will, to the CEO.

MR. SPIVA: It really isn't, Your Honor. And there is no evidence in this record that other than the fact that she, you know, did what any secretary could do, was she sent around an email, of course, that isn't in the record—even if Your Honor were to admit that into the record—

THE COURT: I'm not saying that that makes her one of the individuals that is set out in the rules—

MR. SPIVA: Right.

THE COURT:—to accept service of process.

MR. SPIVA: Right. Yeah. And, yes, that's correct, Your Honor. She clearly is not one of the people set out under the rules who is authorized to accept—

THE COURT: But she is not a low level employee at the DNC.

MR. SPIVA: She's pretty entry level, Your Honor. Had they introduced the pictures they were going to introduce, you would see she's about a couple years out of college and this is a pretty entry level position. There is no evidence on this one way or the other, but she really isn't a high level employee by any manner of speaking, Your Honor.

THE COURT: So the title is somewhat misleading?

MR. SPIVA: Your Honor, in Washington, D.C. there are thousands of special assistants. And, you know, as Your Honor is probably aware, yeah, it's not—it certainly doesn't denote—you know, no disrespect to Ms. Herries but—

THE COURT: No, I understand.
    MR. SPIVA:—but it's like an internship or a clerkship. It's a great thing to do, you know, as a young person out of school, but it is not a high level position.
    Your Honor, unless you have other questions for me, I am content to rest on our papers and what I said before. You know, I think it's very clear from the video, from the affidavits of service that they did not serve these papers on somebody who was authorized under the relevant statutes and rules to accept service of process.
    You know, we are certainly still willing and ready to do a proper

waiver of service, but we don't think the Court should allow them to kind of do a service light, if you will, here where you kind of just go to the office and drop the papers on the first person you can get to come down, you know, the elevator without verifying that that person has any authority to do so.

THE COURT: All right. Thank you.

MR. SPIVA: Thank you, Your Honor.

THE COURT: I think you dropped a piece of paper.

MR. O'BRIEN: Thank you, Your Honor.

MR. SPIVA: Is that yours or mine?

MR. O'BRIEN: Thank you.

THE COURT: Yes, sir.

MR. O'BRIEN: May it please the Court. With respect to my colleague, I just I disagree about what is on the video. I think Your Honor has discretion to find that there was authority by Ms. Herries.

The statements about Ms. Herries' low level or didn't know what was going on or all that, yes, we don't have Ms. Herries here, but we wanted Ms. Herries here. We wanted the security guards here.

I don't think that this Court can accept evidence about Ms. Herries when they haven't brought Ms. Herries here. From the evidence that we have, we have Ms. Herries saying, as Your Honor repeated, perfect, as to Debbie Wasserman Schultz, and to the DNC, okay, as to the DNC on service of process.

I think that when you say service to anybody in this country, they know it's legal process of service of papers. Even in the declaration of Ms. Herries, she talks about having called the COO to find out about legal papers. So even under her own declaration, she knew that this was legal process.

I will say her calculation is troubling because it doesn't mention the conversation that happened with Mr. Lucas. It omits significant details that Your Honor has in evidence.

So I would say to the extent we are relying on Mrs. Herries to counteract the evidence we put in, I don't think she's credible. I just don't think she's credible. To submit a declaration to this Court to not talk about the conversation, I think that renders Ms. Herries not credible.

We wanted her here. We could have asked Ms. Herries all these questions. We could have asked the security guards. We did the best we could. We flew down the videographer. We have the video. We have Mrs. Wilding, the first named plaintiff who watched the video. We've done all we can in terms of evidence.

THE COURT: You have referred to Ms. Herries' declaration. That is not being considered for the purposes of this evidentiary hearing.

MR. O'BRIEN: Correct, Your Honor. And I—Your Honor made a ruling on the motion in limine. I just—my colleague made an argument with respect to what is in the declaration. So we ask Your Honor not to consider anything. But in terms of atmospherics, the reason why it's our burden now to put forward evidence is because of the declaration they submitted which we believe—

THE COURT: To the motion.

MR. O'BRIEN: Excuse me, to the motion to quash.

THE COURT: Right.

MR. O'BRIEN: In support thereof, they filed a declaration of Mrs. Herries that triggered the plaintiffs' burden to put forward evidence as to proper service. But that declaration that triggered the burden now having seen the video is not credible and has, in my opinion, material omissions as to what transpired.

If you read the last paragraph, I just think she should have said what was said. They handed me papers and left. I mean, that's the impression they gave to this Court through this declaration that now require us to put on witnesses and evidence. They won't allow us to bring Mrs. Herries. I think we shouldn't even have to be here. I don't think that declaration should have even triggered the burden.

I have a problem the calculation. They handed me the papers and left.

That's not what happened. They didn't hand her the papers and left. Find the first person. I'm watching a different video.

They asked the security guard—they went into the building. They asked the security guards. There was a lot of conversation. They were trying to find the right person. Somebody came down. Security guards came down. We have no evidence as to why she came down.

Based on the video, it looks like they came down—she came down to accept service of process. I think that's a reasonable conclusion in Your Honor's discretion based on the evidence.

This isn't the first person. Mr. Lucas took his time to say service of process on the DNC, service of process on Debbie Wasserman Schultz, and they brought someone down. It's not like they grabbed someone who was in the elevator bank.

And by the way, this was open for business. They didn't say, hey, sorry, 4th of July weekend, come back after the holiday and someone will be here. They didn't give him that impression, that you can't serve anybody that day. There was no indication that service was improper, not even by Mrs. Herries.

I think they did everything you should do when you are serving a big corporation and the former chairwoman of the corporation in the corporate offices.

I just respectfully disagree with what I am seeing here in the evidence before, Your Honor. So I think Your Honor has the discretion to find that there was actual authority by Mrs. Herries. They have not put forward any evidence to the contrary. Your Honor can make that conclusion.

Whether or not Your Honor rules on the Wikileaks email which we would submit is further evidence contrary to this low level—this non-evidentiary lawyer submission, she's sending an email to the DNC, everybody at the DNC, come to the Wasserman conference room. We've got an all hands on deck meeting. Come to the conference room. That doesn't seem like a low level employee. That sounds like someone who they would entrust, both the DNC and the chairwoman, to come except service.

But if Your Honor doesn't consider the Wikileaks, we would like to submit a memorandum of law on the case we were provided today. I think Your Honor would be making a ruling of first impression on Wikileaks. I don't know that any court has allowed a Wikileaks email in. At least I put it in WestLaw. I didn't find any. So I want to be cautious of that. So we think there's a sufficient record for actual authority.

Process server comes, tells the security guards I'm here to serve process. A lot of security guards talk about it. Someone a white shirt, the head security guard, brings down someone who says, oh, I'm with the DNC upstairs. Okay.

Service of the DNC. Okay. Let me say it correct. Service to the DNC. Okay. And this is for Debbie Wasserman Schultz. Perfect. You guys have been served. Okay.

What else is a process server supposed to do?

I believe that Your Honor also has discretion to find there was apparent authority. If Your Honor in the alternative does not believe that there is actual authority from the record, we have submitted a case, the Kulik case, that we believe allows Your Honor to make that determination.

The case law talks about apparent authority in terms of service of process. And the burden would shift to us to show that someone from the DNC or Debbie Wasserman Schultz gave Mrs. Herries the authority. We don't have Mrs. Herries. We don't have the security guards. But I do believe on this record Your Honor would be within his discretion to determine that when you go into a lobby and you ask security guards about service of process and they bring someone down, I think that's enough for us to meet our burden that the DNC and Debbie Wasserman Schultz gave Mrs. Herries the authority to come down and get it, service of process.

I say that because there is no evidence to the contrary from defendants, and there is no indication whatsoever that something was wrong with service, not from Mrs. Herries, not from the security guards, from no one. So I think the only evidence, in quotes, that Your Honor would have that service was improper would be lawyer argument. I don't think there's any evidence that service was improper. I think it's just lawyer argument that should not be considered as evidence.

THE COURT: And what about service as to Congresswoman Schultz in her individual capacity?

MR. O'BRIEN: I agree, Your Honor, that is a little more gray area. I would say that the DNC, I don't think there's a gray area. The argument we would say, the reason why we think it's a good faith argument respect to Debbie Wasserman Schultz is because she's the chair of the DNC. If you can't serve the chair of the DNC at the DNC headquarters, where else could you serve her? Yeah, we could go to her house or find her on the campaign trail, but she's the chair of the DNC headquarters. I'm sure she doesn't want us going to her house or finding her on the campaign trail. She's the chair. She's not some lower level employee. She's the figurehead of the entire organization with the building that Your Honor saw, Democratic National headquarters. If you can't serve the chair of that building, the stuff that goes on in that building, at the building with the person who comes down and says perfect, I don't know how else to do it.

THE COURT: Am I not bound by Rule 4 of the Federal Rules of Civil Procedure?

MR. O'BRIEN: Your Honor, that is the applicable rule. It would be—

THE COURT:—or the appropriate Florida statute?

MR. O'BRIEN: You are bound. And I think Your Honor has the discretion to find that there is authority, actual authority, based on the interface between the process server and the security guards, the security guards and Mrs. Herries, and Mrs. Herries and the process server, in terms of apparent authority Your Honor has that discretion.

And in Florida law, and if I may submit these cases post hearing, I found a case called Evans versus Thornton under Florida law. The federal rules talk about the law applicable in the district or where the service is. In Florida there is a case called Evans versus Thornton which is 898 So.2d 151 where I would read that case as Florida law allowing apparent authority to serve an individual.

THE COURT: Let me ask the plaintiff, in a case of this nature, this magnitude, if there is—and you have conceded in a way that there is the issue regarding Mrs. Schultz in her individual capacity, that there is a gray area. All right. If there is a gray area regarding service in general and I were to rule in favor of the plaintiff, why would you want that lingering out there for the purposes of appeal at a later point in time?

MR. O'BRIEN: That's a great question, Your Honor.

And the way I would respond to it is the way I responded to my colleagues here when they said just do a waiver of service because—

THE COURT: I'm not saying to give a waiver of service. I'm not suggesting that at all.

MR. O'BRIEN: It's a principled thing. We did it right. We did it the right way. We did not mess up. We don't need to do a waiver of service. That can be used against us as inadequate counsel somehow. We did everything we are supposed to do. When I say gray area, I mean an individual is different than a corporation.

THE COURT: You can turn around and re-serve and clear everything up.

MR. O'BRIEN: You're right, but we served the right way. And just because she's the Democratic National Committee chairperson at the time and just because it's a democratic party, it doesn't mean that they just get to say we messed up when we didn't mess anything up.

THE COURT: I understand. That is a ruling that the Court will eventually make.

MR. O'BRIEN: The reason I say it's a gray area is because individuals are treated differently than corporations, so the step I think Your Honor has the discretion to make is because she's chair, that was proper to serve in that building. We didn't want to get cute with the pleadings. We believe she's sued in her individual capacity.

THE COURT: That's fine. That is not an issue. But it needed to be cleared up for the purposes of the record and for the analysis to take place.

MR. O'BRIEN: Thank you, Your Honor. I would like to rest on the papers unless Your Honor has further questions.

THE COURT: Thank you.

MR. O'BRIEN: Thank you. I would like to be able to submit, if Your Honor would allow, argument regarding Wikileaks at a later point. We could do it in 24 hours if Your Honor would like.

THE COURT: Well, it will have to be quick because this has been now pending, and for the benefit of the parties, I want to give you a ruling on it. So if you can submit it by close of business tomorrow.

MR. O'BRIEN: That's perfect, Your Honor.

THE COURT: Is that fine? Okay.

MR. O'BRIEN: Thank you, Your Honor.

THE COURT: Reply?

MR. SPIVA: Just briefly, Your Honor. Even leaving Ms. Herries' declaration aside which Your Honor has ruled shifted the burden to the other side, there is certainly no evidence and, in fact, I think any evidence that is in the record really is to the contrary, that Ms. Herries fits any of the categories under Rule 4 under the Florida statute, under the D.C. statute for people who are authorized to accept service.

THE COURT: For a corporation.

MR. SPIVA: For a corporation or for Ms. Wasserman, Congresswoman Wasserman Schultz.

THE COURT: Individually.

MR. SPIVA: Individually or in her corporate capacity. We've heard from—

THE COURT: She hasn't been sued in her corporate capacity.

MR. SPIVA: That was our previous understanding until today, Your Honor, was that she was being sued in her corporate capacity. But she hasn't been properly served in either capacity. And Ms. Herries certainly didn't have authority to accept service on her behalf in either capacity.

You know, we have heard that what else is the process server to do. I think one thing to keep in mind here is just based on the affidavits of service themselves and based on the video which I would submit is perfectly consistent with Ms. Herries' declaration in every important respect, the process server, with all due respect, didn't even know who he had left the papers with.

And his affidavit of service doesn't state that. It actually states that he left it with somebody else who also there's certainly no evidence before the Court that Ms. Christopher who he says in his affidavit of service was the person that he served, there is no evidence that she had authority to accept service of process, and she didn't.

And so I think based on that, Your Honor, that they really didn't come close. I think if you take a look at the Sears & Roebuck case in this circuit, as Your Honor knows, service, Rule 4, is strictly construed. They have cited a lot of cases from outside the circuit where some circuits have looser rules on this. I think most of the cases even under looser rules are pretty distinguishable from this case, and we have talked about that in our briefs.

But in this circuit, it is strictly construed. I don't think they even came close. So it's not a matter of, oh, it's kind of a technicality. I mean, they got the first name of the first person who walked down. And her declaration, I did misspeak, I think, when I first got up which I know is the thing that put the burden on them, does talk about what she knew when she came down. She was told somebody was downstairs and they couldn't leave until they could hand some legal papers to someone. It doesn't say that she knew she was being served with a lawsuit and she was accepting service. And certainly the videotape is consistent with that.

I think it's important to strictly construe Rule 4 because otherwise anybody can and will sue, not just the DNC, but potentially the RNC and potentially any corporation in America by simply going to their front offices. Most places have security these days. I have certainly been a plaintiff in many cases, and I know that sometimes you can't get the person you need to serve the first time your service processer goes there. Sometimes they have to go there several times. So sometimes it's not easy.

But here they had alternatives. They had registered mail. And even after we brought to their attention that they had gotten the wrong person, we offered to accept this waiver of service of process.

And I must say, I don't understand this point about we don't want to concede that we did anything wrong. No one is asking them to concede anything. Certainly to just say, look, we want to remove all doubt and move on, it seems like the quicker thing to do would be to send us the waiver of process form.

But one thing we can't concede is that, you know, anybody can just come into the DNC, into the lobby, and essentially hand some legal papers to the first person who comes down and that that's sufficient service, Your Honor.

So we would ask that the motion be granted. Thank you very much.

THE COURT: Do you want time to respond to any written submission that the plaintiff might send?

MR. SPIVA: Yes, Your Honor.

THE COURT: All right. Then I will give you until the close of business on Thursday.

MR. SPIVA: Okay. Thank you, Your Honor. I mean, just if I might, I mean, whichever way Your Honor rules on that email, I don't think it changes the fundamental facts that—

THE COURT: I understand that.

MR. SPIVA: So—

THE COURT: I understand that.

MR. SPIVA: All right. Thank you, Your Honor.

THE COURT: All right. Counsel, thank you very much.

I will wait until I receive the written submissions with the last one being due on the close of business on Thursday. I am going to ask for the lawyers to hold on to your own exhibits.

I really don't think there is any need for the Court to review Plaintiffs' 2 which is the police report. That deals only with Mr. Lucas, and that is not an issue, really. Plaintiffs' 3 is an email again dealing with Mr. Lucas, and that's not an issue. Plaintiffs' 4 I have reserved on. And we have Defendants' 1 and 2 which I have copies of those. Those are docket entry No. 6 and 7 in the court file. And Plaintiffs' 5 is basically the corrected affidavit of service which simply changes a name. So I will ask the lawyers to hold on to your own exhibits then.

MR. O'BRIEN: With respect to Exhibit 1 by the plaintiffs, Your Honor, should we—

THE COURT: You hold on to that thumb drive, yes. You keep that as well. All right. Anything else from the plaintiff?

MR. O'BRIEN: No. Thank you, Your Honor.

THE COURT: From the defense?

MR. SPIVA: No, Your Honor. Thank you.

THE COURT: All right. Counsel, thank you very much. The Court appreciates your argument and your efforts.

There being no further business, this session of the court is the adjourned. Everyone have a great week. Have a safe travel back to your home destinations.

MR. SPIVA: Thank you, Your Honor.

MR. O'BRIEN: Thank you, Your Honor.

THE COURT: Court is in adjournment.

(Thereupon, the hearing concluded at 12:46 p.m.)

CERTIFICATE

I hereby certify that the foregoing is an accurate transcription of the proceedings in the above-entitled matter.

10/13/17   s/ Tammy Nestor
                            Tammy Nestor, RMR, CRR
                            Official Court Reporter 299
                            East Broward Boulevard
                            Fort Lauderdale, Florida 33301
                            tammy_nestor@flsd.uscourts.gov

Appendix III

THE CHARTER & THE BYLAWS
OF THE DEMOCRATIC PARTY
OF THE UNITED STATES

As Amended by
The Democratic National Committee

September 11, 2009

CONTENTS

**CHARTER OF THE DEMOCRATIC PARTY OF
THE UNITED STATES**

BYLAWS

Adopted Pursuant to the Charter of the Democratic Party of the United States

CHARTER OF THE DEMOCRATIC PARTY OF
THE UNITED STATES
PREAMBLE

We, the Democrats of the United States of America, united in common purpose, hereby rededicate ourselves to the principles which have historically sustained our Party. Recognizing that the vitality of the Nation's political institutions has been the foundation of its enduring strength, we acknowledge that a political party which wishes to lead must listen to those it would lead, a party which asks for the people's trust must prove that it trusts the people and a party which hopes to call forth the best the Nation can achieve must embody the best of the Nation's heritage and traditions.

What we seek for our Nation, we hope for all people: individual freedom in the framework of a just society, political freedom in the framework of meaningful participation by all citizens. Bound by the United States Constitution, aware that a party must be responsive to be worthy of responsibility, we pledge ourselves to open, honest endeavor and to the conduct of public affairs in a manner worthy of a society of free people.

Under God, and for these ends and upon these principles, we do establish and adopt this Charter of the Democratic Party of the United States of America.

ARTICLE ONE
The Democratic Party of the United States of America

The Democratic Party of the United States of America shall:

Section 1. Nominate and assist in the election of Democratic candidates for the offices of President and Vice President of the United States;

Section 2. Adopt and promote statements of policy;

Section 3. Assist state and local Democratic Party organizations in the election of their candidates and the education of their voters;

<u>Section 4.</u> Establish standards and rules of procedure to afford all members of the Democratic Party full, timely and equal opportunities to participate in decisions concerning the selection of candidates, the formulation of policy, and the conduct of other Party affairs, without prejudice on the basis of sex, race, age (if of voting age), color, creed, national origin, religion, economic status, sexual orientation, ethnic identity or physical disability, and further, to promote fair campaign practices and the fair adjudication of disputes. Accordingly, the scheduling of Democratic Party affairs at all levels shall consider the presence of any religious minorities of significant numbers of concentration whose level of participation would be affected;

<u>Section 5.</u> Raise and disburse monies needed for the successful operation of the Democratic Party;

<u>Section 6.</u> Work with Democratic public officials at all levels to achieve the objectives of the Democratic Party; and

<u>Section 7.</u> Encourage and support codes of political ethics that embody substantive rules of ethical guidance for public officials and employees in federal, state and local governments, to assure that public officials shall at all times conduct themselves in a manner that reflects creditably upon the office they serve, shall not use their office to gain special privileges and benefits and shall refrain from acting in their official capacities when their independence of judgement would be adversely affected by personal interest or duties.

ARTICLE TWO
National Convention

<u>Section 1.</u> The Democratic Party shall assemble in National Convention in each year in which an election for office of President of the United States is held.

<u>Section 2.</u> The National Convention shall be the highest authority of the Democratic Party, subject to the provisions of this Charter. The National Convention shall recognize the state and other Parties entitled to participate in the conduct of the national affairs of the Democratic Party, including its conventions, conferences and committees. State Party rules or state laws relating to the election of delegates to the National Convention shall be observed unless in conflict with this Charter and other provisions adopted pursuant to authority of the Charter, including the resolutions or other actions of the National

Convention. In the event of such conflict with state laws, state Parties shall be required to take provable positive steps to bring such laws into conformity and to carry out such other measures as may be required by the National Convention or the Democratic National Committee.

<u>Section 3.</u> The National Convention shall nominate a candidate for the office of President of the United States, nominate a candidate for the office of Vice President of the United States, adopt a platform and act upon such other matters as it deems appropriate.

<u>Section 4.</u> The National Convention shall be composed of delegates equally divided between men and women. The delegates shall be chosen through processes which:

(a) assure all Democratic voters full, timely and equal opportunity to participate and include affirmative action programs toward that end,

(b) assure that delegations fairly reflect the division of preferences expressed by those who participate in the Presidential nominating process,

(c) exclude the use of the unit rule at any level,

(d) do not deny participation for failure to pay a cost, fee or poll tax,

(e) allow participation in good faith by all voters who are Democrats and, to the extent determined by a State Party to be in the interests of the Democratic Party in that State, by voters who are not registered or affiliated with any party; and

(f) except with respect to persons referred to in Section 5(b) of this Article, begin within the calendar year of the Convention provided, however, that fairly apportioned and openly selected state Party Committees, elected no earlier than the date of the previous presidential election, shall not be precluded from selecting such portion of their respective state delegations, according to the standards provided in this Charter and the Bylaws and the Delegate Selection Rules, as may be specifically authorized by the Democratic National Committee in the Call to the Convention,

(g) prohibit unpledged and uncommitted delegates, except delegates or alternates expressing an uncommitted preference shall be permitted to be elected at the district level, in which event, if such preference meets the applicable threshold and qualifies for at-large or similar delegates or alternates, such at-large or similar delegates or alternates shall be allocated to that uncommitted preference as if it were a presidential candidate,

(h) notwithstanding any provision to the contrary in this Section:

(i) provide for all of the members of the Democratic National Committee to serve as unpledged delegates,

(ii) provide for each state, territory or commonwealth to select a number of unpledged delegates equal to one (1) such delegate for every four (4) votes on the Democratic National Committee from that state, territory or commonwealth, pursuant to Article Three, Section 2(a) and 2(b) of the Charter, and

(iii) permit unpledged delegates consisting of:

(1) the President and Vice President of the United States, if Democrats,

(2) the Democratic members of the United States Senate and the Democratic members of the House of Representatives,

(3) the Democratic Governors,

(4) former Democratic Presidents and Vice Presidents of the United States,

(5) former Democratic Majority and Minority Leaders of the United States Senate,

(6) former Democratic Speakers and Minority Leaders of the United States House of Representatives,

(7) former Chairs of the Democratic National Committee,

(8) such delegates shall not be permitted to have alternates and such delegates shall constitute an exception to Subsection (b) of this Section 4.

Section 5. The delegate vote allocable to each state shall be determined as provided in the Bylaws, consistent with the formula:

(a) giving equal weight to population, which may be measured by electoral vote, and to the Democratic vote in elections for office of the President; and

(b) giving such additional delegate votes as may be specifically designated by the Democratic National Committee in the Call to the Convention, subject to such conditions as may be set forth by the Democratic National Committee in said Call, for the purpose of providing incentives for scheduling the event constituting the first determining stage in the presidential nominating process in each state later in the year of the Convention than such event would otherwise be scheduled in the absence of such incentive; and

(c) which shall also provide additional delegate positions to members of the Democratic National Committee; and

(d) which may also provide additional delegate positions to Democratic elected public officials specifically designated by the Democratic National Committee in the Call to the Convention, subject to the provisions of Section 4.

ARTICLE THREE
Democratic National Committee

Section 1. The Democratic National Committee shall have general responsibility for the affairs of the Democratic Party between National Conventions, subject to the provisions of this Charter and to the resolutions or other actions of the National Convention. This responsibility shall include:

(a) issuing the Call to the National Convention;

(b) conducting the Party's Presidential campaign;

(c) filling vacancies in the nominations for the office of President and Vice President;

(d) formulating and disseminating statements of Party policy;

(e) providing for the election or appointment of a Chairperson, five Vice Chairpersons, three of whom shall be of the opposite sex of the Chairperson, one of whom shall be the President of the Association of State Democratic Chairs and one of whom shall be the Vice Chairperson for Voter Registration and Participation, a Treasurer, a Secretary, a National Finance Chair and other appropriate officers of the National Committee and for the filling of vacancies; and

(f) all other actions necessary or appropriate in order to carry out the provisions of this Charter and the objectives of the Democratic Party.

Section 2. The Democratic National Committee shall be composed of:

(a) the Chairperson and the highest ranking officer of the opposite sex of each recognized state Democratic Party and of the Democratic Parties of Guam, the Virgin Islands and American Samoa;

(b) two hundred additional members apportioned to the states on the basis set forth in Article Two, Section 5(a) of the Charter, consistent with the full participation goals of Sections 3 and 4 of Article Eight of the Charter; provided that each state shall have at least two such additional members;

(c) two additional members, consisting of one national committeeman and one national committeewoman, from each of Guam, the Virgin Islands and American Samoa;

(d) the Chairperson of the Democratic Governors' Association and two additional governors, of whom, at least one shall be of the opposite sex of the Chairperson, as selected by the Association;

(e) the Democratic Leader in the United States Senate and the Democratic Leader in the United States House of Representatives and one additional member of each body, who shall be of the opposite sex of, and appointed by, the respective leaders;

(f) the Chairperson, the five Vice Chairpersons, the National Finance Chair, the Treasurer, and the Secretary of the DNC;

(g) the Chairperson of the National Conference of Democratic Mayors and two additional mayors, at least one of whom shall be of the opposite sex of the Chairperson, as selected by the Conference;

(h) the President of the Young Democrats of America and two additional members, at least one of whom shall be of the opposite sex as the President, as selected by the organization biennially in convention assembled;

(i) the Chairperson of the Democratic County Officials and two additional county officials, at least one of whom shall be of the opposite sex as the Chairperson, as selected by the organization;

(j) the Chairperson of the Democratic Legislative Campaign Committee and two additional state legislators, at least one of whom shall be of the opposite sex as the Chairperson, as selected by the Committee;

(k) the Chairperson of the National Democratic Municipal Officials Conference and two additional municipal officials, at least one of whom shall be of the opposite sex as the Chairperson, as selected by the Conference;

(l) the President of the National Federation of Democratic Women and two additional members selected by the Federation;

(m) the President of the College Democrats of America and the Vice President, who shall be of the opposite sex, as elected by the organization annually;

(n) the Chairperson of the National Association of Democratic State Treasurers and the Vice Chair who shall be of the opposite sex, as selected by the Association;

(o) the Chairperson of the National Association of Democratic Lieutenant Governors and the Vice Chair who shall be of the opposite sex, as selected by the Association;

(p) the Chairperson of the Democratic Association of Secretaries of State and the Vice Chair who shall be of the opposite sex, as selected by the Association;

(q) the Chairperson of the Democratic Attorneys General Association and one additional attorney general who shall be of the opposite sex of the Chairperson, as selected by the Association;

(r) the Chairperson of the National Democratic Ethnic Coordinating Committee, who is not otherwise a member of the Democratic National Committee and one additional member, who shall be of the opposite sex, as selected by the Coordinating Committee;

(s) the Chairperson of the National Democratic Seniors Coordinating Council, who is not otherwise a member of the Democratic National Committee and one additional member, who shall be of the opposite sex, as selected by the Coordinating Council;

(t) additional members as provided in Article Nine of this Charter. No more than seventy-five additional members of the Democratic National Committee may be added by the foregoing members.

Section 3. Members of the Democratic National Committee apportioned to the states and those provided for in Article Nine who are not otherwise members by virtue of Party office, shall be selected by each state Democratic Party in accordance with standards as to participation established in the Bylaws of the Democratic Party for terms commencing on the day the National Convention adjourns and terminating on the day the next Convention adjourns. Such members shall be selected during the calendar year in which a National Convention is held, through processes which assure full, timely and equal opportunity to participate. Vacancies shall be filled by the state party as provided in the Bylaws. The members of the National Committee from each state shall be divided as equally as practicable between committeemen and committeewomen. Members of the Democratic National Committee who serve by virtue of holding public or Party office shall serve on the Committee only during their terms in such office. Members of the Democratic National Committee added by the other members shall serve a term that runs coterminously with the Chairperson of the Democratic National Committee, through the election of the new Chairperson, and until their successors are chosen; members in this category shall have the right to vote for the new Chairperson. Members of the Democratic National Committee who serve by virtue of holding state Party office shall

be selected by such parties in accordance with standards as to participation established in Bylaws.

Section 4. The Bylaws may provide for removal of members of the Democratic National Committee for cause by a two-thirds vote of the National Committee and may also require continued residence in the
jurisdiction represented by the member and affirmative support for the
Democratic Presidential and Vice Presidential nominees as a condition
of continued membership thereon. The Bylaws may further provide for
a minimum level of attendance at National Committee meetings for
Democratic National Committee members. The Bylaws may establish
that any member of the Democratic National Committee who misses
three consecutive meetings of the Democratic National Committee has
failed to meet the minimum level of attendance and is deemed to have
resigned from the Democratic National Committee.

Section 5. The Democratic National Committee shall meet at least once
each year. Meetings shall be called by the Chairperson, by the Executive Committee of the Democratic National Committee, or by written
request of no fewer than one-fourth of the members of the Democratic
National Committee.

ARTICLE FOUR
Executive Committee

Section 1. There shall be an Executive Committee of the Democratic National Committee, which shall be responsible for the conduct of the
affairs of the Democratic Party subject to this Charter, the National
Convention and the Democratic National Committee.

Section 2. The Executive Committee shall be elected by and serve at the
pleasure of the members of the Democratic National Committee. The
size, composition and term of office shall be determined by the Democratic National Committee, provided that, the number of members
elected by the regional caucuses of members of the Democratic National Committee shall be no fewer than twenty-four less than the number selected by other means.

Section 3. The Executive Committee shall meet at least four times each
year. Meetings shall be called by the Chairperson or by written request
of no fewer than one-fourth of its members. The Executive Committee
shall keep a record of its proceedings which shall be available to the
public.

ARTICLE FIVE
National Chairperson

Section 1. The National Chairperson of the Democratic Party shall carry out the programs and policies of the National Convention and the Democratic National Committee.

Section 2. The National Chairperson, the five Vice Chairpersons, the National Finance Chair, the Treasurer, and the Secretary, shall be elected:

(a) at a meeting of the Democratic National Committee held after the succeeding presidential election and prior to March 1 next, and,

(b) whenever a vacancy occurs. The National Chairperson shall be elected and may be removed by a majority vote of the Democratic National Committee, and each term shall expire upon the election for the following term.

Section 3. The National Chairperson shall preside over meetings of the Democratic National Committee and of the Executive Committee. In the event of a vacancy in the office of the National Chairperson, the designated Vice Chair as provided for in Article Two, Section 12(b) of the Bylaws, or the next highest ranking officer of the National Committee present at the meeting shall preside.

Section 4. The National Chairperson shall serve full time and shall receive such compensation as may be determined by agreement between the Chairperson and the Democratic National Committee. In the conduct and management of the affairs and procedures of the Democratic National Committee, particularly as they apply to the preparation and conduct of the Presidential nomination process, the Chairperson shall exercise impartiality and evenhandedness as between the Presidential candidates and campaigns. The Chairperson shall be responsible for ensuring that the national officers and staff of the Democratic National Committee maintain impartiality and evenhandedness during the Democratic Party Presidential nominating process.

ARTICLE SIX
Party Conference

The Democratic Party may hold a National Party Conference between National Conventions. The nature, agenda, composition, time and place of the Party Conference shall be determined by the Democratic National Committee.

ARTICLE SEVEN
National Finance Organizations

Section 1. The Democratic National Committee shall establish National Finance Organizations which shall have general responsibility for the finances of the Democratic Party. These National Finance Organizations shall raise funds to support the Democratic Party and shall advise and assist state Democratic Parties and candidates in securing funds for their purposes.

Section 2. The National Finance Chair shall be elected or approved by the Democratic National Committee.

ARTICLE EIGHT
Full Participation

Section 1. The Democratic Party of the United States shall be open to all who desire to support the Party and who wish to be known as Democrats.

Section 2. Discrimination in the conduct of Democratic Party affairs on the basis of sex, race, age (if of voting age), color, creed, national origin, religion, economic status, sexual orientation, gender identity, ethnic identity or physical disability is prohibited, to the end that the Democratic Party at all levels be an open party.

Section 3. To encourage full participation by all Democrats, with particular concern for minority groups, Blacks, Native Americans, Asian/Pacifics, Hispanics, women and youth in the delegate selection process and in all Party affairs, as defined in the Bylaws, the National and State Democratic Parties shall adopt and implement an affirmative action program which provides for representation as nearly as practicable of the aforementioned groups, as indicated by their presence in the Democratic electorate. This program shall include specific goals and timetables to achieve this purpose.

Section 4. This goal shall not be accomplished either directly or indirectly by the national or state Democratic Parties' imposition of mandatory quotas at any level of the delegate selection process or in any other Party affairs, as defined in the Bylaws; however, representation as nearly as practicable of minority groups, Blacks, Native Americans, Asian/Pacifics, Hispanics, women and youth, as indicated by their presence in the Democratic electorate, as provided in this Article, shall not be deemed a quota.

Section 5. Performance under an approved affirmative action program and composition of the Convention delegation shall be considered relevant evidence in the challenge of any state delegation. If a state Party has adopted and implemented an approved and monitored affirmative action program, the Party shall not be subject to challenge based solely on delegate composition or solely on primary results.

Section 6. Notwithstanding Section 5 above, equal division at any level of delegate or committee positions between delegate men and delegate women or committeemen and committeewomen shall not constitute a violation of any provision thereof.

ARTICLE NINE
General Provisions

Section 1. Democratic Party means the Democratic Party of the United States of America.

Section 2. The Bylaws shall provide for states in which the Democratic nominee for President or electors committed to the nominee did not appear on the ballot in elections used for apportionment formulae.

Section 3. For the purposes of this Charter, the District of Columbia shall be treated as a state containing the appropriate number of Congressional Districts.

Section 4. For the purposes of this Charter, Puerto Rico shall be treated as a state containing the appropriate number of Congressional Districts.

Section 5. Recognized Democratic Party organizations in areas not entitled to vote in Presidential elections may elect such voting delegates to National Conventions as the Democratic National Committee provides in the Call to the Convention.

Section 6. Democrats Abroad shall have four votes on the Democratic National Committee, which votes shall be shared by the Chairperson, the highest ranking officer of the opposite sex, three National Committeemen and three National Committeewomen except as may otherwise be provided by the Bylaws.

Section 7. The Bylaws shall provide for regional organizations of the Party.

Section 8. To assure that the Democratic nominee for the office of President of the United States is selected by a fair and equitable process, the Democratic National Committee may adopt such statements of policy as it deems appropriate with respect to the timing of Presidential nominating processes and shall work with state Parties to accomplish the objectives of such statements.

Section 9. The Democratic National Committee shall maintain and publish a code of fair campaign practices, which shall be recommended for observance by all candidates campaigning as Democrats.

Section 10. The Democratic Party shall not require a delegate to a Party convention or caucus to cast a vote contrary to his or her expressed preference.

Section 11. Voting by proxy shall not be permitted at the National Convention. Voting by proxy shall otherwise be permitted in Democratic Party affairs only as provided in the Bylaws of the Democratic Party.

Section 12. All meetings of the Democratic National Committee, the Executive Committee, and all other official Party committees, commissions and bodies shall be open to the public, and votes shall not be taken by secret ballot.

Section 13. The Democratic National Committee shall prepare and make available to the public an annual report concerning the financial affairs of the Democratic Party.

Section 14. In the absence of other provisions, Robert's Rules of Order (as most recently revised) shall govern the conduct of all Democratic Party meetings.

Section 15. The text of the Charter and the Bylaws, or portions thereof, shall be made available in other languages as needed upon reasonable request.

Section 16. The membership of the Democratic National Committee, the Executive Committee, Democratic state central committees, and all national official Party Conventions, committees, commissions, and like bodies shall be equally divided between men and women. State Parties shall take provable positive steps to achieve legislative changes to bring the law into compliance with this provision wherever this provision conflicts with state statutes.

Section 17. Democratic Party Credo.

We Democrats are the oldest political party in America and the youngest in spirit. We will remain so, because we enjoy the challenge of government. Time and again, for almost two centuries, the Democratic Party has made government work—to build and defend a nation, to encourage commerce, to educate our children, to promote equal opportunity, to advance science and industry, to support the arts and humanities, to restore the land, to develop and conserve our human and natural resources, to preserve and enhance our built environment, to relieve poverty, to explore space. We have reached difficult and vital goals.

We recognize that the capacity of government is limited but we regard democratic government as a force for good and a source of hope.

At the heart of our party lies a fundamental conviction, that Americans must not only be free, but they must live in a fair society.

We believe it is the responsibility of government to help us achieve this fair society.

- a society where the elderly and the disabled can lead lives of dignity and where Social Security remains an unshakable commitment;
- a society where all people can find jobs in a growing full-employment economy;
- a society where all workers are guaranteed without question the legal right to join unions of their own choosing and to bargain collectively for decent wages and conditions of employment;
- a society where taxes are clearly based on ability to pay;
- a society where the equal rights of women are guaranteed in the Constitution;
- a society where the civil rights of minorities are fully secured and where no one is denied the opportunity for a better life;
- a society where both public and private discrimination based upon race, sex, age, color, creed, national origin, religion, ethnic identity, sexual orientation, gender identity, economic status, philosophical persuasion or physical disability are condemned and where our government moves aggressively to end such discrimination through lawful means;
- a society where we recognize that the strengthening of the family and the protection of children are essential to the health of the nation;
- a society where a sound education, proper nutrition, quality medical care, affordable housing, safe streets and a healthy environment are possible for every citizen;
- a society where the livelihoods of our family farmers are as stable as the values they instill in the American character;
- a society where a strong national defense is a common effort, where promoting human rights is a basic value of our foreign policy, and where we ensure that future by ending the nuclear arms race.

This is our purpose and our promise.

ARTICLE TEN
Amendments. Bylaws. and Rules

Section 1. This Charter may be amended by a vote of a majority of all of the delegates to the National Convention, provided that no such amendment shall be effective unless and until it is subsequently ratified by a vote of the majority of the entire membership of the Democratic National Committee. This Charter may also be amended by a vote of two-thirds of the entire membership of the Democratic National Committee. At least thirty days written notice shall be given of any National Committee meeting at which action will be taken pursuant to this Section, and any proposed amendment shall be given to all members of the National Committee and shall be released to the national news media. This Charter may also be amended by a vote of two-thirds of the entire membership of any Democratic Party Conference called under the authority of this Charter for such purpose.

Section 2. Bylaws of the Democratic Party shall be adopted to provide for the governance of the affairs of the Democratic Party in matters not provided for in this Charter. Bylaws may be adopted or amended by a majority vote of:

(a) the National Convention; or

(b) the Democratic National Committee provided that thirty days written notice of any proposed Bylaw or amendment has been given to all members of the National Committee.

Unless adopted in the form of an amendment to this Charter or otherwise designated, any resolution adopted by the National Convention relating to the governance of the Party shall be considered a Bylaw.

Section 3. Each official body of the Democratic Party created under the authority of this Charter shall adopt and conduct its affairs in accordance with written rules, which rules shall be consistent with this Charter, the Bylaws and other provisions adopted pursuant to authority of the Charter, including resolutions or other actions of the National Convention. The Democratic National Committee shall maintain copies of all such rules and shall make them available upon request.

Section 4. Each recognized state Democratic Party shall adopt and conduct its affairs in accordance with written rules. Copies of such rules and of any changes or amendments thereto shall be filed with the Democratic National Committee within thirty days following adoption.

RESOLUTION OF ADOPTION

Section 1. The Democratic Party of the United States of America, assembled in a Conference on Democratic Party Organization and Policy pursuant to resolution adopted by the 1972 Democratic National Convention and the Call to the Conference hereby adopts for the governance of the Party the Charter attached hereto.

BYLAWS
Adopted Pursuant to the Charter of the Democratic Party of the United States

ARTICLE ONE
Democratic National Convention

Section 1. The National Convention is the highest authority of the Democratic Party, subject to the provisions of the Charter.

Section 2. The National Convention shall adopt permanent rules governing the conduct of its business at the beginning of each Convention, and until the adoption of such permanent rules, the Convention and the activities attendant thereto shall be governed by temporary rules set forth in the Call to the National Convention.

Section 3. Delegates to the National Convention shall be allocated in the Call to the Convention consistent with the Charter.

ARTICLE TWO
Democratic National Committee

Section 1. Duties and Powers. The Democratic National Committee shall have general responsibility for the affairs of the Democratic Party between National Conventions, subject to the provisions of the Charter and to the resolutions or other official actions of the National Convention. This responsibility shall include, but not be limited to:

(a) Issuing the Call to the National Convention;

(b) Conducting the Party's Presidential Campaign;

(c) Filling vacancies in the nominations for the office of the President and Vice President;

(d) Assisting state and local Democratic Party organizations in the election of their candidates and the education of their voters;

(e) Formulating and disseminating statements of Party policy, promoting programs for the systematic study of public policy issues, through participation of members of the Democratic National Committee and through specific projects administered under the authority of the Chairperson of the Democratic National Committee;

(f) Providing for the election or appointment of a Chairperson, five Vice Chairpersons, three of whom shall be of the opposite sex of the Chairperson, one of whom shall be the President of the Association of State Democratic Chairs and one of whom shall be Vice Chairperson for Voter Registration and Participation, a Treasurer, a National Finance Chair, a Secretary and other appropriate officers of the National Committee as shall be determined by the Committee, and for the filling of vacancies;

(g) Establishing and maintaining National Headquarters of the Party;

(h) Promoting and encouraging Party activities at every level, including but not limited to the following:

(i) promoting and encouraging implementation of all Party mandates;

(ii) the fulfillment by the Party of its platform pledge and other commitments;

(iii) establishment and support of an adequate system of political research;

(iv) the preparation, distribution and communication of Party information to its members and the general public;

(v) the development and maintenance of a program of public relations for the Party; and

(vi) development of a program for the coordination of Party committees, organizations, groups, public officials and members.

(i) Devising and executing ways and means of financing activities of the Party;

(j) Taking such other action as may be necessary and proper to carry out the provisions of the Charter, these Bylaws, the resolutions and other official actions to achieve the objectives of the Party and the Convention; and

(k) Approval of the budget of the Democratic National Committee.

<u>Section 2.</u> Membership. The Democratic National Committee shall be composed of:

(a) The Chairperson and the highest ranking officer of the opposite sex of each recognized State Democratic Party as defined by Article Nine of the Charter and of the Democratic Parties of Guam, the Virgin Islands and American Samoa;

(b) Two hundred additional members apportioned to the states on the basis set forth in Article Two, Section 5(a) of the Charter, provided that each state shall have at least two additional members;

(c) Two additional members, consisting of one national committeeman and one national committeewoman, from each of Guam, the Virgin Islands and American Samoa;

(d) The Chairperson of the Democratic Governors' Association and two additional governors, of whom at least one shall be of the opposite sex of the Chairperson, as selected by the Association;

(e) The Democratic Leader in the United States Senate and the Democratic Leader in the United States House of Representatives and one additional member of each body, who shall be of the opposite sex of, and appointed by the respective leaders;

(f) The Chairperson, five Vice Chairpersons, the National Finance Chair, the Treasurer and the Secretary of the Democratic National Committee;

(g) The Chairperson of the National Conference of Democratic Mayors and two additional mayors, at least one of whom shall be of the opposite sex of the Chairperson, as selected by the Conference;

(h) The President of the Young Democrats of America and two additional members, at least one of whom shall be of the opposite sex of the President, as selected by the organization biennially in convention assembled;

(i) The President of the National Federation of Democratic Women and two additional members selected by the Federation;

(j) The Chairperson of the Democratic County Officials and two additional members, at least one of whom shall be of the opposite sex of the Chairperson, as selected by the organization;

(k) The Chairperson of the Democratic Legislative Campaign Committee and two additional state legislators, at least one of whom shall be of the opposite sex of the Chairperson, as selected by the Committee;

(l) The Chairperson of the National Democratic Municipal Officials

Conference and two additional municipal officials, of whom, to the extent possible, at least one shall be of the opposite sex of the Chairperson, as selected by the Conference;

(m) Additional members as provided in Article Nine of the Charter;

(n) The President of the College Democrats of America and the Vice President, who shall be of the opposite sex, as elected by the organization annually;

(o) The Chairperson of the National Association of Democratic State Treasurers and the Vice Chair who shall be of the opposite sex, as selected by the Association;

(p) The Chairperson of the National Association of Democratic Lieutenant Governors and the Vice Chair who shall be of the opposite sex, as selected by the Association;

(q) The Chairperson of the Democratic Association of Secretaries of State and the Vice Chair who shall be of the opposite sex, as selected by the Association;

(r) The Chairperson of the Democratic Attorneys General Association and one additional attorney general who shall be of the opposite sex of the Chairperson, as selected by the Association;

(s) the Chairperson of the National Democratic Ethnic Coordinating Committee, who is not otherwise a member of the Democratic National Committee and one additional member, who shall be of the opposite sex, as selected by the Coordinating Committee;

(t) the Chairperson of the National Democratic Seniors Coordinating Council, who is not otherwise a member of the Democratic National Committee and one additional member, who shall be of the opposite sex, as selected by the Coordinating Council;

(u) No more than seventy-five additional members of the Democratic National Committee may be added by the foregoing members.

Section 3. Selection of Members.

(a) Members of the Democratic National Committee apportioned to the States pursuant to the provisions of Sections 2(b) and 2(c) of this Article and those apportioned pursuant to the provisions of Article Nine of the Charter who are not otherwise members by virtue of Party office shall be selected by each state or territorial Democratic Party in accordance with standards as to participation established under Section 11 of this Article through processes which assure full, timely and equal opportunity to participate. The method of selection for such members shall be described in detail in each state or territory's Party rules and shall be by one of the following methods or any combination thereof:

   (i) by a meeting of the National Convention delegation from the state or territory authorized to elect National Committee members, at an open meeting called within the calendar year of the Convention after effective public notice of the agenda;

   (ii) by state or territorial Primary within the calendar year of the National Convention;

   (iii) by state or territorial Party committees in an open meeting within the calendar year of the National Convention called after effective public notice of the agenda;

   (iv) by a state or territorial convention authorized to select national committee members in an open meeting within the calendar year of the National Convention called after effective public notice of the agenda; and

   (v) by such other method as may be adopted by a state or territorial Party and approved by the Democratic National Committee.

(b) Selection by any of the above methods shall be held to meet the requirements of full, timely and equal opportunity to participate if the selecting body has been established according to law and the Charter and the rules of such body have been approved by the Democratic National Committee.

(c) Members of the Democratic National Committee who serve by virtue of holding Party office shall be selected by each State Party in accordance with standards as to participation appearing in Section 11 of this Article.

(d) When the number of members apportioned to a state or territory pursuant to Section 2(b) of this Article or Article Nine of the Charter is even, there shall be equal division of members between men and women. In such cases where the number is odd, the variance between men and women may not be greater than one.

(e) Members of the Democratic National Committee apportioned pursuant to the provisions of Section 2(u) of this Article shall be elected by the membership provided that notice of any such nomination must be mailed to the membership no less than seven (7) days prior to the election.

Section 4. Certification and Eligibility of Members.

a) Members of the Democratic National Committee provided for in

Section 2 of this Article shall be certified to the National Committee as follows:

(i) those authorized under subsections (a), (b) and (c) of Section 2 shall be certified by the proper Party authority of the state or territory;

(ii) those authorized under subsection (d) of Section 2 shall be certified by the Chairperson of the Democratic Governors' Association;

(iii) those authorized under subsection (e) of Section 2 shall be certified by the Democratic Leader in the United States Senate for the members from that body and by the Democratic Leader in the United States House of Representatives for the members from that body;

(iv) those authorized under subsection (g) of Section 2 shall be certified by the Chairperson of the Conference of Democratic Mayors;

(v) those authorized under subsection (h) of Section 2 shall be certified by the President of the Young Democrats of America;

(vi) those authorized under subsection (i) of Section 2 shall be certified by the President of the National Federation of Democratic Women;

(vii) those authorized under subsection (j) of Section 2 shall be certified by the Chairperson of the Democratic County Officials Conference;

(viii) those authorized under subsection (k) of Section 2 shall be certified by the Chairperson of the Democratic Legislative Campaign Committee;

(ix) those authorized under subsection (l) of Section 2 shall be certified by the Chairperson of the National Democratic Municipal Officials Conference;

(x) those authorized under subsection (n) of Section 2 shall be certified by the President of the College Democrats of America;

(xi) those authorized under subsection (o) of Section 2 shall be certified by the Chairperson of the National Association of Democratic State Treasurers;

(xii) those authorized under subsection (p) of Section 2 shall be certified by the Chairperson of the National Association of Democratic Lieutenant Governors;

(xiii) those authorized under subsection (q) of Section 2 shall be certified by the Chairperson of the Democratic Association of Secretaries of State;

(xiv) those authorized under subsection (r) of Section 2 shall be certified by the Chairperson of the Democratic Attorneys General Association;

(xv) those authorized under subsection (s) of Section 2 shall be certified by the Chairperson of the National Democratic Ethnic Coordinating Committee;

(xvi) those authorized under subsection (t) of Section 2 shall be certified by the Chairperson of the National Democratic Seniors Coordinating Council;

(xvii) those otherwise authorized under Section 2 shall be certified by the Chairperson of the Democratic National Committee.

(b) No person who is not or who does not continue to be a resident for voting purposes of the jurisdiction which he or she represents shall be eligible to hold such office.

(c) No person shall be entitled to vote on a challenge to his or her credentials.

(d) Contests involving membership or challenges to credentials of members shall be heard and adjudicated by the National Committee as determined or provided in Article Two, Section 10(b) of these Bylaws.

Section 5. Resignation or Removal of Members.

(a) A member of the Democratic National Committee may resign by written notice to the Chairperson of the National Committee, and such resignation shall be effective immediately.

(b) After notice and opportunity for public hearing and upon grounds found by the National Committee to constitute good and sufficient cause, the National Committee may remove a member by two-thirds vote of the National Committee.

(c) Failure of any member of the National Committee to declare affirmatively his or her support for the Democratic Presidential and Vice Presidential nominees within thirty (30) days after the adjournment of the National Convention shall constitute good and sufficient cause for removal.

Section 6. Vacancies. Vacancies created by resignation or removal of any member of the National Committee shall be filled as follows:

(a) Vacancies in membership apportioned to the states and territories pursuant to Sections 2(b) and 2(c) of this Article and Article Nine of the

Charter shall be filled by a state or territorial Party in open meeting called after effective public notice of the agenda.

(b) Vacancies created by the removal or resignation of a state Chairperson or highest ranking officer of the opposite sex shall be filled only by their successors in accordance with Section 3(b) of this Article.

(c) Vacancies in the at-large membership of the National Committee shall be filled by the National Committee.

(d) Vacancies in positions filled by the Democratic Governors' Association, the Democratic Mayors Conference, the House and Senate Leadership, the Young Democrats of America, the Democratic County Officials Conference, the Democratic Legislative Campaign Committee, the National Federation of Democratic Women, the National Democratic Municipal Officials Conference, and the College Democrats of America shall be filled by the selecting authority, and in the case where the selecting authority is not in session nor will be in session for a year subsequent to the vacancy, by the body charged with fulfilling the responsibilities operating the organization between meetings of the full group.

Section 7. Meetings.

(a) The National Committee shall meet as soon as possible after the adjournment of the National Convention on the call of the Chairperson. The Committee is authorized to organize with those members already selected, including any person seated temporarily as provided in Section 10(b)(iv) and entitled to serve as of the first meeting of the Committee. They shall select those members of the Executive Committee who are selected by the Regional Caucuses, who shall serve with those who serve by reason of office until the next regular meeting of the Democratic National Committee.

(b) At least two meetings of the National Committee shall be held each year upon call of the Chairperson and after notice to members, unless any such meeting is dispensed with by prior vote of a majority of the full membership of the National Committee.

(c) Special meetings of the National Committee may be held upon the call of the Chairperson with the approval of the Executive Committee with reasonable notice to the members, and no action may be taken at such a special meeting unless such proposed action was included in the notice of the special meeting. The foregoing notwithstanding, a special meeting to fill a vacancy on the National ticket shall be held on the call of the Chairperson, who shall set the date for such meeting in accordance with the procedural rules provided for in Article Two, Section 8(d) of these Bylaws.

(d) No later than thirty (30) days before each regularly scheduled meeting, and as soon as possible before a special meeting of the Democratic National Committee, the Secretary of the Democratic National Committee shall send written notice of the date, time and place of such meeting, and the tentative agenda to all members of the Democratic National Committee.

e) Upon the written request of twenty-five percent or more of the members of the National Committee, filed with the Chairperson within a period of thirty (30) days, it shall be the duty of the Chairperson within fifteen (15) days from receipt of such request to issue a call for a meeting of the National Committee. The date of such meeting shall be fixed by the Chairperson not later than thirty (30) days nor earlier than fifteen (15) days from the date of the call.

Section 8. Attendance and Quorum and Voting.

a) Members of the National Committee apportioned pursuant to the provisions of Section 2 of this Article who miss three consecutive meetings of the Democratic National Committee have failed to meet the minimum level of attendance and shall be deemed to have resigned from the Democratic National Committee. Vacancies created by any member for failing to meet the minimum level of attendance shall be filled in accordance with the provisions of Section 6 of this Article. Proxies shall not be counted at any meeting for the purpose of meeting the minimum level of attendance.

(b) A majority of the full membership of the Democratic National Committee present in person or by proxy shall constitute a quorum, provided that no less than forty percent (40%) of the full membership be present in person for the purpose of establishing a quorum; provided, however, that for purposes of voting to fill a vacancy on the National ticket, a quorum shall be a majority of the full membership present in person.

(c) Forty percent (40%) of the full membership present in person or by proxy, or 50 members present in person, whichever is fewer, shall constitute a quorum for meetings of:

  (i) the DNC standing committees on Credentials, Resolutions, Rules and Bylaws and Budget and Finance;

(ii) the Eastern, Southern, Midwestern, and Western Regional Caucuses;

(iii) the Hispanic, Black, Women's, Asian American and Pacific Islander, and Lesbian, Gay, Bisexual and Transgender American Caucuses; and

(iv) other standing or ad hoc committees created pursuant to the provisions of Section 10(f) of these Bylaws.

(d) Except as otherwise provided in the Charter or in these Bylaws, all questions before the Democratic National Committee shall be determined by majority vote of those members present and voting in person or by proxy.

(i) Up to seventy-five additional members at-large of the Democratic National Committee added by the remaining members pursuant to Article Three, Section 2 of the Charter and eleven members at-large of the Executive Committee selected by the Democratic National Committee pursuant to Article Three, Section 2 of the Bylaws may be elected by plurality vote of the members voting in person or by proxy; and

(ii) A roll call may be requested by a vote of twenty-five percent (25%) of those Democratic National Committee members present and voting.

(e) Each member of the National Committee shall be entitled to one vote on each issue before it, except that Democrats Abroad shall have four votes on the Democratic National Committee, which votes shall be shared by the Chairperson, the highest ranking officer of the opposite sex, three National Committeemen and three National Committeewomen.

(f) Voting to fill a vacancy on the National ticket shall be in accord with procedural rules adopted by the Rules and Bylaws Committee and approved by the Democratic National Committee.

(g) Proxy voting shall be permitted. Proxies may be either general or limited and either instructed or uninstructed. All proxies shall be in writing and transferable if so specified. No DNC member may at any one time hold or exercise proxies for more than one other DNC member; provided, however, that proxy voting shall not be permitted in voting to fill a vacancy on the National ticket.

(h) The Chairperson of the National Committee may refer matters to the members of the National Committee for consideration and vote by mail, provided, however, that if members aggregating more than twenty percent (20%) of the full membership shall so request, the matter shall be presented to the next meeting of the National Committee.

Section 9. Regional Caucuses. There shall be four Regional Caucuses of the members of a Democratic National Committee, comprised as follows:

EASTERN
Connecticut
Delaware
District of Columbia
Maine
Maryland
Massachusetts
New Hampshire
New Jersey
New York
Pennsylvania
Puerto Rico
Rhode Island
Vermont
Virgin Islands
Democrats Abroad (1⁄2 vote)

SOUTHERN
Alabama
Arkansas
Florida
Georgia
Kentucky
Louisiana
Mississippi
North Carolina
South Carolina
Tennessee
Texas
Virginia
West Virginia
Democrats Abroad (1⁄2 vote)

MIDWESTERN
Illinois
Indiana
Iowa
Kansas
Michigan
Minnesota
Missouri
Nebraska
North Dakota
Ohio
Oklahoma
South Dakota
Wisconsin
Democrats Abroad (1⁄2 vote)

WESTERN
Alaska
American Samoa
Arizona
California
Colorado
Guam
Hawaii
Idaho
Montana
Nevada
New Mexico
Oregon
Utah
Washington
Wyoming
Democrats Abroad (1⁄2 vote)

Section 10. Committees.

(a) In addition to the Committees otherwise provided for in the Charter or in these Bylaws, there shall be the following standing committees of the Democratic National Committee:

(i) Credentials Committee;

(ii) Resolutions Committee;

(iii) Rules and Bylaws Committee;

(iv) Budget and Finance Committe.

(b)(i) The Credentials Committee shall receive and consider all challenges to the credentials of Democratic National Committee members.

(ii) Any challenge to the credentials of a member of the Democratic National Committee may be made by any Democrat from the state or territory of the member challenged or any member of the Democratic National Committee and shall be filed by Registered Mail (return receipt requested) within thirty (30) days of the selection of such member.

(iii) The Credentials Committee shall determine the validity of the credentials of those elected to the National Committee, and decide all challenges to the seating of such members. The Credentials Committee shall provide each party to a dispute a reasonable opportunity to be heard, and may give an opportunity for submission of briefs and oral argument and shall render a written report on the issues to the National Committee.

(iv) The National Committee shall proceed to a determination of such contest or contests as its first order of business, if feasible, including the temporary seating of challenged members, in order that the members may participate in other business before the National Committee.

(c)(i) The Resolutions Committee shall receive and consider all resolutions proposed by a member of the Democratic National Committee on matters of policy proposed for adoption by the Democratic National Committee, and shall report in writing. Said report shall contain the text of each resolution recommended by the Committee for adoption, and shall identify resolutions considered but not recommended for adoption; and

(ii) resolutions shall be submitted to the Secretary of the Democratic National Committee at least twenty-one (21) days prior to the meeting of the National Committee, and copies of all such resolutions shall be sent to each member no less than fourteen (14) days prior to the National Committee meeting, provided that the Executive Committee may vote to submit urgent timely resolutions to the National Committee even though not submitted within these time periods.

(c)(i) The Rules and Bylaws Committee shall receive and consider all recommendations for adoption and amendments to the Rules and Bylaws of the National Committee and to the Charter of the Democratic Party of the United States;

(ii) recommendations for amendment to the Charter of the Democratic Party of the United States shall be received by the Rules and Bylaws Committee no less than sixty (60) days prior to a regular meeting of the Democratic National Committee, provided that the Executive Committee may approve direct submission of a recommended amendment to the Charter if the requirements of timeliness of the Charter are otherwise met;

(iii) recommendations for amendment to the Bylaws or adoption of Rules for the Democratic National Committee shall be submitted to the Rules Committee no less than thirty (30) days prior to a meeting of the National Committee, and the Secretary of the National Committee shall mail such proposed recommendations to the members no less than thirty (30) days prior to the National Committee. It shall be the responsibility of the member of the National Committee submitting a Bylaws Amendment to distribute a copy to all members of the Committee within the time required by these Bylaws for consideration, or submit the request to the Secretary with ample time to make such distribution;

(iv) the Executive Committee may refer to the Rules and Bylaws Committee for preliminary consideration the temporary Rules of the National Convention to be included in the Call to the Convention, and the Executive Committee may adopt the recommendations of the Rules and Bylaws Committee as such temporary Convention rules;

(v) the Rules and Bylaws Committee shall conduct a continuing study of the Bylaws, Rules and Charter and make periodic recommendations for amendment, extension or other action,

(vi) provided that any such recommendations by the Rules and Bylaws

Committee be submitted to the members of the National Committee at the time the agenda is presented; and the report of the Rules and Bylaws Committee shall be in writing and shall contain the full text of action recommended and shall identify recommendations not approved by the Committee for adoption.

(e) Budget and Finance Committee

   (i) The Budget and Finance Committee shall be composed of the Treasurer, the National Finance Chair and not more than nine other members of the Democratic National Committee who have training or experience in finance or management;

   (ii) the Budget and Finance Committee shall in full consultation with the National Chairperson of the Democratic National Committee, review the budget of the Democratic National Committee on an on-going basis, make periodic reports including an annual report to the Executive Committee and the full Democratic National Committee on the goals, purposes of expenditures and results of expenditures of the Democratic National Committee and its staff;

   (iii) the Budget and Finance Committee shall, working with the National Chairperson, Chief Financial Officer and counsel, develop and present to the Executive Committee, policies and procedures with respect to:

(a) contracting and procurement of goods and services by the Democratic National Committee, including affirmative action policies; and

(b) avoidance of conflicts of interest;

(vi) meetings of the Budget and Finance Committee shall not be subject to the provisions of Article Nine, Section 12 of the Charter

(f) The National Committee may from time to time create such other standing or ad hoc committees as it shall deem appropriate.

(g) Except as otherwise provided in the Charter or in these Bylaws, the members of all committees of the National Committee shall be appointed by the Chairperson of the Democratic National Committee, in consultation with the Executive Committee, subject to ratification by the Democratic National Committee, and shall be appointed to serve for the tenure of the Chairperson. Notwithstanding the above provision, notice of such pending appointment must be mailed to the Democratic National Committee membership no less than seven (7) days prior to the vote on ratification.

(h) Failure by members to attend three consecutive meetings of the committees of the National Committee shall constitute a failure to meet the minimum level of attendance and shall constitute automatic resignation from the committee. The provisions of Section 8(g) of this Article shall apply to committees of the National Committee, except that proxies shall not be counted at any meeting for the purpose of meeting the minimum level of attendance. Attendance records of committees of the National Committee shall be reported annually to the Executive Committee.

(i) All matters referred to any council, special committee, standing committee, conference or any other sub-group must be acted upon and said action reported to the body which originated the reference.

Section 11. Participation in All Party Affairs.

(a) The Democratic Party of the United States shall be open to all who desire to support the Party and who wish to be known as Democrats. Participation in the affairs of the Democratic Party shall be open pursuant to the standards of non-discrimination and affirmative action incorporated into the Charter of the Democratic Party of the United States.

(b)(i) The National, State, and Local Democratic Party organizations shall undertake affirmative action programs designed to encourage the fullest participation of all Democrats in all Party affairs. All Party affairs shall mean all activities of each official Party organization commencing at the lowest level and continuing up through the National Democratic Party. Such activities shall include but need not be limited to the processes in which delegates are selected to the National Democratic Convention; Party officials are nominated or selected; Party policy, platforms, and rules are formulated; and regular programs of voter registration, public education and public relations. Such programs may be developed and sponsored in cooperation with the Democratic National Committee.

(ii) National and State Democratic Parties shall carry out programs to facilitate and increase the participation of low and moderate income persons. These programs shall include provisions and resources for outreach and recruitment to achieve representation and equitably minimize economic factors which act to bar full participation by such persons.

(iii) State and National Parties shall act affirmatively to develop and implement appropriate education, training, fund-raising and outreach programs directed at low and moderate income Democrats and shall implement rules and regulations of the Party in their most constructive interpretation to effect increased participation and representation by people of low and moderate income. Non-discrimination as it relates to this Section (11(b)) and as provided in Article Eight, Section 2 of the Charter shall be strictly enforced.

(c)(i) Each state or territorial Party shall require each unit of the Party which holds such meetings to publicize effectively and in a timely fashion the dates, times, and places of all such meetings, and the name or names of the person responsible for such meetings.

(ii) Notice of meetings shall be published as required in this Section prior to the meeting. Such notice may appear as legal notice, paid advertisement, news item, direct mail, radio or television announcement, or in such other form as may reasonably be designed to notify Democrats of the meeting provided no state, territorial, or county Party is required to purchase paid advertising; and

(iii) If challenged, a state or territorial Party shall be deemed to be in compliance with this Section upon proof of effective notice from the reporting unit of the Party.

(d) If a county or any local unit of the state or territorial Party fails to comply with the foregoing provisions of this Section, the state or territorial Party may assume responsibility for setting dates, times and places for local meetings and for giving notice of the same as provided in this Section.

(e) Each state or territorial Party may establish such procedures and structures as are necessary to ensure compliance with this Section, including procedures for review of complaints of non-compliance with this Section by any unit of the political process, including the state.

(f) If a state or territorial Party is alleged to have failed to comply with this Section, the alleged non-compliance shall be referred to the Democratic National Committee for review provided that any person alleging non-compliance at any level shall be a resident of the affected jurisdiction and provided that any person alleging non-compliance of a state or territorial Party with this section shall have exhausted all remedies provided by the state or territorial Party.

Section 12. Duties and Responsibilities of the Chairperson.

(a) The Chairperson shall be the chief executive officer of the Democratic National Committee and shall exercise authority delegated to him or her by the Democratic National Committee and the Democratic

National Committee's Executive Committee in carrying out the day-to-day activities of the Committee.

(b) By the time of the next DNC meeting following his or her election, the Chairperson shall designate a Vice Chair who will have authority to act as Chairperson should a vacancy occur or should the Chairperson become incapacitated. In the event of such succession, the designated Vice Chair will serve in the capacity of the Chairperson until a new Chairperson is elected at the next regularly scheduled meeting of the full Democratic National Committee.

ARTICLE THREE
Executive Committee

Section 1. Powers and Duties. The Executive Committee of the Democratic National Committee shall be responsible for the conduct of the affairs of the Democratic Party in the interim between the meetings of the full Committee. This responsibility shall include, but not be limited to:

(a) Authority for the Democratic National Committee between meetings thereof;

(b) Recommending approval of the budget of the Democratic National Committee; and

(c) Reporting all of its proceedings to the Democratic National Committee.

Section 2. Membership. The Executive Committee shall be composed of:

(a) The Chairpersons of the Regional Caucuses of the Democratic National Committee who must be members of the Democratic National Committee;

(b) Four members elected by each of the Regional Caucuses of the Democratic National Committee, who shall be equally divided between men and women and all of whom shall be members of the Democratic National Committee;

(c) The Chairperson, the five Vice Chairpersons, the Treasurer, and the Secretary of the Democratic National Committee;

(d) The National Finance Chair;

(e) The Chairperson of the Democratic Governors' Association or his or her designee from that Association, who must be a member of the Democratic National Committee;

(f) The Democratic Leader of the United States Senate or his or her designee, who must be a member of the Democratic National Committee, and the Democratic Leader from the United States House of Representatives or his or her designee, who must be a member of the Democratic National Committee;

(g) The Chairperson of the National Conference of Democratic Mayors or his or her designee, who must be a member of the Democratic National Committee;

(h) The Chairperson of the Democratic Legislative Campaign Committee or his or her designee from that Committee, who must be a member of the Democratic National Committee;

(i) The Chairperson of the National Democratic County Officials or his or her designee, who must be a member of the Democratic National Committee;

(j) The Chairperson of the National Democratic Municipal Officials Conference or his or her designee, who must be a member of the Democratic National Committee;

(k) The President of the Young Democrats of America or his or her designee, who must be a member of the Democratic National Committee;

(l) Three additional members of the Association of State Democratic Chairs to be selected by the Association;

(m) The President of the National Federation of Democratic Women or her designee, who must be a member of the Democratic National Committee;

(n) The Chairs of the Hispanic, Black, Asian American and Pacific Islander, and Lesbian, Gay, Bisexual and Transgender American Caucuses of the Democratic National Committee or his or her designee, who must be a member of the Democratic National Committee;

(o) The Chair of the Women's Caucus of the Democratic National Committee or her designee, who must be a member of the Democratic National Committee;

(p) The President of the College Democrats of America or his or her designee, who must be a member of the Democratic National Committee;

(q) Eleven members at-large, elected by the Democratic National Committee, who shall be equally divided between men and women, all of whom must be members of the Democratic National Committee;

(r) The Chairs of the standing committees on Credentials, Resolutions, and Rules and Bylaws.

(s) Any designee as provided for in this section, may not otherwise be a member of the Executive Committee and must be a member of the organization or constituency he or she is designated to represent.

Section 3. Election of Members.

(a) Members of the Executive Committee representing the Regional and Constituency Caucuses pursuant to Section 2(b), 2(n) and 2(o) of this Article shall be elected:

    (i) at the second meeting of the Democratic National Committee held after the succeeding presidential election; and

    (ii) whenever a vacancy occurs.

(b) Members of the Executive Committee elected at-large as apportioned pursuant to Section 2(q) of this Article shall be elected:

    (i) at the second meeting of the Democratic National Committee held after the succeeding presidential election; and

    (ii) whenever a vacancy occurs. Notwithstanding the above provisions, notice of any such nomination must be mailed to the Democratic National Committee membership no less than seven (7) days prior to the election.

(c) Members of the Executive Committee shall serve until the election of their successors. Upon the resignation of a member, a successor shall be selected by the original official authority to serve the unexpired portion of the term.

Section 4. Meetings. The Executive Committee shall meet at least four times each year. Meetings shall be called by the Chairperson or by written request of no fewer than one-fourth of its members. All members of the Democratic National Committee shall be notified of meetings of the Executive Committee. The Executive Committee shall keep a record of its proceedings which shall be available to the public.

Section 5. Attendance and Quorum and Voting.

(a) Members of the Executive Committee apportioned pursuant to the provisions of Section 2 of this Article who miss three consecutive meetings of the Democratic National Committee Executive Committee have failed to meet the minimum level of attendance and shall be deemed to have resigned from the Executive Committee. Vacancies created by any member for failing to meet the minimum level of attendance shall be filled by the original authority. Proxies shall not be counted at any meeting for the purpose of meeting the minimum level of attendance.

(b) Notwithstanding the above provision, the provisions of Section 8 of Article Two of these Bylaws shall apply to the Executive Committee.

ARTICLE FOUR
National Finance Organizations

<u>Section 1.</u> Duties and Powers. The National Finance Organizations of the Democratic Party shall have general responsibility for the finances of the Democratic Party for raising funds to support the Democratic Party and the Democratic National Committee to advise and assist State Democratic parties and candidates in securing funds for their purposes. The National Finance Chair and the Treasurer will advise the National Chairperson of the Democratic Party and the Executive Committee of the Democratic National Committee with respect to the finances of the Democratic Party.

ARTICLE FIVE
Amendments

Bylaws may be adopted or amended by majority vote of:

(a) the National Convention; or

(b) the Democratic National Committee provided that thirty (30) days written notice of any proposed Bylaw or amendment has been given to all members of the National Committee. Unless adopted in the form of an amendment to the Charter or otherwise designated, any resolution adopted by the National Convention relating to the governance of the Party shall be considered a Bylaw.

Endnotes

PREFACE

1.   While it is no stretch to say that the election of Abraham Lincoln in 1860 led to secession by the states that would ultimately form the Confederacy and lead to the Civil War, the conflict did not concern the legitimacy of his election. For example, the Richmond Dispatch reported, the day after Election Day in 1860, that "[t]he returns received and published yesterday, left little or no doubt of the election of Abraham Lincoln to the Presidency," but added that, "[t]he event is the most deplorable one that has happened in the history of the country" and "to expect trouble." *See* "Newspapers react to Abraham Lincoln's 1860 presidential win, *Washington Post*" Nov. 7, 2010, http://www.washingtonpost.com/wp-dyn/content/article/2010/11/05/AR2010110502719.html.

2.   *See* CNN Library, "2016 Presidential Campaign Hacking Fast Facts," http://www.cnn.com/2016/12/26/us/2016-presidential-campaign-hacking-fast-facts/index.html.

3.   *See Fox News Insider*, "DNC Chair: Trump 'Didn't Win Election,' GOP 'Doesn't Give a S—t About People,'" http://insider.foxnews.com/2017/04/01/dnc-chair-tom-perez-donald-trump-didnt-win-obamacare-replacement-republicans-dont-give.

4.   *See* Fred Lucas, "Democrat Plans To Impeach Trump Advance On Many Fronts," *Newsweek*, (July 7, 2017), http://www.newsweek.com/democrat-plans-impeach-trump-advance-many-fronts-635032.

5.   Maegan Vazquez, "House Dems introduce articles of impeachment against Trump," CNN (Nov. 26, 2017), http://www.cnn.com/2017/11/15/politics/cohen-articles-of-impeachment/index.html.

6.   While Samuel Tilden also claimed credit as the true winner of the 1876 election, it was as a prelude to his retirement from public life. *See* Jay

Evensen, "Clinton lost despite winning, but the Electoral College must remain," *Deseret News* (Nov. 10, 2016), http://www.deseretnews.com/article/865666806/Clinton-lost-despite-winning-but-the-Electoral-College-must-remain.html (quoting Tilden as saying, "I can retire to private life with the consciousness that I shall receive from posterity the credit of having been elected to the highest position in the gift of the people, without any of the cares and responsibilities of the office").

And although in his concession speech, Al Gore expressed disagreement with the Supreme Court's decision, he urged the country to accept the result "for the sake of our unity as a people and the strength of our democracy" and that "we will stand together behind our new president." *See* https://www.youtube.com/watch?v=GyKlcQ_HiD4.

7.   *See* Hillel Italie, "Hillary Clinton calling new book 'What Happened,'" *Washington Post* (July 27, 2017), https://www.washingtonpost.com/politics/whitehouse/hillary-clinton-calling-new-book-what-happened/2017/07/27/7621141a-72bb-11e7-8c17-533c52b2f014_story.html?utm_term=.67fbbbee7023.

8.   Mike Levine, "What to know about Mueller's use of a grand jury in the Russia probe," ABC News (Aug. 4, 2017), http://abcnews.go.com/Politics/muellers-grand-jury-russia-probe/story?id=49032822.

9.   Matt Zapotosky, Rosalind S. Helderman, Carol D. Leonnig & Spencer S. Hsu, "Three former Trump campaign officials charged by special counsel," *Washington Post* (Oct. 30, 2017), https://www.washingtonpost.com/world/national-security/manafort-and-former-business-partner-asked-to-surrender-in-connection-with-special-counsel-probe/2017/10/30/6fe051f0-bd67-11e7-959c-fe2b598d8c00_story.html?hpid=hp_hp-banner-main_specialcounsel-817am%3Ahomepage%2Fstory&tid=a_inl&utm_term=.cb86254a4fa9.

10. *See* Peter Baker, "Mueller's First Indictments Send a Message to Trump," *New York Times* (Oct. 30, 2017), https://www.nytimes.com/2017/10/30/us/politics/trump-manafort-indictment-analysis.html.

11. *See* Michael D. Shear & Adam Goldman, "Michael Flynn Pleads Guilty to Lying to the F.B.I. and Will Cooperate With Russia Inquiry," *New York Times* (Dec. 1, 2017), https://www.nytimes.com/2017/12/01/us/politics/michael-flynn-guilty-russia-investigation.html.

12. *See, e.g.*, Malcolm Nance, *The Plot to Hack America: How Putin's Cyberspies and WikiLeaks Tried to Steal the 2016 Election* (Skyhorse, 2016);

Dan Kovalik, *The Plot to Scapegoat Russia: How the CIA and the Deep State Have Conspired to Villify Russia* (Skyhorse, 2017); Patrick Lawrence, "A New Report Raises Big Questions About Last Year's DNC Hack," *The Nation* (Aug. 9, 2017), https://www.thenation.com/article/a-new-report-raises-big-questions-about-last-years-dnc-hack/.

OPENING STATEMENT: "Democracy Demands the Truth"

13. Sanders quoted in Emily Schultheis & Kylie Atwood, "Bernie Sanders talks "political revolution of 2016," CBS News (June 16, 2016), https://www.cbsnews.com/news/bernie-sanders-to-supporters/.

14.

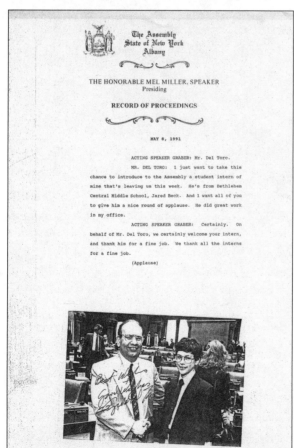

Assemblyman Angelo Del Toro (l) with the author in 1991.

The Author twenty-five years later, in Philadelphia during the Democratic National Convention.

15. *See* Jared Beck, "Student on 'shaky ground with Clinton at U-Albany," *The Spotlight*, Nov. 9, 1994, http://www.bethlehempubliclibrary.org/webapps/spotlight/years/1994/1994-11-09.pdf, 1.

16. *See* Jared Beck, "A one-house legislature could end gridlock," *The Spotlight*, July 6, 1994, http://www.bethlehempubliclibrary.org/webapps/spotlight/years/1994/1994-07-06.pdf, 6.

17. *See, e.g.*, Jared Beck, "Snap, Crackle, Pop Culture: The Politicization Of Pop Culture," *Harvard Political Review* 10 vol. XXIII, no. 2 (Spring 1996).

18. The Department of Government is Harvard's somewhat atypical name for its department of political science. It is not affiliated with the John F. Kennedy School of Government, which is the name for Harvard's graduate school of public policy.

19. Mainstays of the Harvard government faculty during my time in Cambridge, Hoffmann and Huntington were both leading experts on

international relations and American foreign policy. Huntington is probably best known for his theory of post–Cold War international conflict as set forth in *The Clash of Civilizations and the Remaking of World Order* (Touchstone, 1996).

20. *See* Jim Saksa, "You Can Do Anything With a Law Degree," *Slate* (May 14, 2014), http://www.slate.com/articles/life/culturebox/2014/05/you_can_do_anything_with_a_law_degree_no_no_you_cannot.html.

    Writing in 2014, Saksa noted that over 11percent of recent American law school graduates could not even find employment.

21. *See* David S. Law & Mila Versteeg, "The Declining Influence of the United States Constitution," *NYU Law Rev.* 87, no. 3 (June 2012): 762, https://papers.ssrn.com/sol3/papers.cfm?abstract_id=1923556##.

    Law and Versteeg note that while according to a 1987 study, "160 of the 170 nations then in existence had modeled their constitutions upon our own," as of 2012, the U.S. Constitution is "increasingly far from the global mainstream." *See id.* at 762-64.

22. Our starting salary right out of law school in 2004 was $125,000 a year per associate, not including bonuses.

23. The company, Mortgage Electronic Services, Inc. ("MERS"), has been the subject of considerable litigation. *See, e.g.,* Brad Swanson, "MERS wins in four Pennsylvania county lawsuits, Housing Wire (May 8, 2017), https://www.housingwire.com/articles/40068-mers-wins-in-four-pennsylvania-county-lawsuits ; Elliot Njus, "11 Oregon counties sue private mortgage registry MERS," *The Oregonian* (Nov. 3, 2016), http://www.oregonlive.com/front-porch/index.ssf/2016/11/11_oregon_counties_sue_private.html; "Beshear reaches $2.8M settlement with national mortgage recording company," *Lexington Herald Leader* (Feb. 28, 2017), http://www.kentucky.com/news/politics-government/article135416529.html.

24. *See, e.g.,* Robert Rich, "The Great Recession," Federal Reserve History (Nov. 22, 2013), https://www.federalreservehistory.org/essays/great_recession_of_200709.

25. *See* Abby Goodnough, "As Condos Rise in South Florida, Nervous Investors Try to Flee," *New York Times* (May 26, 2007), http://www.nytimes.com/2007/05/26/us/26condo.html?mcubz=0.

26. *See id.*

27. *See id.*

28.   Preconstruction contracts in the relevant period typically set the deposit at 20 percent of the condominium's total purchase price.

29.   The easing of credit that fueled the overheated real estate market, not just in but across the country, was a direct result of the continual deregulation of the U.S. banking industry starting with the Reagan administration. *See* Joseph Stiglitz, "Capital Fools," *Vanity Fair* (Dec. 10, 2008), https://www. commondreams.org/views/2008/12/10/capitalist-fools.

30.   *See, e.g.*, Bernie Sanders Campaign Press Release, "The Rigged Economy," (Nov. 13, 2015), https://berniesanders.com/press-release/the-rigged-economy/.

31.   This line of cases will be discussed further in Act II.

32.   *See* Stephen C. Yeazell, *From Medieval Group Litigation to the Modern Class Action* (Yale University Press, 1987), 221.

33.   The Federal Rules of Civil Procedure are the body of procedural rules governing all civil proceedings in federal district courts.

34.   *See generally* Brian T. Fitzpatrick, "The Ironic History of Rule 23," Vanderbilt Law Research Paper No. 17-41 (Aug. 10, 2017), https://papers. ssrn.com/sol3/papers.cfm?abstract_id=3020306##.

35.   Arthur R. Miller, "The Preservation and Rejuvenation of Aggregate Litigation: A Systemic Imperative," *Emory Law Journal* 64 (2014): 293, 295. http://law.emory.edu/elj/_documents/volumes/64/2/articles/miller.pdf.

36.   *See* Maureen Carroll, "Class Action Myopia," *Duke Law Journal* 65, no. 5 (Feb. 2016): 862, note 111 (citation omitted), http://scholarship.law. duke.edu/cgi/viewcontent.cgi?article=3835&context=dlj.

37.   *See* Fitzpatrick, *supra* at 17 (quoting American College of Trial Lawyers, Report and Recommendation of the Special Committee on Rule 23 of the FRC). Curiously, the corporate bar failed to anticipate the potential effects of the new class action rule six years earlier when it "did little to nothing to stop" the amendments from taking effect. *See* Fitzpatrick at 15.

38.   Miller, *supra* at 296.

39.   *See* Miller, *supra* at 296-303. The two asbestos cases discussed by Miller are *Amchem Products, Inc. v. Windsor*, 521 U.S. 591 (1997) and *Ortiz v. Fireboard Corp.*, 527 U.S. 815 (1999).

40.   Corporations have also successfully pushed anti–class action legislation through Congress. Examples include the Private Securities Litigation Reform Act, signed by Bill Clinton in 1995, which imposed new procedural burdens on securities class action plaintiffs, as well as the Class

Action Fairness Act of 2005, which required most class actions to be filed in federal court, where they are then subject to the growing federal precedent restricting the procedure's usefulness.

41. 564 U.S. 338 (2011).

42. *See id.* at 346, 354-55.

43. "Commonality" refers to one of four basic prerequisites for any class to be certified. For commonality to exist, there must be "questions of law or fact common to the class." The other requirements are "numerosity" ("the class is so numerous that joinder of all members is impracticable"); "typicality" ("the claims or defenses of the representative parties are typical of the claims or defenses of the class"); and "adequacy" ("the representative parties will fairly and adequately protect the interests of the class"). *See* Fed. R. Civ. P. 23(a).

44. *Id.* at 356.

45. 563 U.S. 333 (2011).

46. Jessica Silver-Greenberg & Robert Gebeloff, "Arbitration Everywhere, Stacking the Deck of Justice," *New York Times* (Oct. 31, 2015), https://www.nytimes.com/2015/11/01/business/dealbook/arbitration -everywhere-stacking-the-deck-of-justice.html?mcubz=0.

47. *See id.*

48. *Concepcion*, 563 U.S. at 347.

49. *Carnegie v. Household Int'l, Inc.*, 376 F.3d 656, 661 (7th Cir. 2004) (Posner, J.).

50. *See* Silver-Greenberg & Gebeloff, *supra.*

51. *See Concepcion*, 563 U.S. at 345-46 (stating that the Federal Arbitration Act was "designed to promote arbitration" and "embod[ies] a national policy favoring arbitration" (citation omitted)).

52. I had a similar sense of incongruity when I first read *Citizens United.* The maxim that corporate spending amounts to free expression—key legal underpinnings of our political system as constructed by the Supreme Court—was scarcely addressed in my constitutional law class, the casebook of which devoted just twenty-two pages to "Money and Political Campaigns." The book spends more pages pontificating upon the supposed marvels of *Marbury v. Madison*, an otherwise obscure nineteenth century decision regarding whether a justice of the peace for the District of Columbia had been properly appointed. *See* Kathleen Sullivan & Gerald Gunther, *Constitutional Law* 2-29, 1369-92 (14th ed. 2001).

53. *See generally* Arthur R. Miller, "The Pretrial Rush To Judgment: Are The 'Litigation Explosion,' 'Liability Crisis,' and Efficiency Clichés Eroding Our Day In Court And Jury Trial Commitments," *NYU Law Review* 78, no. 982 (2003), http://www.nyulawreview.org/sites/default/files/pdf/2.pdf ; *id.* at 1134 ("Taking decision-making authority from juries runs counter to basic and long-cherished principles of our system."); *see also* Arthur R. Miller, "Simplified Pleading, Meaningful Days In Court, And Trials On The Merits: Reflections On The Deformation Of Federal Procedure, *NYU Law Review* 88, no. 286 (2013), http://www.nyulawreview.org/sites/default/files/pdf/NYULawReview-88-1-Miller.pdf.

54. *See generally* Arthur R. Miller, "From *Conley* to *Twombly* to *Iqbal*: A Double Play On The Federal Rules Of Civil Procedure" *Duke Law Journal 60, no.* 1 (2010), http://scholarship.law.duke.edu/cgi/viewcontent.cgi?article=1472&context=dlj.

55. *Id.* at 2.

56. *See* Asher Schechter, Richard Posner: "The Real Corruption Is the Ownership of Congress by the Rich," *Pro-Market* (the blog of the Stigler Center at the University of Chicago Booth School of Business) (Mar. 28, 2017), https://promarket.org/richard-posner-real-corruption-ownership-congress-rich/ . The article contains a link to video of Posner's entire address.

57. *Id.*

58. *Id.* As a lawyer who has prosecuted antitrust cases on behalf of consumers, I wholeheartedly agree with Posner's view. Along with judicially heightened pleading standards demanding that plaintiffs plead the actual details of an antitrust claim without having access to any discovery, the Supreme Court's endorsement of arbitration clauses as a means of banning class actions has, for all intents and purposes, rendered the litigation of antitrust lawsuits extraordinarily difficult if not impossible altogether. *See Bell Atl. Corp. v. Twombly*, 550 U.S. 544, 570-97 (2007) (Stevens, J., dissenting) (criticizing the Court for creating a "heightened pleading burden" in an antitrust case "where the proof is largely in the hands of the alleged conspirators" while noting that "[t]he transparent policy concern that drives the decision is the interest in protecting antitrust defendants—who in this case are some of the wealthiest corporations in our economy" (citations and internal quotation marks omitted)); *Am. Express*

Co. v. Italian Colors Restaurant, 133 S. Ct. 2304, 2320 (2013) (Kagan, J., dissenting) (criticizing the Supreme Court for upholding a contractual class action ban in a small restaurant's merchant agreement with American Express and thereby depriving the restaurant of "any effective opportunity to challenge monopolistic conduct allegedly in violation of the Sherman Act").

59. John Fabian Witt, "The Provocative Life of Judge Richard Posner," *New York Times* (Oct. 7, 2016), https://www.nytimes.com/2016/10/09/books/review/richard-posner-biography-william-domnarski.html.

60. *Id.*

61. *See also* Jason Meisner & Patrick M O'Connell, Richard Posner, acerbic legal mind, retires from federal appeals court in Chicago, *Los Angeles Times* (Sept. 3, 2017), ("Posner's biting and often brilliant written opinions as well as his unrelenting questioning from the bench have made him an icon of the court for years."), http://www.latimes.com/nation/la-na-richard-posner-20170902-story.html.

    Posner retired from the bench on September 2, 2017. *See id.* Upon stepping down, Posner reiterated his dim outlook regarding the federal judiciary. *See* Adam Liptak, "An Exit Interview With Richard Posner, Judicial Provocateur," *New York Times* (Sept. 11, 2017), (quoting Posner as stating of pro se litigants, "most judges regard these people as kind of trash not worth the time of a federal judge"), https://www.nytimes.com/2017/09/11/us/politics/judge-richard-posner-retirement.html?mcubz=0.

62. *See, e.g.*, "Getting Big Money Out of Politics and Restoring Democracy," https://berniesanders.com/issues/money-in-politics/, ("Six years ago, as a result of the disastrous *Citizens United* Supreme Court decision, by a 5-to-4 vote, the U.S. Supreme Court essentially said to the wealthiest people in this country: you already own much of the American economy. Now, we are going to give you the opportunity to purchase the U.S. Government, the White House, the U.S. Senate, the U.S. House, Governors' seats, legislatures, and State judicial branches as well").

63. Glenn Greenwald, "The Untouchables: How the Obama administration protected Wall Street from prosecutions," *The Guardian* (Jan. 23, 2013), https://www.theguardian.com/commentisfree/2013/jan/23/untouchables-wall-street-prosecutions-obama.

64. *See* Philip Rucker & Robert Barnes, "Trump to inherit more than 100 court vacancies to reshape judiciary," *Washington Post* (Dec. 25, 2016), https://www.washingtonpost.com/politics/trump-to-inherit-more -than-100-court-vacancies-plans-to-reshape-judiciary/2016/12/25/ d190dd18-c928-11e6-85b5-76616a33048d_story.html?utm_term=. ab793054dea7.

65. *See* Adam Liptak, "Study Calls Snub of Obama's Supreme Court Pick Unprecedented," *New York Times* (June 13, 2016), https://www.nytimes. com/2016/06/14/us/politics/obama-supreme-court-merrick-garland. html, (stating that before Senate Republicans refused to consider Obama's Supreme Court appointee Judge Merrick B. Garland, the Senate had "never before transferred a president's appointment power in comparable circumstances to an unknown successor[.]").

   While obstruction by the Republican Senate was the proximate cause of Obama's historic inability to appoint a Supreme Court Justice, his lackluster performance on judicial appointments was apparent even when Democrats controlled the Senate. According to a Brookings Institution study on judicial nomination during Obama's first four years in office, his first term ended with "more vacancies than when it started because of, comparatively, fewer nominees, later submission dates, and a weaker district nominee confirmation rate." In addition, "elapsed times for making district court nominations and confirming them [grew] to eye-popping levels." *See* Russell Wheeler, *Judicial Nominations and Confirmations in Obama's First Term*, Governance Studies at Brookings Institution 1 (Dec. 13, 2012), https://www.brookings.edu/wp-content/ uploads/2016/06/13_obama_judicial_wheeler.pdf.

66. *See* S. 987—112th Congress: Arbitration Fairness Act of 2011, www. GovTrack.us, https://www.govtrack.us/congress/bills/112/s987 (last visited Oct. 3, 2017).

67. Between August 12, 2015 and May 24, 2016, we donated $2,403.00.

68. *USA Today* described one "Bernstorm" organized by the Sanders campaign in Johnson City, Tennessee as a gathering of two hundred at a "hipster" coffeehouse "to learn how to help get the Vermont senator into the White House." *See* Amanda Florian, "'Bernstorm' hits East Tennessee coffeehouse," *USA Today College* (Feb. 13, 2016), at http://college.usato- day.com/2016/02/13/bernstorm-hits-east-tennessee-coffeehouse/.

69.

70. The Magna Carta was forged from the conflict between the notoriously weak King John and a cabal of aristocrats who, in 1215, captured the city of London after King John's army, raised with baronial funds, lost to the French at the Battle of Bouvines, ending the Anglo-French War of 1202-1214. At a meadow named Runnymede along the River Thames, the cabal forced John to accede to a list of demands mainly concerning their grievances regarding property rights, taxes, and the royal justice system. *See* Claire Breay & Julian Harrison, "Magna Carta: an introduction," British Library (Jul. 28, 2014), https://www.bl.uk/magna-carta/articles/magna-carta-an-introduction.

    For the full text of the Magna Carta, see https://www.bl.uk/magna-carta/articles/magna-carta-english-translation.

71. The procedural history of *Citizens United* shows the Supreme Court's decision to be a stunning example of "aggressive conservative judicial activism." *See* Jeffrey Toobin, "Money Unlimited," *The New Yorker* (May 21, 2012), https://www.newyorker.com/magazine/2012/05/21/money-unlimited.

    While the case originally presented the Court with a narrow issue of interpretation pertaining to a narrow issue of statutory interpretation under a relatively obscure provision of the Bipartisan Campaign Reform Act of 2002 (otherwise known as the McCain-Feingold Act), the Court took the highly unusual step of ordering that the case be reargued so that it could rule on the constitutionality of limiting expenditures by corporations. *See id.* As Justice John Paul Stevens wrote in his ninety-page dissenting opinion, "Essentially, five Justices were unhappy with the limited nature of the case before us, so they changed the case to give themselves an opportunity to change the law." *Citizens United*, 558 U.S. at 398.

72. *Id.* at 365.

73. *Id.* at 337.

74. *See* Matea Gold, "Can super PACs be put back in the box?," *Washington Post* (July 6, 2016), https://www.washingtonpost.com/politics/can-super-pacs-be-put-back-in-the-box/2016/07/06/9beb18ba-43b1-11e6-8856-f26de2537a9d_story.html?utm_term=.40dd56dfe324.

    The precise legal basis for Super PACs came into being two months after *Citizens United*, when the D.C. Circuit Court of Appeals removed limits on contributions to independent expenditure-only political action committees on the ground that such limits violate the right to free speech as articulated in *Citizens United*. *See SpeechNow.org v. Federal Election Comm'n*, 599 F.3d 686, 692-96 (D.C. Cir. 2010).

75. *See* Libby Watson, "The final stretch: The big-spending super PACs behind Hillary Clinton," Sunlight Foundation (Nov. 1, 2016), https://sunlightfoundation.com/2016/11/01/the-final-stretch-the-big-spending-super-pacs-behind-hillary-clinton/.

76. Michelle Ye Hee Lee, "Sanders's claim that he 'does not have a super PAC,'" *Washington Post* (Feb. 11, 2016), https://www.washingtonpost.com/news/fact-checker/wp/2016/02/11/sanderss-claim-that-he-does-not-have-a-super-pac/?utm_term=.a9987875fba9; National Nurses United, Center for Responsive Politics (OpenSecrets.org), https://www.opensecrets.org/pacs/lookup2.php?strID=C00490375 (last visited Sept. 14, 2017).

77. Miller, *supra,* 306.

78. *See* Zachary R. Miller, "Lawyer Insulted by Trump for Breast-Pumping Sets Up Super-PAC," *Bloomberg Politics* (Feb. 23, 2016), https://www.bloomberg.com/news/articles/2016-02-23/lawyer-insulted-by-trump-for-breast-pumping-sets-up-superpac.

   The *Florida Record* published an account of JamPAC's origins on its two-month anniversary. *See* Taryn Phaneuf, "Attorney couple starts 'progressive and independent' super-PAC; Bernie Sanders is favored candidate," *Florida Record* (Apr. 22, 2016), http://flarecord.com/stories/510718660-attorney-couple-starts-progressive-and-independent-super-pac-bernie-sanders-is-favored-candidate.

79. *See* http://docquery.fec.gov/cgi-bin/forms/C00609750/1051735/ (last visited Oct. 6, 2017).

80. *See* Nancy Tartaglione, "Spike Lee's 'Chi-Raq' Panel Dominated By Talk Of Diversity, Gun Violence & Donald Trump—Berlin," *Deadline Hollywood* (Feb. 16, 2016), http://deadline.com/2016/02/spike-lee-chi-raq-diversity-donald-trump-gun-violence-berlin-1201703370/(reporting that "Lee drew some huzzahs when he said he was for 'Bernie Sanders from Brooklyn, New York'").

81. The name "JamPAC" was originally suggested by our creative director, Dan DeVivo, and refers to "culture jamming"—which may be defined as "a form of semiological guerrilla warfare. . . . In Culture Jamming the signs

and significations of the mass media are hijacked and diverted to both draw attention to the original message and create new messages with radically different intent." Tim Cresswell, "Night discourse: producing/consuming meaning on the street," in *Images of the Street: Planning, Identity, and Control in Public Space,* Nicholas R. Fyfe, ed., (London: Routledge, 1998), https://books.google.com/books?id=w0TSfW4MU4QC&pg=PA274#v=onepage&q&f=false.

82. *See* Jared Beck, "JamPAC: A Hack For An Ailing Political System," (Apr. 14, 2016), https://beckandlee.wordpress.com/2016/04/14/jampac-a-hack-for-an-ailing-political-system/.

83. I want to express gratitude to Dr. Vinay Gupta, who provided his unique brand of consulting services to JamPAC free of charge, as well as Ernst Valery who offered valuable early-stage advice.

84. Both Elizabeth and I became much more active users of Facebook and Twitter as a result of our activism on behalf of Bernie Sanders. Before the 2016 election season, my online presence mainly entailed a sporadically updated blog that had focused on legal issues arising out of the 2007-08 real estate market crash in Florida. *See* Jared Beck, *Beck's Law,* at https://beckandlee.wordpress.com.

85. Gil Troy, "Why Black Voters Don't Feel the Bern," *Politico Magazine* (Mar. 7, 2016), http://www.politico.com/magazine/story/2016/03/why-black-voters-dont-feel-the-bern-213707.

86. *See* Philip Rucker, "Can Bernie Sanders win over Latino voters?," *Washington Post* (Nov. 9, 2015), https://www.washingtonpost.com/politics/can-bernie-sanders-win-over-latino-voters/2015/11/09/b3947a36-86fd-11e5-9a07-453018f9a0ec_story.html?utm_term=.3c440ad8ed93 (characterizing a Bernie Sanders rally in North Las Vegas, Nevada as a "sea of white people" while stating that "Clinton has been cultivating relationships in the Latino community for decades" and Martin O'Malley "built strong ties with Latinos[.]" The article goes on to state that, "[f]or Sanders, the kind of coalition politics practiced by Clinton and O'Malley is somewhat foreign").

87. *See* Jan Jennings, "Award-Winning Documentary Film, Crossing Arizona, Examining Illegal Immigration to Screen April 12 at UCSD," University of California, San Diego News Center (Mar. 27, 2017), http://ucsdnews.ucsd.edu/archive/newsrel/events/03-07CrossingArizona.asp; Stephen Lemons, "Joe Arpaio Doc *Two Americans* Rocks

Harkins for One Week Only," *Phoenix New Times* (Oct. 26, 2012), http://www.phoenixnewtimes.com/blogs/joe-arpaio-doc-two-americans-rocks-harkins-for-one-week-only-6501166.

88. "Vote Your Conscience," https://www.youtube.com/watch?v=FsmgpV5pRjs (last visited Oct. 7, 2017).

89. JamPAC produced films directed by John Haas, Reed Lindsay, and Washington Digital Media (Ricardo Villalba and Christopher Schrack).

90. https://www.youtube.com/channel/UCxq7sQfX7dj4ipVUAR1m7Fg/videos.

91. JamPAC also produced an election-themed game ("Election Fighter") with GamePrez LLC, run by my friends Daniel Korenblum and Tom Birdsey. *See* Beck *supra*.

92. JamPAC, "Proud Latinos For Bernie," https://www.youtube.com/watch?v=gD5Mil-p_dE&t=17s (last visited Oct. 7, 2017); JamPAC, "Sabies quien apoya una reforma migratoria?," https://www.youtube.com/watch?v=755g3gqrj6A (last visited Oct. 7, 2017); JamPAC, "A mi commidad Latina, les digo," https://www.youtube.com/watch?v=UnA_zwmp-sWU (last visited Oct. 7, 2017).

93. At least one study of what makes a video "go viral" suggests that mainstream media exposure can be a significant factor. *See* Lindsey Elliott, "What Makes A Non-Professional Video Go Viral: A Case Study Of 'I'm Farming And I Grow It,'" Master's Thesis as submitted to Kansas State University 58-59 (2013), http://jmc.k-state.edu/graduate/LindseyElliott2013.pdf.

94. For a brief period during the summer of 2015, we experienced intense media scrutiny arising from an incident in one of our condominium deposit cases, where Donald Trump was a defendant. From 2009 through 2014, Beck & Lee had represented the purchasers of condominium hotel units in the never-built Trump International Hotel & Tower in Fort Lauderdale in a federal lawsuit against the developers of the failed project, which included (or so our clients were led to believe, by the project's advertising), Donald Trump. (Trump, as it turned out, had made a deal only to license his name on the hotel and was not one of the project's developers.)

During Trump's deposition in one of our cases in 2011, the witness got into a shouting match with Elizabeth over a prearranged break to use her breast pump and abruptly departed the room, requiring us to complete the deposition at another time and place. The deposition was not videotaped and there was only a written transcript of the deposition which was filed into the court record. *See Trilogy Partners LLC et al. v. SB Hotel Associates LLC et al.*, Case No. 09-21406-CIV, Docket Entry 230-1 (S.D. Fla., entered on docket June 4, 2012), https://www.scribd.com/document/275942466/Transcript-of-Donald-Trump-s-Deposition.

In the summer of 2015, as Trump was dominating the polls for the Republican nomination, a reporter at the *New York Times* named Michael Barbaro got hold of the transcript and must have divined that something had gone awry that day back in November 2011. He called our office; we returned his call and each gave him our recollection of the deposition and surrounding events. At the time, I wondered about the newsworthiness of the incident, given that bad behavior by deponents is not entirely unusual, but that was not my determination to make. The resulting article led to a media frenzy: within forty-eight hours of its appearance on the front page of the *New York Times* website, Elizabeth had been interviewed on CNN, MSNBC, and several international TV stations. Hundreds of articles about the incident appeared on the Internet, many with their own unique political spin. For my own perspective on the media frenzy at the time, see Jared Beck, "The Breast Pump That Stumped Trump: Notes From Inside A Media Maelstrom," *Beck's Law* (Aug. 27, 2015), https://beckandlee.wordpress.com/2015/08/27/the-breast-pump-that-stumped-trump-notes-from-inside-a-media-maelstrom/.

For the *New York Times* article about the underlying incident in the litigation against Trump, see Michael Barbaro & Steve Elder, "Under Oath, Donald Trump Shows His Raw Side," *New York Times* (July 28, 2015), https://www.nytimes.com/2015/07/29/us/politics/depositions-show-donald-trump-as-quick-to-exaggerate-and-insult.html?mtrref=undefined&assetType=nyt_now.

95. The only mainstream coverage of JamPAC came out the day after Elizabeth created with the FEC and was a very short item highlighting (predictably enough) the widely covered fact that Elizabeth had once gotten into verbal fracas with Trump over a request to use her breast pump. *See* Zachary R. Milder, "Lawyer Insulted by Trump for Breast-Pumping Sets Up Super-PAC," *Bloomberg Politics* (Feb. 23, 2016), https://www.bloomberg.com/news/articles/2016-02-23/lawyer-insulted-by-trump-for-breast-pumping-sets-up-superpac.

96. Email from Charles Jones to Elizabeth Beck, Jared Beck, and Dan De-
Vivo dated March 17, 2016 (on file with the author).

97. *See* Barbara With, "Saboteurs of Sanders Campaign Lead to Clinton
National Security Think Tank," Wisconsin Media Cooperative (Apr. 1,
2016), forty-eight https://wcmcoop.com/2016/04/01/saboteurs-of-sanders
-campaign-lead-to-clinton-national-security-think-tank/.

98. *See* Jason Horowitz, "Bernie Sanders Courts Black Voters in South Carolina After Criticism on Racial Issues," *New York Times* (Aug. 22, 2015),
https://www.nytimes.com/2015/08/23/us/politics/a-shift-in-tone-as-
bernie-sanders-speaks-on-criminal-justice-in-south-carolina.html   (de-
picting Niko House at a Bernie Sanders rally in Sumter, South Carolina).

99. *See* Alex Daugherty, "Sanders leaders on campus turning their
backs on Clinton campaign," *McClatchy* DC Bureau (Sept. 22, 2016),
http://www.mcclatchydc.com/news/politics-government/election/
article103315202.html (interviewing Niko House and other campus or-
ganizers).

100. *See, e.g.*, "Exposing internal corruption in the Bernie Sanders campaign"
(posted on Mar. 18, 2016), https://www.youtube.com/watch?v=hbR2IN-
Jtkfo&t=3s;   https://www.facebook.com/nikoforthepeople/videos/
vb.1664743843800306/1704063983201625/?type=2&theater (video posted
to Niko House's Facebook page).

101.

Niko, Elizabeth, and Jared's meeting.

102. *See* Alan Yuhas, "Bernie Sanders: Clinton 'creamed us' in south but
west coast will be better," *The Guardian* (Mar. 20, 2016), https://www

.theguardian.com/us-news/2016/mar/20/bernie-sanders-hillary-clinton-south-west-coast-us-election-2016.

103. *See* Video Transcript of Press Conference and Interview of Niko House at Beck & Lee, P.A, Miami, Florida (Mar. 20, 2016) (on file with author). Niko's account of infiltration is briefly summarized in With, *supra*.

104. *See* Dan Merica, "Fired Sanders aide: I wasn't peeking at Clinton data files," CNN (Dec. 18, 2015), http://www.cnn.com/2015/12/18/politics/sanders-dnc-data-breach-josh-uretsky/index.html.

105. *See* TPM Livewire, "Sanders Campaign Maintains DNC Holds Responsibility For Data Breach," *Talking Points Memo* (Dec. 26, 2015), http://talkingpointsmemo.com/livewire/sanders-adviser-dnc-josh-uretsky.

    After the DNC suspended its access to the voter database based on Uretsky's actions, the Sanders campaign sued the DNC in federal court. At the time, Sanders's campaign manager, Jeff Weaver, stated that by restricting the campaign from access to voter data, "the leadership of the Democratic National Committee is actively trying to undermine our campaign." *See* Catherine Treyz, "Sanders campaign sues DNC after database breach," CNN (Dec. 21, 2015), http://www.cnn.com/2015/12/18/politics/bernie-sanders-campaign-dnc-suspension/index.html.

    While the DNC and Sanders's campaign quickly agreed to restore the campaign's access to the data, the lawsuit continued until April 29, 2016, when the campaign announced it would be dropped. *See* John Wagner, "Sanders campaign drops lawsuit against DNC stemming from December data-breach flap," *Washington Post* (Apr. 29, 2016), https://www.washingtonpost.com/news/post-politics/wp/2016/04/29/sanders-campaign-drops-lawsuit-against-dnc-stemming-from-december-data-breach-flap/?utm_term=.cd34c3b0add6.

106. *See* Niko House Interview Video Tr. (on file with author).

107. *See* "House on Fire"—Investigative Documentary Series, Generosity.com, https://www.generosity.com/fundraising/house-on-fire-investigative-documentary-series (last visited Oct. 10, 2017).

108. Craig C. Donasanto & Nancy L. Simmons, *Federal Prosecution of Election Offenses* (7th ed., May 2007), https://www.justice.gov/sites/default/files/criminal/legacy/2013/09/30/electbook-0507.pdf.

109. *See* AJ Vicens, "The Election in Arizona Was a Mess," *Mother Jones* (Mar. 24, 2016), http://www.motherjones.com/politics/2016/03/arizona-primary-long-lines-voting-restrictions/.

110. *See* Matt Pearce, "'It was just chaos': Broken machines, incomplete voter rolls leave some wondering whether their ballots will count," *Los Angeles Times* (June 7, 2014).

111. *See* Reuters Staff, "New York City watchdog decries 'irregularities' in primary voting," Reuters (Apr. 19, 2016), http://www.reuters.com/article/us-usa-election-new-york-comptroller/new-york-city-watchdog-decries-irregularities-in-primary-voting-idUSKCN0XG2ML.

112. *See* Harper Neidig, "Sanders campaign accuses Puerto Rico Dem officials of fraud," *The Hill* (June 4, 2016), http://thehill.com/blogs/ballot-box/dem-primaries/282228-sanders-campaign-accuses-puerto-rico-dem-officials-of-fraud.

113. For comprehensive reporting on the numerous irregularities in the 2016 Democratic primaries encompassing registration tampering, voter purging, and inaccurate voting machine counts, see Election Justice USA, "*Democracy Lost:* A Report on the Fatally Flawed 2016 Democratic Primaries," July 30, 2016, http://www.p2016.org/chrnothp/Democracy_Lost_Update1_EJUSA.pdf.

   For a rigorous statistical analysis of Democratic primary data detecting "suspect statistical patterns giving Clinton inflated percentages, that in all likelihood are not fully based on actual votes; and leaving Sanders with what appear to be artificially depressed totals," see lulu Fries'dat & Anselmo Sampietro in collaboration with Fritz Scheren, "An Electoral System in Crisis" (July 25, 2016), available at https://static1.squarespace.com/static/579f40a01b631bd12f10c29e/t/58375666c534a52c855d9648/1480021608216/000+An+Electoral+System+in+Crisis.pdf.

114. *See* Nate Cohn and Toni Monkovic, "Bernie Sanders and Rigged Elections: Sometimes You Just Lose," *New York Times* (June 1, 2016), https://www.nytimes.com/2016/06/02/upshot/bernie-sanders-and-rigged-elections-sometimes-you-just-lose.html.

115. Guccifer 2.0 should not be confused with Guccifer, the pseudonym of Romanian hacker Marcel Lehel Lazar who, on September 16, 2016, was sentenced in federal court on charges of hacking into email accounts belonging to Hillary Clinton confidant Sidney Blumenthal and former secretary of state Colin Powell, among others. *See* Joe Uchill, "'Guccifer' hacker sentenced to 52 months in prison," *The Hill* (Sept. 1,

2016), http://thehill.com/policy/cybersecurity/294116-marcel-guccifer
-lazar-leher-sentenced-to-52-months.

There is no known connection between Lazar and Guccifer 2.0.

116. One day before the Guccifer 2.0 website was established, it was reported that hackers affiliated with the Russian government had breached the DNC's servers and stolen files. *See* Ellen Nakashima, "Russian government hackers penetrated DNC, stole opposition research on Trump," *Washington Post* (June 14, 2016), https://www.washingtonpost.com/world/national-security/russian-government-hackers-penetrated-dnc-stole-opposition-research-on-trump/2016/06/14/cf006cb4-316e-11e6-8ff7-7b6c1998b7a0_story.html.

The claim that Guccifer 2.0 was working on behalf of Russia has been largely unquestioned and repeated as fact in the U.S. mainstream media. *See, e.g.*, "Trump adviser Roger Stone admits contact with Guccifer 2.0 during campaign," CBS News (Mar. 14, 2017), https://www.cbsnews.com/news/trump-adviser-roger-stone-admits-contact-with-guccifer-2-0-during-campaign/ ; Michael Weiss, "Roger Stone's moment of truth?," CNN (Sept. 24, 2017), http://www.cnn.com/2017/09/24/opinions/roger-stone-moment-of-truth-opinion-weiss/index.html.

In contrast, an independent study based on interviews and communications with the person claiming to be Guccifer 2.0 and close analysis of the metadata in the electronic document files released by Guccifer 2.0 suggests it is far more likely that Guccifer 2.0 was a persona created by someone inside the DNC itself, with the aim of preempting news about the impending publication of internal DNC documents by WikiLeaks—Julian Assange had announced on June 12 that WikiLeaks would be publishing documents from the DNC—so that responsibility for this leak might be pinned on Russian hackers. *See* Adam Carter, "Guccifer 2.0: Game Over," http://g-2.space/#12 (last visited Oct. 11, 2017).

Adam Carter's conclusions find corroboration in another independent analysis focusing on the metadata in locked files from the DNC published by Guccifer 2.0, and which concludes that the files were transferred from the DNC's servers by someone on the East Coast of the United States and, based on file transfer speeds recorded within the files, probably by downloading the files directly from the server onto a thumb drive rather than over an Internet connection. *See* Patrick Lawrence, "A New Report Raises Big Questions about "Last Year's DNC Hack," *The Nation*

(Aug. 9, 2017), https://www.thenation.com/article/a-new-report-raises-big-questions-about-last-years-dnc-hack/.

From the perspective of holding the DNC accountable for its rigging of the nomination process against Bernie Sanders, the identity of Guccifer 2.0 is irrelevant. The DNC has never disputed the authenticity of the documents that were published (whether obtained by "hack" or "leak"); instead, their genuineness as DNC documents has been folded into a prevailing mainstream media narrative condemning Russia for "interference" in the 2016 elections. *See, e.g.*, Eugene Scott, "10 most damning findings from report on Russian interference," CNN (Jan. 7, 2017), http://www.cnn.com/2017/01/07/politics/intelligence-report-russian-interference/index.html.

From the perspective of laying waste to this mainstream narrative, however, the evidence strongly pointing to Guccifer 2.0 as an inside job is potent stuff, and certainly exceeds the conclusory public "findings" of any of the U.S. intelligence agencies, which, in any event, have not had access to the DNC's servers for purposes of conducting their analysis. *See* Alex Diaz, "Hacked DNC servers: Will government ever be given access," Fox News (July 7, 2017), http://www.foxnews.com/politics/2017/07/07/hacked-dnc-servers-will-government-ever-be-given-access.html.

117. The case was *In re Peregrine Systems, Inc. Securities Litigation*, Case No. 02-CV-0870-BEN (RBB) (S.D. Cal.). From 2004 to 2005, Elizabeth and I practiced law as associates at the Los Angeles office of Quinn Emanuel, a large firm with a substantial docket of cases defending large companies in fraud matters.

118. For details on the accounting fraud at Peregrine Systems, Inc., see Bruce Bigelow, "11 indicted in fraud at Peregrine," *San Diego Union-Tribune* (Oct. 7, 2004), http://legacy.sandiegouniontribune.com/uniontrib/20041007/news_1n7peregrine.html.

119. Preliminary questions such as standing are especially important in light of cases involving the conduct of government officials, because the Supreme Court has long prohibited the concept of "generalized grievance" standing, *i.e.,* permitting individuals to sue "if their only injury is as a citizen or a taxpayer concerned with having the government follow the law." *See* Erwin Chemerinsky, Federal Jurisdiction 89 § 2.3 (Aspen 4th ed. 2003).

120. *See Danvers Motor Co. v. Ford Motor Co.*, 432 F.3d 286, 293 (3d Cir. 2005).

121. *See, e.g.*, Edward-Isaac Dovere & Marc Caputo, "Wasserman Schultz's divided loyalties," *Politico* (Sept. 3, 2015), http://www.politico.com/story/2015/09/debbie-wasserman-schultz-joe-biden-hillary-clinton-2016-loyalty-213294 (quoting Wasserman Schultz as stating "it's my job to run a neutral primary process and that's what I committed to doing[.]"); Tribune news services, "Sanders says he is backing opponent of DNC chair Wasserman Schultz," *Chicago Tribune* (May 21, 2016), http://www.chicagotribune.com/news/nationworld/politics/ct-sanders-dnc-chair-20160521-story.html (Wasserman Schultz: "Even though Senator Sanders has endorsed my opponent, I remain, as I have been from the beginning, neutral in the presidential Democratic primary.")

122. *See* Philip Bump, "Bernie Sanders keeps saying his average donation is $27, but his known numbers contradict that," *Washington Post* (Apr. 18, 2016), https://www.washingtonpost.com/news/the-fix/wp/2016/04/18/bernie-sanders-keeps-saying-his-average-donation-is-27-but-it-really-isnt/?utm_term=.10331263083a.

123. Elsewhere, I have likened the DNC and its conduct to that of a "political Ponzi scheme": "it was purporting to be 'selling' a fair primary process but in reality was serving as a front for the Hillary Clinton campaign. People lost well over $200 million as a result." *See* Ian Mason, "Exclusive: Attorney For Bernie Donor Class Action Calls DNC 'The Ultimate Ponzi Scheme,'" Breitbart (June 20, 2017) (quoting Jared H. Beck), http://www.breitbart.com/big-government/2017/06/20/exclusive-attorney-for-bernie-donor-class-action-against-dnc-talks-with-breitbart-news.

124. Elizabeth Beck, "DNC Fraud Class Action Lawsuit," JamPAC (June 21, 2016), http://jampac.us/2016/06/21/dnc-fraud-class-action-lawsuit/.

      Upon filing the lawsuit, we established a dedicated Facebook page. *See* https://www.facebook.com/DNCfraudlawsuit/ (last visited Oct. 12, 2017). To the best of my knowledge, it is the first Facebook page established for a civil lawsuit that has generated a significant amount of online activity. As of today, the page has over 59,000 "likes" and its posts have been shared thousands of times, often generating hundreds of comments on the page.

125. At one point, our firm's email service became overloaded and stopped working.

126. A sample of emails follows:

6 donations to the Bernie Sanders campaign since the primaries, totaling $50. I don't have much to give, actually I don't have anything to give. I've been between addresses since leaving my job to care for my mother a year ago. I'm preparing my truck to live in with my two dogs. . . As I saw it, I couldn't afford not to support Bernie Sanders. He's the only candidate whom may actually help people like me. And he never had a chance. Thank you for trying to help correct this corrupt system. Please let me know what I can do, I haven't wholly sacrificed my hope just yet.

—T, "Homeless Student Defrauded by the DNC," email sent on July 24, 2016

Hi!

My name is M . . . I am a Social Worker who full heartedly saw the need for a President like Bernie Sander, not only to give my children a better world to grow up in but also because he addresses the Social needs that I encounter in my work daily working with mentally ill individualls, elderly, those on Social Security, the homeless and so many more.

I not only supported Bernie by getting others (including those across party lines and undecided) to agree to vote for Bernie Sanders, but also supported him with time and money . . . I see the importance in his movement but am heavy hearted at the deception and coruption which I have seen amplified over the last 6 months; but now know started just after he announced that he was running thanks to WikiLeaks. I would like to be a class representative for the lawsuit as I am a CURRENT member of the Democratic Party and have decided to remain intact as a member. I fully believe that the DNC Had/has an obligation to its members to run a fair and unbiased election and they have betrayed the member's trust to further one candidate over another. THIS MUST BE RECTIFIED! There needs to be consequences for their actions and justice needs to be served. I know many other people who have also donated to Bernie Sanders (both time and money) and feel that we deserve to see the DNC follow their rules and bylaws and give us a fair opportunity to allow the candidate of the PEOPLE'S choosing to be elected, whether this happens now or in future elections is to be seen but it needs to happen.

Thank you for putting together this law suit against DWS & the DNC. Please let me know what items are needed to prove that the DNC's

Behavior cause me financial loss as this can be proved with e-mails or bank/credit card statements.

—M, "Class representative," email sent on July 30, 2016

I have donated several times to Bernie Sanders campaign. My name is B. I would like to be added to the DNC lawsuit.

—Dr. B, email sent on August 2, 2016

I am a former DNC donor as well as a Bernie donor.

—Dr. M, "Want to join class," email sent on July 1, 2016

I would like to join this class action. I donated the legal maximum to an ind. Campaign (2700).

—D, "Dnc class action," email sent on August 30, 2016

Hello, I donated the maximum of $2,700 to the Bernie campaign, and I'd be interested in joining your class action.

—T, "DNC Lawsuit," email sent on August 1, 2016

Hi! Thank you so much for your lawsuit on behalf of us Bernie supporters. It was devastating to learn that the thousands of dollars and unpaid hours I sacrificed to campaign for Bernie Sanders was nothing more than a rigged carnival game with a predetermined outcome.

I am an attorney (named a Super Lawyer in 2016) . . .

—K, "Bernie Sanders - Class-Action Lawsuit - Request for inclusion," email sent June 24, 2016

Hello.

I am an attorney from Indiana . . . I have been volunteering for and supporting Bernie Sanders presidential run since he announced last year. . . . When I have had the ability, I have donated to his campaign through ActBlue and I have left a "tip" to ActBlue a couple of times . . . before the election fraud become apparent.

First, is there anything I can do to help? Second, are you attempting to make a nation-wide class? If so, I would be glad to participate. If I can be of assistance in another way, please let me know. I have a busy schedule, but I am dedicated to my ideals and one of those is actual democracy.

Thank you for taking this on. I am from a small town and have a small town general practice . . . election law (as well as class action suits) are outside my usual domain. I would have had no idea where to even begin!

Question . . . I saw that you are planning to use the leaks from Guccifer 2.0 . . . how do you plan to authenticate these pieces of evidence? That is the big hurdle I see, but I really hope you have a way to overcome it!

—S, "Indiana Attorney," email sent on July 1, 2016

Please add me to the lawsuit against the dnc. Further, I am an attorney in Colorado, if I can ever be of assistance. Thanks! —K, "Add" email sent July 24, 2016.

127. We have litigated a number of class actions with Tony and Cullin.

128. Like all class actions litigated by our firm, the suit against the DNC is being pursued on a "contingency" ("No win, No fee") basis. In addition, the lawyers are advancing all the costs of the suit out of their own funds.

129. *See, e.g.,* Elizabeth Vos, "BREAKING: DNC Fraud Lawsuit Dismissed," *Disobedient Media* (Aug. 25, 2017), https://disobedient media.com/2017/08/breaking-dnc-fraud-lawsuit-dismissed/.

130. The judicial district encompasses Wasserman Schultz's congressional district.

131. Three of the original 120 named plaintiffs were national Sanders delegates, who were dropped from the caption after they were threatened with de-credentialing—which would have made them ineligible to attend the Democratic National Convention and cast their votes for Sanders—unless they ceased participating in the lawsuit. *See* Amended Complaint, *Wilding*, Case No. 16-cv-61511-WJZ (filed July 13, 2016), http://jampac. us/wp-content/uploads/2016/07/8-D.E.-8-Amd-Complaint-7-13-16.pdf.

132. *See* Complaint, *Wilding*, Case No. 16-cv-61511-WJZ (filed June 28, 2016), http://jampac.us/wp-content/uploads/2016/06/1-CLASS-ACTION -COMPLAINT-6-28-16.pdf.

The Complaint alleges these claims on behalf of three distinct proposed classes: (1) donors to the Sanders campaign; (2) donors to the DNC; and (3) members of the Democratic Party. The first five claims pertain to the DNC's failure to live up to the obligation of neutrality. The sixth claim, for negligence, concerns the DNC's failure to safeguard the data of its own donors (among the items published by Guccifer 2.0 were spreadsheets containing the private information of donors). *See Krottner v. Starbucks Corp.* 628 F.3d 1139 (9th Cir. 2010) (recognizing claim against a corporation based on the failure to protect personal data).

133. http://jampac.us/wp-content/uploads/2016/06/1-1-EXHIBIT-1-TO-CLASS-ACTION-COMPLAINT.pdf.

134. *See* Paul Rosenberg, "A look at the year's top 10 bombshell news stories that barely made the news," *Monterey County Weekly* (Oct. 5, 2017), http://www.montereycountyweekly.com/news/cover/a-look-at-the-year-s-top-bombshell-news-stories/article_758fedb8-a944-11e7-866b-ff39834ea8d2.html (featuring the DNC fraud lawsuit as one of "the top 10 censored stories of the year").

However, the lawsuit *has* received intense attention at all stages from non-mainstream media, including a series of pieces by Michael Sainato published in the *Observer* (formerly, the *New York Observer*). *See, e.g.*, Michael Sainato, "Debbie Wasserman Schultz Served Class Action Lawsuit for Rigging Primaries," *Observer* (June 30, 2016), http://observer.com/2016/06/debbie-wasserman-schultz-served-class-action-lawsuit-for-rigging-primaries/.

Other journalists to have covered the DNC lawsuit include Jordan Chariton of *The Young Turks* network, Lee Camp of *Russia Today*, Ian Mason of Breitbart, Alex Jones and Owen Shroyer of *InfoWars*, Liz Wheeler of One America News Network, William Craddick and Elizabeth Vos of *Disobedient Media*, H.A. Goodman, Zach Haller, Caitlin Johnstone, and Stefan Molyneux. *See, e.g.*, Jordan Chariton, "DNC Lawsuit: Digging Into Plaintiffs' Legal Argument," (interview with Jared Beck), TYT Politics (May 8, 2017), https://www.youtube.com/watch?v=uoVQy0MGHb0 ; Lee Camp, "The Lawyer Bringing The Lawsuit Against The DNC Speaks Out," *Redacted Tonight* (interview with Jared Beck), May 18, 2017, https://www.youtube.com/watch?v=F-B72rzgCxAQ ; Ian Mason, "Exclusive: Attorney For Bernie Donor Class Action Calls DNC 'The Ultimate Ponzi Scheme,'" Breitbart (June 20, 2017), http://www.breitbart.com/big-government/2017/06/20/exclusive-attorney-for-bernie-donor-class-action-against-dnc-talks-with-breitbart

-news/ ; Alex Jones, "Elizabeth Beck, The Lawyer Who Exposed Election Theft By Hillary Tells All," *Info Wars* (interview with Elizabeth Beck), Aug. 29, 2017, https://www.youtube.com/watch?v=1dmGeZd31LA ; Owen Shroyer, "DNC Fraud Lawsuit Counsel Speaks Out On Lawsuit, Seth Rich" (interview with Jared Beck), *Info Wars* (June 23, 2017, https://www.youtube.com/watch?v=Sz_dRxwEmDM&t=5s; Liz Wheeler, "This guy is suing the DNC for rigging the primary!," One America News Network (My 24, 2017), https://www.youtube.com/watch?v=Xl_6Mppncxo ; Elizabeth Vos, "Breaking: DNC Lawsuit Attorneys File Notice Of Appeal," https://disobedientmedia.com/2017/09/breaking-dnc-lawsuit-attorneys-file-notice-of-appeal/ ; H.A. Goodman, "DNC Lawsuit Attorney Jared Beck Expose Debbie Wasserman Schultz" (interview with Jared Beck), https://www.youtube.com/watch?v=ve2rMl7scC8&t=2472s; Zach Haller, "7 Jaw-Dropping Revelations From Hearings on the Motion to Dismiss the DNC Fraud Lawsuit," (Apr. 30, 2017), https://medium.com/@zachhaller/7-jaw-dropping-revelations-from-hearings-on-the-motion-to-dismiss-the-dnc-fraud-lawsuit-bee1723b713f ; Caitlin Johnstone, "The DNC Fraud Lawsuit Has Been Dismissed. Dismiss The Democratic Party," (Aug. 25, 2017), https://medium.com/@caityjohnstone/the-dnc-fraud-lawsuit-has-been-dismissed-dismiss-the-democratic-party-7413e4de0b43 ; Stefan Molyneux, "DNC Fraud: Bernie Sanders Donors File Lawsuit," (interview with Jared Beck) (Aug. 23, 2016), available at https://www.youtube.com/watch?v=2ktseCdBnyg.

135. For exceptions, see Eric DuVall, "Bernie Sanders supporters sue Debbie Wasserman Schultz, DNC for 'fraud,'" UPI (June 30, 2016), https://www.upi.com/Top_News/US/2016/06/30/Bernie-Sanders-supporters-sue-Debbie-Wasserman-Schultz-DNC-for-fraud/7411467293953/ ; Jacob Gersham, "DNC Seeks Dismissal of Lawsuit Alleging Donor Deception," *Wall Street Journal* (July 25, 2016), https://blogs.wsj.com/law/2016/07/25/dnc-seeks-dismissal-of-lawsuit-alleging-donor-deception/.

136. *See* https://www.facebook.com/DNCfraudlawsuit/?pnref=lhc ; https://twitter.com/dncfraudlawsuit?lang=en ; https://twitter.com/JaredBeck ; https://twitter.com/eleebeck ; https://www.facebook.com/jaredbeck ; https://www.facebook.com/elizabethbeck.

137. "The traditional manner of providing notice" of a lawsuit "is 'personal service'—in hand delivery of the summons to the defendant by a sheriff,

marshal or someone similarly authorized by law. . . . Personal service remains a sufficient, and in some ways, the preferred form of notice giving." Jack H. Friedenthal, Mary Kay Kane & Arthur R. Miller, *Civil Procedure*, 170 § 3.20 (West Publishing Co., 2d ed. 1993).

138. *See* Ricardo O. Villalba, "Serving at the DNC," DNC Fraud Lawsuit Facebook page, (July 1, 2016), https://www.facebook.com/DNC fraudlawsuit/videos/617773348385477/.

Ricardo O. Villalba, "Serving the Lawsuit at the DNC live," DNC Fraud Lawsuit Facebook page, (July 1 , 2016), https://www.facebook. com/DNCfraudlawsuit/videos/617778231718322/.

As of the time of writing, video of the live-stream has been viewed over 350,000 times on Facebook and over 625,000 times on YouTube. *See* "YOU GOT SERVED!" DNC and Debbie Wasserman Schultz get served in Wilding class action, JamPAC YouTube page (July 3, 2016), https://www.youtube.com/watch?v=D3FMgZruOXE (last visited Oct. 14, 2017). I am not aware of any other service of process event having received a comparable degree of attention.

139. These comments are still visible on Villalba, "Serving the Lawsuit at the DNC live," DNC Fraud Lawsuit Facebook page, (July 1 , 2016), at https://www.facebook.com/DNCfraudlawsuit/videos/617778231718322/.

140. *See* Defendant's Memorandum of Law In Support Of Defendants' Motion To Dismiss For Insufficient Service Of Process Or, In The Alternative, Extend Time To Answer Or Respond To Complaint in *Wilding* (filed July 22, 2016), http://jampac.us/wp-content/uploads/2016/07/11-D.E.-11-Memo-ISO-Ds-MTD-Complaint-7-22-16.pdf.

141. *See* Declaration Of Rebecca C. Herries In Support Of Defendants' Motion To Dismiss For Insufficient Service Of Process Or, In The Alternative, Extend Time To Answer Or Respond To Complaint in *Wilding* (filed July 22, 2016), http://jampac.us/wp-content/uploads/2016/07/10-D.E.-10-Declaration-of-R.-Herries-7-22-16.pdf.

142. One might ask why we didn't try to re-serve the lawsuit at the DNC headquarters. But the issue isn't as simple as it might seem at first. For one, the DNC was clearly a tightly secured facility, and there was no guarantee we would get an "authorized" person on the next attempt. Furthermore, once we received the Rebecca Herries affidavit, we felt that we had already caught the DNC in bad faith conduct. Either Herries was

being deceptive to Shawn when she gave him every impression that she had been sent down precisely to receive the legal papers without giving any indication that the "right" person was not in the office at the time, or her affidavit was untruthfully swearing, under penalty of perjury, that she was never "authorized" to the receive the papers. An effective part of any litigation strategy involves holding your opponent to the consequences of their representations before the court, and, given the stakes, we wanted to set the tone from the very onset.

143. *See* Joseph Morton, "27-year-old Creighton grad, DNC staffer shot dead in D.C. wanted 'to try to save the world,'" *Omaha World-Herald* (July 13, 2016), http://www.omaha.com/news/crime/year-old -creighton-grad-dnc-staffer-shot-dead-in-d/article_023644eb-87b4-5c36 -be7b-3edf96d02ebe.html.

144. *See, e.g.*, Emily Zanotti, "Still No Clues in Murder of DNC's Seth Rich, As Conspiracy Theories Thicken," *Heat Street* (July 29, 2016), https://web.archive.org/web/20170311045247/https://heatst.com/pol itics/still-no-clues-in-murder-of-dncs-seth-rich-as-conspiracy-theories -thicken//.

145. *See* William Craddick, "Questions Linger About Seth Rich Murder Details," *Disobedient Media* (June 7, 2017), https://disobedientmedia. com/2017/06/questions-linger-about-seth-rich-murder-details/; Michael Yoder, "My 2 cents: Murder of Seth Rich remains unsolved," *Reading Eagle* (May 31, 2017), http://www.readingeagle.com/life/article /my-2-cents-murder-of-seth-rich-remains-unsolved; Cassandra Fairbanks, "Audio: Seymour Hersh States Seth Rich Was WikiLeaks Source," Big League Politics (Aug. 1, 2017), https://bigleaguepolitics.com/audio -seymour-hersh-states-seth-rich-wikileaks-source/.

146. Approximately two months later, Elizabeth would receive an email from the D.C. Department of Forensic Sciences and Office of the Chief Medical Examiner stating that Shawn Lucas's death was accidental and caused by "[c]ombined adverse effects of fentanyl, cyclobenzaprine, and mitragynine." *See* email from LaShon Beamon to Elizabeth Lee Beck dated Nov. 1, 2016, available at http://jampac.us/wp-content/ uploads/2017/05/11-10-16.pdf.

   "Fentanyl is a strong opioid pain medication, sometimes used as part of anaesthesia. Cyclobenzaprine is a muscle relaxant, while mitradynine is a substance found in Kratom." Elizabeth Vos, "DNC Lawsuit Exposes Corruption, Data Breaches, Raises Questions About Death Of Shawn Lucas," *Disobedient Media* (May 30, 2017), https://disobedientmedia. com/2017/05/dnc-lawsuit-exposes-corruption-data-breaches-raises-questions-about-death-of-shawn-lucas/.

147. Plaintiffs' Response In Opposition To The Defendants' Motion To Dismiss And Alternative Motion To Extend Time Ex. 1 in *Wilding* (filed Aug. 5, 2016), http://jampac.us/wp-content/uploads/2016/08/ 24-1-D.E.-24-1-Exh-1-8-5-16.pdf.

148. Plaintiffs' Response In Opposition To The Defendants' Motion To Dismiss And Alternative Motion To Extend Time in *Wilding* (filed Aug. 5, 2016), http://jampac.us/wp-content/uploads/2016/08/24-D.E.-24-Ps-Opp-to-Ds-MTD-8-5-16.pdf.

149. Order Setting Evidentiary Hearing in *Wilding* (filed Aug. 10, 2016), http://jampac.us/wp-content/uploads/2016/08/25-D.E.-25-Order -Setting-Evidentiary-Hrg-8-10-16.pdf.

150. *See id.*

151. Authentication is the process by which any proffered evidence is deemed genuine—that is, in the case of a video, shown to be a true and accurate depiction of what it purports to show. Testimony by a witness with knowledge about the item of evidence being proffered is one of the chief vehicles for authentication. *See* Fed. R. Evid. 901(b)(1).

152. *See* https://wikileaks.org/dnc-emails/.

153. In addition to having worked for large defense and plaintiffs' firms, Cullin spent years as a Florida state public defender in Broward County.

154. *See* Appendix II.

155. *Id.* at 200-201.

156. *See id.* at 213-214.

157. In particular, while Herries testified in her declaration that the two men she met in the lobby simply "handed me papers and left," the video actually shows Shawn introducing himself, shaking Herries's hand, confirming that she works for the DNC, then telling her, "[T]his is going to be a service to the DNC, and this is for Debbie Wasserman Schultz. You guys have been served! Thank you so much. We'll see you in Court." *Compare* Declaration Of Rebecca Herries In Support Of Defendants' Motion To Dismiss For Insufficient Service Of Process

Or, In The Alternative, Extend Time To Answer Or Respond To Complaint in *Wilding* (filed July 22, 2016), available at http://jampac.us/wp-content/uploads/2016/07/10-D.E.-10-Declaration-of-R.-Herries-7-22-16.pdf; *with* "YOU GOT SERVED! DNC and Debbie Wasserman Schultz get served in Wilding class action, JamPAC YouTube page (Jul. 3, 2016) 11:58-12:15 at https://www.youtube.com/watch?v=D3FMgZruOXE.

158. At one point, Spiva asserted in response to the Court's suggestion that Herries's title of "special assistant to the CEO" might be "somewhat misleading" that "in Washington D.C. there are thousands of special assistants." *See* Appendix II at 213-214.

159. *See* Plaintiffs' Exhibit 8—May 11, 2016 email from Rebecca Herries to HQStaff_D@dnc.org, Intern_D@dnc.org in *Wilding* (filed Aug. 19, 2016), available at http://jampac.us/wp-content/uploads/2016/08/33-5-D.E.-33-5-Exh-8-8-19-16.pdf.

Relying on the theory that WikiLeaks had published emails obtained by Russian hackers, Spiva objected to the plaintiffs' introduction of the email on the basis that it was "stolen." *See* August 23. 2016 transcript at 10. Judge Zloch reserved ruling on this issue at the hearing and ultimately never reached it.

160. *See* Appendix II.

161. *See* Patrick Healy & Jonathan Martin, "Democrats Make Hillary Clinton a Historic Nominee," *New York Times* (July 26, 2016), https://www.nytimes.com/2016/07/27/us/politics/dnc-speakers-sanders-clinton.html.

162. *See* Victor Morton, "Wasserman Schultz immediately joins Clinton campaign after resignation," *Washington Times* (July 24, 2016), http://www.washingtontimes.com/news/2016/jul/24/debbie-wasserman-schultz-immediately-joins-hillary/.

163. Ultimately, Judge Zloch ordered the plaintiffs to re-serve the defendants. In his order, the judge admonished the DNC about "subsequent attempts by Plaintiffs to effect service. No evidence at the Hearing explains Ms. Herries's conduct; however, the Court hereby advises Defendant DNC that it will not tolerate the conduct in which Defendant DNC engaged in this instance." Order filed Aug. 30 2016 in *Wilding*, available at http://jampac.us/wp-content/uploads/2016/08/40-D.E.-40-Order-Granting-Ds-Mtn-to-Quash-Service-8-30-16.pdf.

164. Defendants' Motion To Dismiss Plaintiffs' First Amended Complaint And Memorandum Of Law In Support, *Wilding* (filed Sept. 21, 2016), at http://jampac.us/wp-content/uploads/2016/09/44-D.E.-44-Ds-MTD-FAC-9-21-16.pdf.

165. *See* Defendants' Motion To Dismiss Plaintiffs' First Amended Complaint And Memorandum Of Law In Support, at 6. A clear example of a court rejecting this type of claim is *Berg v. Obama*, 574 F. Supp. 2d 509, 529 (E.D. Pa. 2008), where the court dismissed a donor's claim against the DNC and President Obama for failing to live up to promises in the 2008 Democratic National Platform.

   For more on Bush's ill-fated promise, see Opinion, "The Problem With 'Read My Lips,'" *New York Times* (Oct. 15, 1992), http://www.nytimes.com/1992/10/15/opinion/the-problem-with-read-my-lips.html ; Michael Levenson, "Former president Bush honored for '90 tax hikes," *Boston Globe* (May 4, 2014), https://www.bostonglobe.com/metro/2014/05/04/former-president-george-bush-honored-for-breaking-new-taxes-pledge/gTMnk2hGmIbx4dlPsx8zTM/story.html.

166. *See* Transcript of Hearing held April 25, 2017 in *Wilding* at 34, at http://jampac.us/wp-content/uploads/2016/07/042517cw2.pdf.

167. April 25, 2017 Transcript at 35-37 (emphasis added). *See* Appendix I.

168. *Id.* at 132.

169. *See id.* at 169-170.

170. *Id.* at 125.

171. *Id.* at 114.

172. Mind you, the hearing was being conducted three months into the Trump administration.

173. *Id.* at 7.

174. The entire hearing lasted approximately three hours. For discussion of key points, see Zach Haller, "7 Jaw-Dropping Revelations From Hearings on the Motion to Dismiss the DNC Fraud Lawsuit," *Medium* (Apr. 30, 2017), at https://medium.com/@zachhaller/7-jaw-dropping-revelations-from-hearings-on-the-motion-to-dismiss-the-dnc-fraud-lawsuit-bee1723b713f ; *see also* Brook Hines, "DNC Lawsuit: 'You're Morons To Believe Us'—Part 1 Of 3" (May 1, 2017), *Florida Squeeze*, https://thefloridasqueeze.com/2017/05/01/dnc-lawsuit-youre-morons-to-believe-us-part-1-of-3/ ; Michael Sainato, "DNC Lawyers Argue DNC Has Right

to Pick Candidates in Back Rooms," *New York Observer* (May 1, 2017), http://observer.com/2017/05/dnc-lawsuit-presidential-primaries-bernie-sanders-supporters/.

175. *Id.* at 107.

176. *See id.* at 108-09.

177. *Id.* at 109.

ACT I: STORIES WITH NO FINGERPRINTS

178. *See* Dan Merica, "Bernie Sanders is running for president," CNN Politics (Apr. 30, 2015), http://www.cnn.com/2015/04/29/politics/bernie-sanders-announces-presidential-run/.

179. Available at https://wikileaks.org/podesta-emails/emailid/1120. The authenticity of the documents released by Guccifer 2.0 and WikiLeaks has never been disputed. Indeed, the Russian hacking narrative promoted by the Hillary Clinton campaign and Democratic Party following the election *depends* on the authenticity of these documents, *i.e.*, insofar as they claim that Russian actors wrongfully obtained these internal files and then released them to the public. And some, including John Podesta, have publicly confessed to the authenticity of their emails as published by WikiLeaks. *See, e.g.*, Amy Chozick, "John Podesta Says Russian Spies Hacked His Emails to Sway Election," *New York Times* (Oct. 11, 2016), at https://www.nytimes.com/2016/10/12/us/politics/hillary-clinton-emails-wikileaks.html.

180. The Charter and Bylaws are attached as Appendix III.

181. Ben Norton, "How the Hillary Clinton campaign deliberately 'elevated' Donald Trump with its 'pied piper' strategy," *Salon* (Nov. 9, 2016), http://www.salon.com/2016/11/09/the-hillary-clinton-campaign-intentionally-created-donald-trump-with-its-pied-piper-strategy/.

182. This document was released by Guccifer 2.0 to the public on June 15, 2016, and the original can be accessed at https://guccifer2.wordpress.com/2016/06/15/dnc/.

183. Nor, for that matter, do the names of any other potential Democratic candidates other than Clinton, including Joe Biden, Lincoln Chaffee, Martin O'Malley, Elizabeth Warren, and Jim Webb—each of whom either formally entered the race or were reported to be considering entering at some point.

184. Ben H. Bagdikian, *The New Media Monopoly,* 20th ed. (Beacon Press, 2004).

185. *Id.* at 2.

186. Bagdikian identifies these moguls as the heads of Time Warner, Disney, Rupert Murdoch's News Corporation, Viacom, and Bertelsmann. *Id.* at 30-50. A more recent assessment of the astonishing concentration of the media industry states that "more than 90 percent of the media is owned by just six companies: Viacom, News Corporation, Comcast, CBS, Time Warner and Disney." Michael Corcoran, "Twenty Years of Media Consolidation Has Not Been Good For Our Democracy," Truthout (Feb. 11, 2016), http://www.truth-out.org/news/item/34789-democracy-in-peril-twenty-years-of-media-consolidation-under-the-telecommunications-act.

187. Other examples discussed by Bagdikian include the absence of legitimate business reporting that could have detected the accounting frauds being perpetrated at companies such as Enron, Tyco, and WorldCom in the years before those companies collapsed, and, less recently, the American mainstream media's failure to accurately report on the Vietnam War, U.S.-backed coups in Guatemala and Chile, as well as American support of Indonesia's brutal suppression in East Timor.

188. "Bernie Sanders confirms presidential run and damns America's inequities," *The Guardian* (Apr. 29, 2015), https://www.theguardian.com/us-news/2015/apr/30/bernie-sanders-confirms-presidential-run-and-damns-americas-inequities (quoting Bernie Sanders).

189. Sanders in interview with Katie Couric (June 2, 2015), transcript available at https://www.reddit.com/r/BernieSpeaks/wiki/bernie-katie-couric-2015-0602.

190. Thomas E. Patterson, "Pre-Primary News Coverage of the 2016 Presidential Race: Trump's Rise, Sanders' Emergence, Clinton's Struggle," (June 2016), https://shorensteincenter.org/wp-content/uploads/2016/06/Pre-Primary-News-Coverage-Trump-Sanders-Clinton-2016.pdf.

191. *Id.* at 3.

192. *Id.*

193. *Id.*

194. The eight outlets studied are CBS, Fox, the *Los Angeles Times,* NBC, the *New York Times, USA Today,* the *Wall Street Journal,* and the *Washington Post. Id.* at 4.

195. *Id.* at 11-12 (footnotes omitted).

196. Bagdikian at 26, 49.

197. Ed O'Keefe & John Wagner, "100,000 people have come to recent Bernie Sanders rallies. How does he do it?" *Washington Post* (Aug. 11, 2015), https://www.washingtonpost.com/politics/how-does-bernie-sanders-draw-huge-crowds-to-see-him/2015/08/11/4ae018f8-3fde-11e5-8d45-d815146f81fa_story.html?utm_term=.c91c1515febe. *See also* Alex Seitz-Wald, "Bernie Sanders draws biggest crowd of any 2016 candidate yet," MSNBC (July 22, 2015), (reporting crowd of nearly 10,000 at a Sanders rally in Wisconsin), http://www.msnbc.com/msnbc/bernie-sanders-draws-biggest-crowd-any-2016-candidate-yet.

198. Tamara Keith on *Morning Edition*, "Campaign Mystery: Who Don't Bernie Sanders' Big Rallies Lead to Big Wins?," NPR (April 26, 2016), http://www.npr.org/2016/04/26/475681237/campaign-mystery-why-dont-bernie-sanders-big-rallies-lead-to-big-wins.

199. The NPR piece ruminates that Sanders failed to attain "big wins" due to one or more of the following factors: (1) the visible enthusiasm of his supporters was an "optical illusion"; (2) Sanders's enormous rallies were actually staged to look more crowded than they actually were; (3) Sanders's supporters were akin to fans of the Grateful Dead and Phish and not seriously representative of the electorate; and (4) Sanders's support base was simply not a "winning coalition." *See id.*

200. Gregory Krieg, "These Charts Show Just How Impressive Bernie Sanders' Fundraising Haul Is," *Mic* (Oct. 1, 2015), https://mic.com/articles/126147/these-charts-show-just-how-impressive-bernie-sanders-fundraising-haul-is#.ytCivz9DY.

201. *See e.g.*, Patrick Healy, "Bernie Sanders's Campaign, Hitting Fund-Raising Milestone, Broadens Focus," *New York Times* (Oct. 1, 2015) at https://www.nytimes.com/2015/10/02/us/politics/bernie-sanders-election-campaign.html?hp&action=click&pgtype=Homepage&module=photo-spot-region&region=top-news&WT.nav=top-news.

Meanwhile, the mainstream media closely tracked Hillary Clinton's fundraising activities throughout summer of 2015. *See, e.g.*, Gabriel Debenedetti, "Exclusive: Hillary's jam-packed fundraising schedule," *Politico* (June 2, 2015), at http://www.politico.com/story/2015/06/exclusive-hillary-clintons-jam-packed-fundraising-schedule-118562; Rich Pearson, "Bull Ruthhart & John Chase, Major donor to Obama, Emanuel to host Hillary Clinton fundraiser in Chicago," *Chicago Tribune* (July 21, 2015), at http://www.chicagotribune.com/news/local/politics/ct-hillary-clinton-chicago-fundraiser-20150721-story.html.

202. Patterson, *supra*.

203. The term "Bernie Bro" was coined in an article appearing in *The Atlantic* on October 17, 2015. *See* Robinson Meyer, "Here Comes the Berniebro," *The Atlantic* (Oct. 17, 2015), at https://www.theatlantic.com/politics/archive/2015/10/here-comes-the-berniebro-bernie-sanders/411070/.

204. Glenn Greenwald, "The 'Bernie Bros' Narrative: a Cheap Campaign Tactic Masquerading as Journalism and Social Activism," *The Intercept* (Jan. 31, 2016), https://theintercept.com/2016/01/31/the-bernie-bros-narrative-a-cheap-false-campaign-tactic-masquerading-as-journalism-and-social-activism/.

205. *Id.*

206. Clinton's quest to become the first woman president was a central element of her campaign from the beginning, and, as such, rendered the mainstream media reticent to report on issues complicating her appeal to women voters. But three days after the New Hampshire primary, *Politico* did take note of her apparent "woman problem," noting that Sanders had received 53 percent of the female vote to Clinton's 46 percent, including an "astonishing" 82 percent of women under the age of 30. *See* "Hillary's Woman Problem," *Politico* (Feb. 12, 2016), at http://www.politico.com/magazine/story/2016/02/hillary-clinton-2016-woman-problem-213621.

207. *See* Greenwald, *supra*, note 37.

208. *Id.*

209. *See id.*; "Bernie Sanders supporters get a bad reputation online," BBC (Jan. 28, 2016), at http://www.bbc.com/news/blogs-trending-35422316.

    As it turns out, Nussbaum was characterizing all of Bernie Sanders's supporters based on a tweet she had received from @RepStevenSmith, a parody account pretending to be a fictitious "Tea Party Patriot" Congressman from Georgia. *See* Greenwald; "Bob Cusack, Fake congressman fools people on Twitter," *The Hill* (Feb. 25, 2014), at http://thehill.com/blogs/in-the-know/in-the-know/199111-fake-congressman-fools-people-on-twitter.

210. Sally Kohn, "Are accusations that Bernie Sanders is sexist fair?," CNN (Nov. 3, 2015), http://www.cnn.com/2015/11/03/opinions/kohn-bernie-sanders-sexism/index.html.

211. Annie Karni, "Clinton allies shout 'sexism' at Sanders," *Politico* (Oct. 20, 2016), https://www.politico.com/story/2015/10/hillary-clinton-sexism-bernie-sanders-215375.

212. *See* Robinson Meyer, "Here Comes the Berniebro," *The Atlantic* (Oct. 17, 2015), https://www.theatlantic.com/politics/archive/2015/10/here-comes-the-berniebro-bernie-sanders/411070/.

213. *See* Neil A. Lewis, "Man in the News: Bernard William Nussbaum; Litigator on a Tightrope," *New York Times* (Feb. 5, 1994), http://www.nytimes.com/1994/02/05/us/man-in-the-news-bernard-william-nussbaum-litigator-on-a-tightrope.html?pagewanted=all; "Paid Notice: Deaths NUSSBAUM, TOBY A.," *New York Times* (Jan. 5, 2006), http://www.nytimes.com/2006/01/05/classified/paid-notice-deaths-nussbaum-toby-a.html.

214. Thus, while Greenwald suggests that the cardinal sin of the Bernie Bro Myth is the mythmakers' failure to disclose that they were acting as Clinton operatives rather than journalists ("I see nothing wrong with journalists being vehemently devoted to a political candidate. But it's important to know what it is."), the problem is much more insidious than that. If the production of journalism is ungoverned by ethical constraints requiring journalists to disclose conflicts of interests or precluding them from serving as campaign operatives (whether disclosed or not), then it would seem that the very function of the free press—what Thomas Jefferson called "the only security of all" —is thereby jeopardized.

Curiously, Greenwald also omits discussion regarding the actual etymology of "Bernie Bro"—which, according to Wikipedia, was coined in the October 17, 2015 article in The Atlantic. *See* Bernie Bro, Wikipedia, https://en.wikipedia.org/wiki/Bernie_Bro (last visited Aug. 20, 2017).

At the time, Atlantic Media Company (*The Atlantic*'s publisher) was owned by David G. Bradley, a wealthy tycoon and Clinton donor. *See* Howard Kurtz, "*The Atlantic*'s Owner Ponies Up," *Washington Post* (Aug. 6, 2007), http://www.washingtonpost.com/wp-dyn/content/article/2007/08/05/AR2007080501576.html.

Nearly one year after injecting the Bernie Bro Myth into the public discourse, and while still under Bradley's control, *The Atlantic* endorsed Clinton in the general election—marking just the third presidential endorsement in the magazine's over 150-year history, and its first since it endorsed Lyndon B. Johnson in 1964 (the magazine also endorsed Abraham

Lincoln in 1860). *See* Kelsey Sutton, "*The Atlantic* endorses Hillary Clinton," *Politico* (Oct. 5, 2016) at http://www.politico.com/blogs/on-media/2016/10/the-atlantic-endorses-hillary-clinton-for-president-229209. Bradley has since sold a majority in *The Atlantic* to outspoken "Hillary Clinton supporter Laurene Powell Jobs. *See* Tim Graham, "Hillary's Biggest Fan Is Buying *The Atlantic* Magazine," Newsbusters (July 28, 2017) https://www.newsbusters.org/blogs/nb/tim-graham/2017/07/28/hillarys-biggest-fan-buying-atlantic-magazine.

215. Max Ehrenfreund, "Why Bernie Sanders' problems with black voters go much deeper than him just blaming the media," *Washington Post* (Sept. 14, 2015), https://www.washingtonpost.com/news/wonk/wp/2015/09/14/why-bernie-sanders-problems-with-black-voters-go-much-deeper-than-him-just-blaming-the-media/?utm_term=.04c3d7bdb932.

216. Maryalice Parks, "Bernie Sanders' Problem With Hispanics," ABC News (Aug. 4, 2015), http://abcnews.go.com/Politics/bernie-sanders-problem-hispanics/story?id=32871315.

217. https://wikileaks.org/podesta-emails/emailid/5205.

218. *See* Jim Newell, "Hacked Email Appears to Show That Donna Brazile Fed Clinton Campaign a Town Hall Question," *Slate* (Oct. 11, 2016), at http://www.slate.com/blogs/the_slatest/2016/10/11/donna_brazile_may_have_fed_clinton_campaign_town_hall_question.html.

219. https://wikileaks.org/podesta-emails/emailid/5205.

220. The question and Clinton's answer may be viewed here: https://www.youtube.com/watch?v=9FWYzMSKl2c. In her answer to Rick Jackson (who had been wrongly convicted of and served a 39-year sentence for murder), Clinton voiced support for elimination of the death penalty at the state level, a position in conflict with statements she made on the campaign trail in New Hampshire just months earlier. *See* Amy Chozick, "Hillary Clinton Comes Out Against Abolishing the Death Penalty," *New York Times* (Oct. 28, 2015), at https://www.nytimes.com/politics/first-draft/2015/10/28/hillary-clinton-comes-out-against-abolishing-the-death-penalty/?mcubz=0.

This was not the only instance of Brazile passing along debate questions to the Clinton camp. Eventually, she admitted to "shar[ing] potential town hall topics with the Clinton campaign," including one regarding lead poisoning in Flint, Michigan. *See* Adam Shaw, "Brazile admits she forwarded town hall questions to Clinton camp," Fox News (Mar. 17, 2017), http://www.foxnews.com/politics/2017/03/17/brazile-admits-forwarded-debate-questions-to-clinton-camp.html.

221. Brazile obtained the question from Roland Martin, a former CNN contributor who at the time was working with TV One, CNN's partner in producing the Ohio debate. *See* Hadas Gold, "New email shows Brazile may have had exact wording of proposed town hall question before CNN," *Politico* (Oct. 12, 2016), available at http://www.politico.com/blogs/on-media/2016/10/roland-martin-cnn-email-donna-brazile-wikileaks-229673.

222. In announcing its acceptance of Brazile's resignation from the network, CNN maintained that while it had never granted Brazile access to the questions, "[w]e are completely uncomfortable with what we have learned about her interactions with the Clinton campaign while she was a "CNN contributor[.]" *See* Michael M. Grynbaum, "CNN Parts Ways With Donna Brazile, a Hillary Clinton Supporter," *New York Times* (Oct. 31, 2016), at https://www.nytimes.com/2016/11/01/us/politics/donna-brazile-wikileaks-cnn.html?mcubz=0 (quoting CNN spokeswoman Lauren Pratapas).

CNN's attempt to disclaim any responsibility for the Brazile leak seems more than a little disingenuous given the longstanding relationship between CNN and Brazile's apparent source, Roland Martin, who generated the death penalty question on behalf of TV One—CNN's partner in cohosting the Ohio town hall debate. *See* Hadas Gold, "New email shows Brazile may have had exact wording of proposed town hall question before CNN," *Politico* (Oct. 12, 2016), at http://www.politico.com/blogs/on-media/2016/10/roland-martin-cnn-email-donna-brazile-wikileaks-229673. Indeed, the very narrative that Brazile "resigned" from CNN due to the WikiLeaks revelations (as presented in CNN's October 2015 announcement) is itself dubious, given that CNN had already severed ties with Brazile to allow her to become interim Chair of the DNC in the wake of Wasserman Schultz's resignation. *See* Hadas Gold, "CNN," ABC cut ties with Donna Brazile, freeing her up for DNC Job," *Politico* (July 24, 2016), at http://www.politico.com/blogs/on-media/2016/07/cnn-cuts-ties-with-donna-brazile-226096.

223. Callum Borchers, "Donna Brazile is totally not sorry for leaking debate questions to Hillary Clinton," *Washington Post* (Nov. 7, 2016), https://www.washingtonpost.com/news/the-fix/wp/2016/11/07/donna-brazile-is-totally-not-sorry-for-leaking-cnn-debate-questions-to-hillary-clinton/?utm_term=.5e031f9b47fa.

By March 2017, Brazile had changed her tune, writing in *Time* that "sending those emails was a mistake I will forever regret." Donna Brazile, "Russian DNC Narrative Played Out Exactly As They Hoped," *Time* (Mar. 17, 2017), http://time.com/4705515/donna-brazile-russia-emails-clinton/. However, Brazile's essay made it clear she was not sorry owing to any qualms about the legality or morality of leaking the questions; rather, she regretted that the emails were disseminated during the general election and fueled opposition against Clinton. *See id.* ("By stealing all the DNC's emails and then selectively releasing those few, the Russians made it look like I was in the tank for Secretary Clinton"). But even if one were to credit Brazile's claim that public disclosure of the emails was a result of Russian hacking, it is hard to deny that her complaint ultimately boils down to displeasure at being portrayed in an accurate light. Brazile's own public comments show she was always "in the tank for Secretary Clinton"—and avowedly so!

224. *Black's Law Dictionary* at 1347 (7th ed. 1999). In criminal proceedings, scienter is often equivalent to the *mens rea* (state of mind) of the defendant necessary to prove he or she committed a crime. In civil litigation, scienter is typically required as an element of torts based on fraudulent conduct.

225. *In re Intelligroup Securities Litigation*, 527 F. Supp. 2d 262, 283 (D.N.J. 2007); *see also United States v. Lynch*, 611 F.3d 932, 935 (8th Cir. 2010) ("[i]ntent is a state of mind difficult of proof by direct evidence. It may, however, be established by circumstantial evidence and by inferences reasonably to be drawn from the conduct of the defendant and from all the attendant circumstances in the light of human behavior and experience").

226. While illuminating, the WikiLeaks DNC email database is hardly a comprehensive library of DNC correspondence, as it is drawn from the accounts of just seven DNC employees over a seventeen-month time span. *See* https://wikileaks.org/dnc-emails/.

At 44,053 emails and 17,761 attachments, the collection is, in fact, comparatively miniscule when one weighs the typical document production in a major securities fraud class action. *See, e.g.*, Erin Coe, "JPMorgan Puts Up $388M To End MBS Class Action, Law360" (July 17, 2015), at https://www.law360.com/articles/680873/jpmorgan-puts-up-388m-to-end-mbs-class-action, ("Discovery by itself was a massive undertaking, involving the production of over 80 million pages of documents. . .").

227. CEO Amy Dacey, communications director Luis Miranda, and press secretary Mark Paustenbach. The email chain is available at https://wikileaks.org/dnc-emails/emailid/11508.

228. Id.

229. The email chain can be read at https://wikileaks.org/dnc-emails/emailid/10403.

230. Maria Cardona, "Why Sanders must take the high road," CNN (May 18, 2016), http://www.cnn.com/2016/05/18/opinions/unrest-at-dem-convention-must-not-happen-maria-cardona/.

231. Eric Wemple, "WikiLeaks emails: Pro-Clinton CNN political commentator pre-checked op-ed with DNC," *Washington Post* (July 24, 2016), https://www.washingtonpost.com/blogs/erik-wemple/wp/2016/07/24/wikileaks-emails-pro-clinton-cnn-political-commentator-pre-checked-op-ed-with-dnc/?postshare=2121469397273100&tid=ss_tw&utm_term=.131b17de6a13.

Ironically, Wemple's own paper was no stranger to seemingly going out of its way to bash Sanders at critical junctures during the campaign. During a sixteen-hour window encompassing the Flint, Michigan, debate of March 7, 2016, and its attendant coverage, the *Washington Post* ran sixteen negative stories on Sanders "[i]n what has to be some kind of record[.]" Adam Johnson, "*Washington Post* Ran 16 Negative Stories on Bernie Sanders in 16 Hours," Fairness & Accuracy in Reporting (FAIR) (Mar. 8, 2016), http://fair.org/home/washington-post-ran-16-negative-stories-on-bernie-sanders-in-16-hours/.

232. *See* Wemple (emphasis added). This was not the only example of "pre-clearance" revealed by WikiLeaks, which also published emails showing *Politico* reporter Ken Vogel to have violated his publication's policy by sending a complete draft of an article on the DNC's joint fundraising agreement with Hillary Clinton's campaign to the DNC for comments prior to publication. *See* Joe Concha, "*Politico* reporter sent story to Dem committee for prepubli-

cation review," *The Hill* (July 25, 2016), http://thehill.com/blogs/blog
-briefing-room/289150-politico-reporter-sent-story-to-dem-committee
-for-pre-publication.

233. *See* Cardona, note 56 *supra*.

234. *See* Doug Johnson Hatlem, "The Faux Fracas in Nevada: How a Reporter
Manufactured a Riot," *CounterPunch* (May 18, 2016), at https://www.
counterpunch.org/2016/05/18/the-faux-fracas-in-nevada-how-a-report-
ers-pack-of-lies-ran-riot-in-the-fact-averse-media/.

235. *See* "The Chair Thrown 'Round the World, Snopes," http://www.snopes.
com/did-sanders-supporters-throw-chairs-at-nevada-democratic-conven-
tion/ (last visited Aug. 22, 2017). This wasn't the only false narrative to
circulate about Bernie Sanders in relation to the Nevada caucus. *Time*,
for example, falsely reported that Sanders had chanted "English only"
in Nevada. *See* Alex Griswold, "*TIME* Magazine Now Falsely Claiming
Bernie Sanders *Himself* Yelled 'English Only,'" *Mediaite* (Feb. 24, 2016) at
https://www.mediaite.com/online/time-magazine-now-falsely-claiming-
bernie-sanders-himself-yelled-english-only/.

236. https://www.youtube.com/watch?v=R8w5wY_wT9M.

237. https://wikileaks.org/dnc-emails/emailid/9999.

238. Shane Goldmacher, "Bernie's legacy: One of the most valuable donor lists
ever," *Politico* (June 6, 2016), http://www.politico.com/story/2016/06/
bernie-sanders-actblue-donor-lists-223964.

239. *Id.*; "Summary for Bernie Sanders, Candidate Summary, 2016 Cycle:
Fundraising Details," OpenSecrets.org, https://www.opensecrets.org/
pres16/candidate.php?id=N00000528 (last visited Aug. 23, 2017).

240. *See, e.g.*, "Bernie bucks: Sanders smashes Obama record with $33mn
from individual donors," RT (Jan. 3, 2016), at https://www.rt.com/us-
a/327801-sanders-record-individual-donors/; Tessa Berenson, "Bernie
Sanders Breaks Fundraising Record," *Time* (Dec. 21, 2015), at http://
time.com/4157904/bernie-sanders-fundraising-donations-record/.

241. Josep M. Colomer, "The electoral college is a medieval relic. Only the
U.S. still has one," *Washington Post* (Dec. 11, 2016), https://www.wash
ingtonpost.com/news/monkey-cage/wp/2016/12/11/the-electoral-college
-is-a-medieval-relic-only-the-u-s-still-has-one/?utm_term=.af52cf5c6e47.

242. *Encyclopedia Britannica*, s.v. "Comitia Centuriata," https://www.britan-
nica.com/topic/Comitia-Centuriata.

243. Hannah Arendt, "Philosophy and Politics," *Social Research* 57, no. 1 (Spring 1990) at 94, https://zetesisproject.files.wordpress.com/2015/05/arendt-phi-and-politics.pdf.

244. *Id.* at 94.

ACT II: A BANKRUPT INSTITUTION

245. Charter at Art. 3, § 1.

246. Charter at Art. 1, § 4.

247. *Id.* at Art. 1, § 7.

248. *Id.* at Art. 2, § 4.

249. *Id.* at Art. 8, § 3.

250. Bylaws at Art. 2, §11(a).

251. *Id.* at Art. 2, §11(b)(i).

252. *Id.* at Art. 2, § 11(b)(ii).

253. Lisa Jane Disch, *Tyranny of the Two-Party System* (Columbia University Press, 2002).

254. *See* Disch at 4.

255. *Id.*

256. *See id.* at 4-5.

257. *Id.* at 34.

258. *See id.* at 35.

259. *See id.* at 34 (discussing James Madison's "architecture for a system that was to frustrate 'communication and concert' of the people, to insulate representatives against the vagaries of public opinion, and to disperse popular majorities" as set forth in *Federalist* no. 10).

260. *Id.* at 35 (emphasis in original).

261. *Id.* at 35-37.

262. "Fusion," also known as "cross-endorsement" or "multiple party nomination," is an electoral practice whereby two or more parties are allowed to run a single candidate on multiple party lines. Until the mid-1890s, when the practice was outlawed in most states, fusion enabled third parties to play a vital role in U.S. elections by engaging in strategic nominations that could either spoil the chances of major party candidates or, alternatively, tip the balance of power in their favor. *See* Dietsch at 12-13.

263. *Id.* at 45.

264. *Id.* (quoting Peter H. Argersinger, *The Limits of Agrarian Radicalism: Western Populism and American Politics*, 136 (Lawrence: UP of Kansas, 1995)). Before the adoption of the modern-day "Australian ballot," where state the prints a single ballot listing the official candidates for each office, voters would typically drop filled-out ballots printed by partisan newspapers into a box.

265. Argersinger at 136.

266. Disch at 55.

267. Detroit Evening News (Mar. 20, 1895) (quoted in Disch at 55-56).

268. Theresa Amato, "The two party ballot suppresses third party change," *The Harvard Law Record* (Dec. 4, 2009), http://hlrecord.org/2009/12/the-two-party-ballot-suppresses-third-party-change/.

269. Walter Dean Burnham, "The Changing Shape of the American Voting Universe," *American Political Science Review* 59 (1965): 23-26 (cited in Disch at 44 n.63).

270. Drew Desilver, "US trails most developed countries in voter turnout," Pew Research Center (May 15, 2017), http://www.pewresearch.org/fact-tank/2017/05/15/u-s-voter-turnout-trails-most-developed-countries/.

    According to the Pew Research Center, approximately 55.7% of the U.S. voting-age population voted in the 2016 presidential election. This compares to voting rates of 87.2%, 79%, 66.1%, and 62.1% in recent elections in Belgium, Australia, Germany, and Canada, respectively.

271. *See* Michael D. Regan, "Why is voter turnout so low in the U.S.?," *PBS Newshour* (Nov. 6, 2016), at http://www.pbs.org/newshour/updates/voter-turnout-united-states/ ; Voter Turnout in Presidential Elections: 1828-2012, The American Presidency Project at the University of California, Santa Barbara, http://www.presidency.ucsb.edu/data/turnout.php (last visited Aug. 30, 2017).

272. *See* Gregory Wallace, "Voter turnout at 20-year low in 2016," CNN, http://www.cnn.com/2016/11/11/politics/popular-vote-turnout-2016/index.html.

273. *See generally* Walter Dean Burnham, "Party Systems and the Political Process (1967), "collected in Walter Dean Burnam, *The Current Crisis in American Politics* (Oxford University Press, 1982).

274. *Id.* at 92-93.

275. Robert D. Putnam, *Bowling Alone* (New York: Simon & Schuster, 2000), 37-38.

276. *Timmons v. Twin Cities Area New Party*, 520 U.S. 351 (1997).

277. *Id.* at 367.

278. For example, to support the notion that the two-party system promotes "political stability," *Timmons* cites Justice Antonin Scalia's dissenting opinion, in a prior case, that "The stabilizing effects of such a [two-party] system are obvious." *Id.*, quoting *Rutan v. Republican Party of Ill.*, 497 U.S. 62, 107 (1990) (Scalia J. dissenting).

279. At one point, the Court cites a declaration submitted by Professor Burnham to help the trial judge case for the proposition that the two-party system is "traditional" while ignoring how Professor Burnham describes, *in the very same declaration*, how this supposed "tradition" has actually been fostered by election laws. *Compare id.* at 367 *with* Declaration of Walter Dean Burnham filed on Sept. 2, 1994 in *Twin Cities Area New Party v. Lou McKenna et al.*, Case No. Cv. 3-94-953 (D. Minn.).

280. Chief Justice William Rehnquist wrote the majority opinion in *Timmons*, and was joined by Justices Sandra Day O'Connor, Antonin Scalia, Anthony Kennedy, Clarence Thomas, and Stephen Breyer.

281. Disch at 42.

282. *See* Scott Piroth, "Selecting Presidential Nominees: The Evolution of the Current System and Prospects for Reform," *Social Education* 64, no. 5 (Sept. 2000), https://www.uvm.edu/~dguber/POLS125/articles/piroth.htm.

283. *See* Joshua Mound, "What Democrats Still Don't Get About George McGovern," *New Republic* (Feb. 29, 2016), at https://newrepublic.com/article/130737/democrats-still-dont-get-george-mcgovern.

284. *Id.*

285. *Id.* The anti-McGovern campaign was led by the governor of Georgia at the time, Jimmy Carter. *See id.*

286. R.W. Apple Jr., "Democrats Adopt A Party Charter; Walkout Avoided," *New York Times* (Dec. 8, 1974), http://www.nytimes.com/1974/12/08/archives/democrats-adopt-a-party-charter-walkout-avoided-12article-charter.html.

287. 291 *See* Mound, 110, *supra*.

288. 292 Nate Silver (writing as poblano), "A Brief History of Superdelegates," *Daily Kos* (Feb. 15, 2008), https://www.dailykos.com/stories/2008/2/15/457181/.

289. Jake Miller, "The Strange History of Superdelegates: What They Mean for Super Tuesday and Beyond," *Mic* (Mar. 1, 2016), https://mic.com/articles/136627/the-strange-history-of-superdelegates-what-they-mean-for-super-tuesday-and-beyond#.PeeBkWTnE.

290. Branko Marcetic, "The Secret History of Super Delegates," *In These Times* (May 16, 2016), http://inthesetimes.com/features/superdelegates_bernie_sanders_hillary_clinton.html.

291. "Hunting The Hunt Commission," *In These Times* (May 16, 2016), http://inthesetimes.com/features/hunt_commission_what_are_superdelegates.html#part1.

292. Silver, *supra*.

293. Charter, Art. 5 § 4.

294. Charter at Art. 2, § 4.

295. Indeed, it is questionable whether these were *ever* vital principles of the Charter, given that, as we have seen, by the time it was adopted in 1974, the backlash against McGovern's candidacy was already in full swing.

296. Hope Yen, Stephen Ohlemacher, Lisa Lerer, & Catherine Lacey, "AP count: Clinton has delegates to win Democratic nomination," Associated Press (June 6, 2016), http://elections.ap.org/content/ap-count-clinton-has-delegates-win-democratic-nomination-0.

297. Interestingly, the date of the announcement (June 6, 2016) was the day before the eight-year anniversary of Clinton having formally ended her last presidential campaign, thus making Barack Obama the Democrats' presumptive nominee. *See* AP, "Clinton ends historic bid, endorses Obama" (June 7, 2008), http://www.nbcnews.com/id/24993082/ns/politics-decision_08/t/clinton-ends-historic-bid-endorses-obama/#.Wa3Ge7KGOUk.

298. Wilson Andrews, Kitty Bennett, and Alicia Parlapiano, "2016 Delegate Count and Primary Results," *New York Times*, https://www.nytimes.com/interactive/2016/us/elections/primary-calendar-and-results.html.

     Taken together, these primaries accounted for over 17 percent of the unpledged delegates.

299. Philip Bump, "Why the Associated Press called the race for Hillary Clinton when nobody was looking," *Washington Post* (June 7, 2016), https://www.washingtonpost.com/news/the-fix/wp/2016/06/07/

why-the-associated-press-called-the-race-for-hillary-clinton-when
-nobody-was-looking/?utm_term=.2f44d04eac15.

300. Of the 713 superdelegates in 2016, there were 432 members of the DNC, 193 U.S. representatives, 47 U.S. senators, 21 governors, and 20 "distinguished party leaders." *See* Bump *supra*.

301. *See* Linda Qui, "No, Donald Trump, Bernie Sanders wouldn't have won even if super delegates were nixed," PolitiFact (July 25, 2016), at http://www.politifact.com/truth-o-meter/statements/2016/jul/25/donald-trump/no-donald-trump-bernie-sanders-wouldnt-have-won-ev/.

Before counting superdelegates (who favored Clinton over Sanders by a tally of 570.5 to 44.5), Clinton topped Sanders in pledged delegates, 2,200 to 1,831.

302. *See* David Nather, "Leaping Voters In a Single Bound," *CQ Weekly* (Feb. 25, 2008), at https://web.archive.org/web/20081127130726/http://public.cq.com/docs/cqw/weeklyreport110-000002675899.html.

303. Thomas E. Patterson, "Pre-Primary News Coverage of the 2016 Presidential Race: Trump's Rise, Sanders' Emergence, Clinton's Struggle," (June 2016), https://shorensteincenter.org/wp-content/uploads/2016/06/Pre-Primary-News-Coverage-Trump-Sanders-Clinton-2016.pdf.

304. *Id.* at 11-12. *See, e.g.,* Doyle McManus, "Why Bernie Sanders is truly a long-shot candidate," *Los Angeles Times* (May 29, 2015), http://www.latimes.com/opinion/readersreact/la-le-0530-bernie-sanders-electability-postscript-20150530-story.html.

305. Michele Gorman, "Over Half Of Democratic Superdelegates Support Hillary Clinton: Report," *Newsweek* (Nov. 13, 2015), http://www.newsweek.com/half-superdelegates-support-hillary-clinton-393776.

306. *Id. See also* Domenico Montarno, "Clinton Has 45-To-1 'Superdelegate' Advanctage Over Sanders," NPR (Nov. 13, 2015), at http://www.npr.org/2015/11/13/455812702/clinton-has-45-to-1-superdelegate-advantage-over-sanders (reporting that "What's more, superdelegates have a greater importance than raw numbers. That's because the way they lean, political scientists have found, is one of the best predictors of who will become the nominee").

307. *See* Gregory Krieg, "These Charts Show Just How Impressive Bernie Sanders' Fundraising Haul Is," *Mic* (Oct. 1, 2015), at https://mic.com/articles/126147/these-charts-show-just-how-impressive-bernie-

sanders-fundraising-haul-is#.ytCivz9DY; Ed O'Keefe & John Wagner, "100,000 people have come to recent Bernie Sanders rallies. How does he do it?" *Washington Post* (Aug. 11, 2015), https://www.washingtonpost.com/politics/how-does-bernie-sanders-draw-huge-crowds-to-see-him/2015/08/11/4ae018f8-3fde-11e5-8d45-d815146f81fa_story.html?utm_term=.c91c1515febe.

308. *See* Drew DeSilver, "Turnout was high in the 2016 primary season, but just short of 2008 record," Pew Research Center (June 10, 2016), http://www.pewresearch.org/fact-tank/2016/06/10/turnout-was-high-in-the-2016-primary-season-but-just-short-of-2008-record/.

309. Josh Stewart, "Following the money behind the nearly $500 million 2016 Democratic primary," Sunlight Foundation (June 21, 2016), https://sunlightfoundation.com/2016/06/21/following-the-money-behind-the-nearly-500-million-2016-democratic-primary/.

This includes money spent by the Clinton, Sanders, and O'Malley campaigns, as well as their allied Super PACs and other groups.

310. Eli Clifton & Joshua Holland, "Bernie's Fundraising Was Revolutionary. How He Spent His Money Was Not.," *Slate* (July 13, 2016), http://www.slate.com/articles/news_and_politics/politics/2016/07/how_bernie_spent_his_millions_was_anything_but_revolutionary.html.

311. *See id.,* noting that the firm of one consultant (who previously worked for the campaigns of Al Gore and John Kerry) received just under $4.8 million for video and media production services and split $10 million in commissions with another company.

312. Sam Stein & Paul Blumenthal, "Hillary Clinton and Donna Brazile Left The DNC Without Debt. Was That Wise?," *Huffington Post* (Mar. 14, 2017), http://www.huffingtonpost.com/entry/dnc-no-debt-clinton-brazile_us_58c805a2e4b0428c7f134148.

313. *See id.* Donna Brazile's latest revelations, however, indicate that the Clinton campaign was choking the DNC behind the scenes. *See* https://www.politico.com/magazine/story/2017/11/02/clinton-brazile-hacks-2016-215774.

314. *See* "Joint fundraising by political party committees," Federal Election Commission, at https://www.fec.gov/help-candidates-and-committees/making-disbursements-political-party/joint-fundraising-political-party-committees/ (last visited Sept. 7, 2017).

315. *See* "Hillary Victory Fund," Center for Responsive Politics (OpenSecrets. org), at https://www.opensecrets.org/jfc/summary.php?id=C00586537 (last visited Sept. 7, 2017).

   A draft of the Joint Fundraising Agreement forming the Hillary Victory Fund can be found at https://wikileaks.org/podesta-emails/fileid/28674/7815.

316. *See* "2016 Campaign Contribution Limit," Center for Responsive Politics (OpenSecrets.org), at https://www.opensecrets.org/overview/limits.php (last visited Sept. 7, 2017).

317. *See* Ted Johnson, "Hillary Clinton Raises Huge Sums at Homes of George Clooney, Jeffrey Katzenberg," *Variety* (Apr. 16, 2016), at http://variety.com/2016/biz/news/hillary-clinton-george-clooney-fundraiser-jeffrey-katzenberg-1201755147/ ; Annie Karni & Kenneth Vogel, "Clinton asks for $353K to sit with the Clooneys," *Politico* (Mar. 24, 2016), at http://www.politico.com/story/2016/03/hillary-clinton-george-clooney-fundraiser-221207.

   Two Clooney-hosted fundraisers in California raised over $15 million on their own. *See* Dominic Patten, "Hillary Clinton Snags $15M+ From George Clooney-Hosted SF & LA Fundraisers," *Deadline Hollywood* (Apr. 15, 2016), at http://deadline.com/2016/04/george-clooney-hillary-clinton-fundraisers-jeffrey-katzenberg-steven-spielberg-bernie-sanders-1201738559/.

318. C. Eugene Emery Jr., "George Clooney: Bulk of the money collected at Clinton fundraiser will go to down-ballot," PunditFact (May 5, 2016), http://www.politifact.com/punditfact/statements/2016/may/05/george-clooney/george-clooney-decries-big-money-politics-says-mos/.

319. *See* Bob Biersack, "How wealthy donors fund the national party by giving to the states," Center for Responsive Politics (OpenSecrets.org) (July 24, 2017), https://www.opensecrets.org/news/2017/07/wealthy-donors-fund-national-party-giving-to-states/.

320. *See id. See also* "Contribution Limits For 2017-2018 Federal Elections," Federal Election Commission, at https://transition.fec.gov/pages/brochures/contriblimitschart.htm (last visited Sept. 8, 2017).

321. While the financial gains from the Hillary Victory Fund posed an obvious conflict of interest impeding the DNC's neutrality obligation, that didn't stop reports in the mainstream media from trying to

defend the arrangement as just a "regular part of presidential campaigning." *See, e.g.*, Peter Overby, "Clinton Fundraising Violations? A Breakdown Of Sanders' Claims," NPR (Apr. 19, 2016), at http://www.npr.org/2016/04/19/474851697/explainer-bernie-sanders-on-hillary-clintons-joint-fundraising-committee.

A National Public Radio report, for example, defended the Hillary Victory Fund by pointing to the existence of the Bernie Victory Fund—a joint fundraising committee between the Sanders campaign and the DNC. *See id.* However, the Bernie Victory Fund—which raised a grand total of $1000—only proves the point that the Hillary Victory Fund created a situation of extreme financial dependency by the DNC on the Clinton campaign. *See* "Bernie Victory Fund," Center for Responsive Politics (OpenSecrets.org), at https://www.opensecrets.org/jfc/summary.php?id=C00592568&cycle=2016 (last visited Sept. 8, 2017).

322. *See* Margot Kidder, "How Hillary Clinton Bought the Loyalty of 33 State Democratic Parties," *CounterPunch* (Apr. 1, 2016), https://www.counterpunch.org/2016/04/01/how-hillary-clinton-bought-the-loyalty-of-33-state-democratic-parties/ ("One could reasonably infer that the tacit agreement between the signatories was that the state parties and the Hillary Clinton Campaign would act in unity and mutual support. And that the Super Delegates of these various partner states would either pledge loyalty to Clinton, or, at the least, not endorse Senator Sanders. Not only did Hillary's multi-millionaire and billionaire supporters get to bypass individual campaign donation limits to state parties by using several state parties apparatus, but the Clinton campaign got the added bonus of buying that state's Super Delegates with the promise of contributions to that Democratic organization's re-election fund").

323. Nate Silver (writing as poblano), "A Brief History of Superdelegates," *Daily Kos* (Feb. 15, 2008), https://www.dailykos.com/stories/2008/2/15/457181/.

324. *Buckley v. Valeo*, 424 U.S. 1 (1976).

325. Andy Kroll, "Follow the Dark Money," *Mother Jones* (July/August 2012), http://www.motherjones.com/politics/2012/06/history-money-american-elections/.

326. *See id.*; *Buckley*, 424 U.S. at 45.

327. *Buckley*, 424 U.S. at 45.

328. *Id.* at 19.

329. *See id.* at 16.

330. 391 U.S. 367 (1968).

331. *Id.* at 376.

332. *Buckley,* 424 U.S. at 26-29, 45.

333. *Id.* at 27.

334. *Id.* at 29.

335. *Id.* 47.

336. 558 U.S. 310 (2010).

337. The procedural history of *Citizens United* shows the Supreme Court's decision to be a stunning example of "aggressive conservative judicial activism." *See* Jeffrey Toobin, "Money Unlimited," *The New Yorker* (May 21, 2012), https://www.newyorker.com/magazine/2012/05/21/money-unlimited.

While the case originally presented the Court with a narrow issue of interpretation pertaining to a narrow issue of statutory interpretation under a relatively obscure provision of the Bipartisan Campaign Reform Act of 2002 (otherwise known as the McCain-Feingold Act), the Court took the highly unusual step of ordering that the case be reargued so that it could rule on the constitutionality of limiting expenditures by corporations. *See id.* As Justice John Paul Stevens wrote in his ninety page dissenting opinion, "Essentially, five Justices were unhappy with the limited nature of the case before us, so they changed the case to give themselves an opportunity to change the law." *Citizens United*, 558 U.S. at 398.

338. *Id.* at 365.

339. *Id.* at 337.

340. *Id.,* (citation and internal quotation marks omitted).

341. *See* Matea Gold, "Can super PACs be put back in the box?," *Washington Post* (July 6, 2016), https://www.washingtonpost.com/politics/can-super-pacs-be-put-back-in-the-box/2016/07/06/9beb18ba-43b1-11e6-8856-f26de2537a9d_story.html?utm_term=.40dd56dfe324.

The precise legal basis for Super PACs came into being two months after *Citizens United*, when the D.C. Circuit Court of Appeals removed limits on contributions to independent expenditure-only political action committees on the ground that such limits violate the right to free speech as articulated in *Citizens United. See SpeechNow.org v. Federal Election*

Comm'n, 599 F.3d 686, 692-96 (D.C. Cir. 2010). Note that the holding of *SpeechNow.org* takes the money-speech equivalency introduced in *Buckley* even further down the slippery slope. *Buckley* identified the act of *spending money* on campaign communications to be a form of speech. But with its creation of the Super PAC, the D.C. Circuit identified the act of *giving money* to a political action committee as a form of speech.

342. *See* Libby Watson, "The final stretch: The big-spending super PACs behind Hillary Clinton," Sunlight Foundation (Nov. 1, 2016), at https:// sunlightfoundation.com/2016/11/01/the-final-stretch-the-big-spending-super-pacs-behind-hillary-clinton/.

343. Michelle Ye Hee Lee, "Sanders's claim that he 'does not have a super PAC,'" *Washington Post* (Feb. 11, 2016), https://www.washingtonpost.com/news/fact-checker/wp/2016/02/11/sanderss-claim-that-he-does-not-have-a-super-pac/?utm_term=.a9987875fba9 ; National Nurses United, Center for Responsive Politics (OpenSecrets.org), https://www.opensecrets.org/pacs/lookup2.php?strID=C00490375 (last visited Sept. 14, 2017).

344. 134 S. Ct. 1434 (2014).

345. *Id.,* at 1450 (citation and internal quotation marks omitted).

346. *Id.,* (citation omitted).

347. Availableathttp://docquery.fec.gov/cgi-bin/forms/C00586537/1024437/.

348. *Id.* at 1454-55.

349. Eric Johnson, "Full transcript: Hillary Clinton at Code 2017," Recode (Mar. 31, 2017), https://www.recode.net/2017/5/31/15722218/hillary-clinton-code-conference-transcript-donald-trump-2016-russia-walt-mossberg-kara-swisher.

350. The Court's blessing of joint fundraising committees such as the Hillary Victory Fund may have come just in the nick of time. The year before *McCutcheon*, the DNC was reported to be "nearly broke" and "so deeply in the hole from spending in the last election that it is struggling to pay its vendors." *See* Tory Newmyer, "The DNC is nearly broke," *Fortune* (Sept. 30, 2013), http://fortune.com/2013/09/30/the-dnc-is-nearly-broke/ (discussing impediments to fundraising experienced by the DNC).

351. "Bankrupt" derives from the Italian, *banca rotta*, meaning "a broken bank or bench." Frank O. Loveland, *A Treatise on the Law and Proceedings in Bankruptcy,* vol. 1 (The W. Anderson Co., 1912) Ch. 1 § 3. "It is said to

have been the custom in Italy to break the bench, or counter, of a money-changer upon his failure[.]" *Id.* n.8 (citation omitted).

352. While going out of its way to protect the right of corporations to spend unlimitedly on campaigns, the Supreme Court under Chief Justice John Roberts has also endorsed onerous voter-identification requirements and rolled back the protections of the Voting Rights Act. *See* Thomas B. Edsall, "Supreme Injustice," *New York Times* (May 6, 2014) at https://www.nytimes.com/2014/05/07/opinion/edsall-supreme-injustice.html?mcubz=0.

353. *Citizens United*, 558 U.S. at 354 (citation omitted).

354. *Id.* at 364.

355. *McCutcheon*, 134 S.Ct. at 1451.

SUMMATION: Rule of Law Demands Consequences

356. Donna Brazile, "Inside Hillary Clinton's Secret Takeover of the DNC," *Politico* (Nov. 2, 2017), https://www.politico.com/magazine/story/2017/11/02/clinton-brazile-hacks-2016-215774.

357. *Id.*

358. *Id.*

359. *See* Alex Seitz-Wald, "Memo Reveals Details of Hillary Clinton-DNC Deal," (Nov. 3, 2017), https://www.nbcnews.com/politics/elections/memo-reveals-details-hillary-clinton-dnc-deal-n817411.

360. The memorandum setting forth the fundraising agreement can be accessed at http://msnbcmedia.msn.com/i/TODAY/z_Creative/DNC-Memo%20(002).pdf.

361. *See* Brazile, note 335, *supra.*

362. *See* Final Order of Dismissal entered Aug. 8, 2017 in *Wilding*, 12, http://jampac.us/wp-content/uploads/2017/08/62-D.E.-62-Ord-of-Dismissal-8-25-17.pdf.

363. *Id.* at 16, 18.

364. The appellate court docket can be viewed at http://jampac.us/dnclawsuit/.

365. *See* "Just the Facts: U.S. Courts of Appeals," Administrative Office of the U.S. Courts (Dec. 20, 2016), http://www.uscourts.gov/news/2016/12/20/just-facts-us-courts-appeals.

366. *See* Zach Haller, "7 Jaw-Dropping Revelations From Hearings on the Motion to Dismiss the DNC Fraud Lawsuit," *Medium* (Apr. 30, 2017),

https://medium.com/@zachhaller/7-jaw-dropping-revelations-from-hearings-on-the-motion-to-dismiss-the-dnc-fraud-lawsuit-bee1723b713f ; Battle of Blair, "From the official transcripts of the DNC lawsuit," Caucus99percent (May 18, 2017), https://caucus99percent.com/content/official-transcripts-dnc-lawsuit.

367. *See* Andrew Berger, "Brandeis And The History Of Transparence," Sunlight Foundation (May 26, 2009), https://sunlightfoundation.com/2009/05/26/brandeis-and-the-history-of-transparency/.

368. *Id.*

369. *See* Ciara McCarthy, "Is Sunlight Actually the Best Disinfectant?" *Slate* (Aug. 9, 2013), at http://www.slate.com/articles/health_and_science/explainer/2013/08/sunlight_is_the_best_disinfectant_not_exactly.html.

370. *See id.*

371. *See id.*

372. *See* Peter Scott Campbell, "Democracy v. Concentrated Wealth: In Search of a Louis D. Brandeis Quote," *Greenbag* 16, no. 2D (2013): 251, http://greenbag.org/v16n3/v16n3_articles_campbell.pdf.

373. *See id.* at 251.

374. *See* Walter Dean Burnham, "The Changing Shape of the American Voting Universe," *American Political Science Review* 59 (1965): 23-26 (cited in Disch at 44 n.63).

375. *See* Asher Schechter, Richard Posner: "The Real Corruption Is the Ownership of Congress by the Rich," *Pro-Market* (The blog of the Stigler Center at the University of Chicago Booth School of Business) (Mar. 28, 2017), https://promarket.org/richard-posner-real-corruption-ownership-congress-rich/.

376. *See Thom Hartmann Program*, "Bernie Sanders: The United States is an Oligarchy!," (Aug. 5, 2015), https://www.youtube.com/watch?v=qhvxk0xJhXM.

377. Jeffrey A. Winters & Benjamin I. Page, "Oligarchy in the United States?," *Perspectives on Politics*, 7, no. 4 (Dec. 2009): 744, at https://www.researchgate.net/publication/231898807_Oligarchy_in_the_United_States.

378. "Study: US is an oligarchy, not a democracy," BBC News (Apr. 17, 2014), http://www.bbc.com/news/blogs-echochambers-27074746.

379. *See* Andrew Prokop, "Lawrence Lessig quits Democratic race, says party changed rules to exclude him from debate," Vox (Nov. 2, 2015),

https://www.vox.com/2015/11/2/9659014/lawrence-lessig-quits
-presidential.

380. *See* Lawrence Lessig, "We the People, and the Republic we must reclaim,"
TED (Apr. 3, 2013), https://www.youtube.com/watch?v=mw2z9lV3W1g.

381. (University of Illinois Press 2017).

382. Winters & Page at 744.

383. *Schneiderman v. U.S.*, 320 U.S. 118, 136 (1943).

384. "Democracy," U.S. Department of State official website, https://www.
state.gov/j/drl/democ/ (last visited No. 7, 2017).

385. Plato, *Republic* (G.M.A. Grube trans.) (Hackett, 1992), at Bk. VII, 187.

386. *See* Melissa Lane, "Ancient Political Philosophy," *Stanford Encyclopedia
of Philosophy* (footnote omitted), https://plato.stanford.edu/entries/an-
cient-political/.

387. Aristotle, *The Politics* (Carnes Lord trans.) Bk. 4, Ch. 4 at 122-23 (Univ. of
Chicago 1984).

388. *See id.* Bk. 4, Chs. 4-6, at 122-28.

389. *Id.* at Bk. 4, Ch. 4, at 125.

390. *Id.* at Bk. 4, Ch. 5, at 127.

391. See in particular, Aristotle, *Nicomachean Ethics* (Terence Irwin trans.)
(Hackett 1985). For specific references to how law is intertwined with Ar-
istotelian ethics, refer to "law" at pages 413-14 of the glossary.

392. *See, e.g.*, Plato, *Statesman;* Plato, *The Laws;* Plato, *The Laws* (trans. Trevor
J. Saunders) (Penguin rev. ed., 1975). The translator's introduction to the
latter provides an overview of the role of law in Plato's political philosophy as well as career as political advisor.

393. Final Order of Dismissal in *Wilding*, available at http://jampac.us/
wp-content/uploads/2017/08/62-D.E.-62-Ord-of-Dismissal-8-25-17.pdf.

394. Donna Brazile, "Inside Hillary Clinton's Secret Takeover of the
DNC," *Politico* (Nov. 2, 2017), https://www.politico.com/magazine/
story/2017/11/02/clinton-brazile-hacks-2016-215774.

395. Summaries of the manifold election irregularities, including related
legal actions that will ultimately prove futile in obtaining any meaningful relief, can be found at Election Justice USA, *"Democracy Lost:
A Report on the Fatally Flawed 2016 Democratic Primaries,"* http://
www.p2016.org/chrnothp/Democracy_Lost_Update1_EJUSA.
pdf, as well as lulu Fries'dat & Anselmo Sampietro in collaboration
with Fritz Scheuren, "An Electoral System in Crisis," (July 25, 2016),

https://static1.squarespace.com/static/579f40a01b631bd12f10c29e/t/
58375666c534a52c855d9648/1480021608216/000+An+Electoral+System+
in+Crisis.pd.

In just one particularly egregious example, the New York City Board
of Elections has acknowledged it illegally purged more than 200,000 voters from city rolls; while the New York state attorney general announced a
"settlement" with the Board, there is no relief provided for those actually
injured by the illegal voter purge. *See* Andrew Keshner, "NYC's Board of
Elections will admit it purged more than 200,000 voters from city rolls," *New
York Daily News* (Oct. 24, 2017), http://www.nydailynews.com/news/poli-
tics/board-elections-admit-purged-200-000-voters-rolls-article-1.3586490.

Suffice to say, the unresolved and unaddressed irregularities characterizing the 2016 primaries are hardly atypical of U.S. elections, nor
should they be surprising given that, "Compared with equivalent Western democracies, rather than regulating uniform standards across all
polling places and establishing independent and non-partisan authori-
ties, American elections have allowed exceptionally partisan control and
highly decentralized arrangements." Pippa Norris, "Why American Elections Are Flawed (And How to Fix Them)," Faculty Research Working
Paper Series, Harvard Kennedy School 8-9 (Sept. 2016), https://papers.
ssrn.com/sol3/papers.cfm?abstract_id=2844793.

396. I have written at length on the Hillary Clinton email server investigation.
See Jared Beck, "Why Hillary Clinton's Emails Matter: A Legal Analysis," (June 6, 2016), https://beckandlee.wordpress.com/2016/06/06/why-
hillary-clintons-emails-matter-a-legal-analysis/ ; "Comey's Volley, Or The
Indictment That Wasn't," (July 11, 2016), https://beckandlee.wordpress.
com/2016/07/11/comeys-volley-or-the-indictment-that-wasnt/ ; Jared
Beck, "On Corruption, Our Coming Election And Beyond," (Oct. 23,
2016), https://beckandlee.wordpress.com/.

Since the FBI closed its investigation (after briefly reopening it in
October 2016 in relation to emails found on Anthony Weiner's laptop),
documents have surfaced showing Comey's statement to have been revised from an earlier draft finding Clinton's conduct to have been
"grossly negligent"—*i.e.*, the exact standard set forth under 18 U.S.C.
793(f). *See* John Solomon, "Early Comey draft accused Clinton of
gross negligence on emails," *The Hill* (Nov. 6, 2017), http://thehill.com/

homenews/senate/358982-early-comey-memo-accused-clinton-of-gross
-negligence-on-emails.

397. *See* Matt Zapotosky, Rosalind S. Helderman & Tom Hamburger,
"FBI agents pressed Justice unsuccessfully for probe of Clinton Foundation," *Washington Post* (Oct. 30, 2016), https://www.
washingtonpost.com/world/national-security/fbi-agents-pressed-justice
-unsuccessfully-for-probe-of-clinton-foundation/2016/10/30/98c823
ec-9ee9-11e6-8d63-3e0a660f1f04_story.html?utm_term=.f98b9236961c.

The case that there exists ample evidence to prosecute the Clinton
Foundation for the crime of inurement as well as in connection with "pay
to play" transactions facilitated while *Clinton was secretary of state has been
cogently set forth in Peter Schweizer, Clinton Cash: The Untold Story of How and
Why Foreign Governments and Businesses Helped Make Bill and Hillary Rich*
(Harper, 2015); and Jerome Corsi, *Partners in Crime: The Clintons' Scheme
to Monetize the White House* (WND Books, 2016).

Recently, public interest in Clinton's email server as well as the
dealings of the Clinton Foundation reignited with the announcement of
Congressional investigations into the subjects, along with reports that
the FBI had uncovered a Russian bribery plot before Secretary Clinton
exercised approval over a controversial transaction granting Russia control over 20 percent of America's main uranium production capacity. *See*
Miles Park, "House Republicans Launch New Investigations Into Clinton Email Probe, Uranium Deal," NPR (Oct. 24, 2017), https://www.
npr.org/2017/10/24/559854924/house-republicans-launch-new-investi-
gations-into-clinton-email-probe-uranium-dea; John Solomon & Alison
Spann, "FBI uncovered Russian bribery plot before Obama administration approved controversial nuclear deal with Moscow," *The Hill* (Oct.
17, 2017), http://thehill.com/policy/national-security/355749-fbi-un-
covered-russian-bribery-plot-before-obama-administration.

398. *See* Marc Caputo, "Blowback from staffer scandal burns Wasserman Schultz," *Politico* (Aug. 10, 2017), https://www.politico.com/
story/2017/08/10/debbie-wasserman-schultz-scandal-241466.

399. *See* Anthony Man, "Wasserman Schultz warns Capitol police chief
to expect 'consequences,'" *Sun Sentinel* (May 25, 2017), http://www.
sun-sentinel.com/news/politics/fl-reg-wasserman-schultz-police-chief-
threat-20170525-story.html.

400. *See* "Imran Awan case: Lawmaker calls 'massive' data transfers from Wasserman Schultz aide a 'substantial security threat,'" Fox News (Oct. 11, 2017), http://www.foxnews.com/politics/2017/10/11/imran-awan-case-lawmaker-calls-massive-data-transfers-from-wasserman-schultz-aide-substantial-security-threat.html.

401. *See, e.g.*, Zephyr Teachout, *Corruption in America: From Benjamin Franklin's Snuff Box to Citizens United* (Harvard University Press, 2016) for a comprehensive study of how the United States legal order has evolved from one that rigorously criminalized corruption to one that "treats corruption lightly and in a limited way." *Id.* at 7.

402. Philip Rucker, "Donna Brazile: I considered replacing Clinton with Biden as 2016 Democratic nominee," *Washington Post* (Nov. 4, 2016), https://www.washingtonpost.com/politics/brazile-i-considered-replacing-clinton-with-biden-as-2016-democratic-nominee/2017/11/04/f0b75418-bf4c-11e7-97d9-bdab5a0ab381_story.html?utm_term=.af11d5abcecd.

403. These events are summarized in an unsuccessful motion filed by the *Wilding* plaintiffs seeking an order of protection from the trial court. *See* Elizabeth Vos, "Attorneys in DNC Fraud Lawsuit Seek Court's Protection, Cite Seth Rich," *Disobedient Media* (June 13, 2017), https://disobedientmedia.com/2017/06/watch-attorneys-in-dnc-fraud-lawsuit-seek-courts-protection-cite-seth-rich/.

404. *See, e.g.*, David Weigel, "In one corner of the Internet, the 2016 Democratic primary never ended," *Washington Post* (Aug. 29, 2016), https://www.washingtonpost.com/news/powerpost/wp/2017/08/29/in-one-corner-of-the-internet-the-2016-democratic-primary-never-ended/?utm_term=.a450fc0d3a6c; David Weigel, "The Seth Rich conspiracy shows how fake news still works," *Washington Post* (May 20, 2016), https://www.washingtonpost.com/news/the-fix/wp/2017/05/20/the-seth-rich-conspiracy-shows-how-fake-news-still-works/?utm_term=.7e24ee34908e (labeling the *Wilding* action "largely frivolous").

405. *The Politics* at Bk. 4, Ch. 11, 135.

406. *Republic* at Bk. VIII, 220.

Acknowledgments

Many people worked to make this book a reality.

A large number of them are friends and interlocutors of mine on social media, who provided invaluable support and vigorous discussion during the intense, roughly four-month period it took to write the manuscript. While they are too numerous to list by name, one of these friends merits special recognition: Alan Smithee (a/k/a Actual Flatticus), who tragically and unexpectedly passed away shortly after I began the project. In the spirit of Smithee's zeal for deep, relentless and principled testing of evidence and argumentation, I hope that readers of this work will be inspired to join the conversation and follow me on Twitter (https://twitter.com/JaredBeck) and Facebook (https://www.facebook.com/jaredbeck).

I am also deeply grateful to The Philomathean Society, and Jeffrey Green, professor of political science at the University of Pennsylvania. They invited me to Philadelphia, at a critical moment in the writing process, to give a talk on the class action against the Democratic National Committee as part of the Andrea Mitchell Center for the Study of Democracy's "Politics on the Edge" series. This talk, and the ensuing question-and-answer session, proved instrumental in clarifying my thoughts. I am also grateful to Jason Goodman of Crowdsource the Truth for livestreaming the event, and bringing the talk to a wider audience.

My editors, Mark Gompertz and Caroline Russomanno of Skyhorse Publishing, provided careful and probing comments and plenty of patience and tough love.

I am also indebted to the Sholl family, who, behind the scenes, offered their camaraderie and good spirits, often at times when it seemed like finishing this book was an insurmountable task.

My parents, Mary Ellen and Roger Beck, have supported their son from day one and encouraged him in all his endeavors, no matter where life takes him.

My wife Elizabeth is also my law partner, business partner, agent, editor, and best friend. During the writing of this book, she somehow managed to juggle managing our law firm and running the family, not to mention providing invaluable edits and commentary on the book itself, so that I could enjoy the seclusion necessary to actually write it. How she manages, I'll never know, but I have never felt so loved, and I love her with all my heart.

Finally, my daughters Vesper and Myfanwy endured too many days of not being able to play with Daddy because his office door was closed. I hope one day they will understand why their father felt the urgency to write this book at the time he did.